from the briar patch...

Roger (signature)

A practical guide to successful Christian living.

Roger Alan Faber

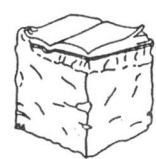

White Stone Books
Publishing Company
Beaufort, Missouri 63013

First Printing — September 1991

Most scriptures taken from the New American
Standard Bible, © 1960, 1962, 1963, 1968, 1971, 1972,
1973, 1975, 1977 by The Lockman Foundation. Used by
Permission.

*All other quoted scriptures as
indicated in footnotes.*

ISBN 1-880122-00-4

Manufactured entirely in the State of Missouri
United States of America

DEDICATION

This book is dedicated to my
parents, Lester and Florence Faber
who gave me both a love for the
Bible and demonstrated how to
apply it to life.

PREFACE

This book grew *from the briar patches* originally written for the congregations I pastored. Each was limited to what would fit on the back of our Sunday Bulletin. The name came from the blackberry patch I had on the property at the time. The idea is that when one passes through a *briar patch* he often gets caught on a briar.

There are three things we get from a *briar patch*: succulent berries, pricks from the briars, and chigger bites. As you pass through these *briar patches* you will delight your spiritual taste buds with God's promises and encouragement. You will also get caught on some of the briars that call your attention to needed changes in your life. Finally, there will be chigger bites. Those things the Holy Spirit has been urging you to do but you've been putting off.

A variety of topics, teachings, and themes are repeated throughout the year in this devotional commentary. How like the scriptures which teach us line upon line, precept upon precept. Each scripture carries in its bosom multiple applications.

With any work of man not everyone likes it or agrees with it. The *briar patches* in this book that raise your hackles will get strong "Amens" from other folks. You may not agree with my interpretation or application of the scriptures. Good! It's so boring when everyone agrees with you.

While teaching English in the St. Louis City public schools for over two decades I spent a lot of time trying to get my students to disagree so they would think, reason, defend their positions. Often I would state something contrary to my own belief. You are safe in this book, what I've written here I DO AGREE WITH. The point is you may not agree with me and are invited to write and tell me so.

All quoted scripture is *italics* and most is taken from New American Standard Bible because for me it is the most accurate translation in modern English. When other translations are quoted it is noted in the text. Your translation may not use the exact same words but the concepts, teaching, and principals are the same.

There is at least one *briar patch* for every book of the Bible. *from the briar patch* is indexed by scripture so you can use it as a commentary.

I've also left space at the bottom of each page for you to write your comments, keep a brief diary, record prayer reminders or whatever.

My prayer is this: by the time you've worked your way through a year's worth of *briar patches* you will be changed, more committed, better equipped to live for Jesus Christ. To Him be the honor, glory, and victory. Amen.

Scripture: Psalm 104:19-23

"Time has no divisions to mark its passage, there is never a thunderstorm or blare of trumpets to announce the beginning of a new month or year. Even when a new century begins it is only we mortals who ring bells and fire off pistols." So wrote Thomas Mann.

The division and measuring of time is not for God but for man. God provided the stars, the moon, and the seasons. *"And God said, 'Let there be lights in the expanse of the sky to separate the day from the night, and let them serve as signs to mark seasons and days and years...'"* (Genesis 1:14). By these we measure and count our days and years.

Everything we do is affected by the clock. We have advanced in our scientific measure of time to the division of seconds into nanoseconds; that is one billionth of a second. God knew this when He hurled the stars into the heavens; but with Him there is no time for He is eternal.

As children of the eternal God through the blood of Jesus Christ in what way should we celebrate the passing of time from one year to the next? Might we do well to mark the passing with renewed commitment to spiritual things; seeking those things which are above instead of those things here below?

Mark the beginning of this new year with renewed commitment to live for Him who died for you.

Scripture: Psalm 15

A cheery greeting and hearty wave does wonders to dispel the gloom of doom-sayers. If we listen to the uglies, those evil words others speak against us, pretty soon we feel rather worthless. We begin to feel unloved and insignificant.

We notice detractors because they're so vocal. Detractors are those people who diminish us with their cutting words. They relish stealing our self-esteem and reputation. Often their words are wrapped in the pretense of being helpful, protective, or as a warning. Dynamite destroys regardless the wrapper.

David asked who may abide in the Lord's tent? He who, "...*does not slander with his tongue, Nor does evil to his neighbor, Nor takes up a reproach against his friend.*" Psalm 15:3 Solomon wrote, "...*he who spreads slander is a fool...*" Proverbs 10:18. Jesus said slander comes from the heart, (Mark 7:21f).

The redeemed need to be vocal in uplifting, encouraging, and comforting one other. Paul wrote, "...*comfort those who are in any affliction...*" (2 Corinthians 1:4). Affliction is not limited to physical suffering. Words hurt. Be on the alert to share comfort with those afflicted by wagging tongues. We must be busy binding up the broken hearted.

A wagging tongue is not from the Lord. So if you know anyone who robs others of their self-esteem, joy, peace, or reputation pray for them to be redeemed by the blood of Jesus Christ.

Who knows you may be next on their hit list.

Scripture: Psalm 66:5-16

Reporting from Amman, Jordan, January 18, 1991 CBS reporter, Allen Pizzey said, "If you only had a phone line you could tell people something of your experience that you want them to know." He was telling of the frustration of trying to get information out of Baghdad during the initial bombing in the Gulf War. Allen Pizzey was in danger of his life.

As I listened I wondered how many Christians are that anxious to tell about their deliverance unto life that they are experiencing in Jesus Christ. Is your experience with Jesus less exciting than being in a war? If so, how come?

David wrote, "*Come and hear, all who fear God, And I will tell of what He has done for my soul. My mouth shall tell of Thy righteousness, And of Thy salvation all day long; For I do not know the sum of them. But as for me, the nearness of God is my good; I have made the Lord God my refuge, That I may tell of all Thy works. And men shall speak of the power of Thine awesome acts; And I will tell of Thy greatness.*" (Psalms 66:16; 71:15; 73:28; and 145:6).

Allen Pizzey was very frustrated because he couldn't get a phone line to tell about what he was experiencing. Do you have the desire of David? Do you have a phone line?

Scripture: Matthew 23:23-28

"Amerika (sic) is full of castles," the visitor said. "Look at the wealth, the affluence, the clean faces and clean hands." To a visitor America looks great. Similar to the impression a visitor to Jerusalem gets of the white-washed tombs. The descendants keep the tombs white-washed. They glisten in the sun making a very pretty sight. It is grand until someone asks, "Why do people white-wash graves?"

A Christian visitor to America might ask, "Why do Americans build castles over trash and garbage heaps?" We do. Have you noticed?

Millions of Americans have built beautiful castles of 'good works' to hide even from themselves the rottenness of death within. You are familiar with the scenario. A person realizes he has not been living up to his capacities so he gets involved in busy work at the church or some humanitarian organization. He feels good about his 'new' quality of life but he has not done anything about his inner self. *"The wages of sin is death but the free gift of God is eternal life through Jesus Christ our Lord."* (Romans 6:23). All the external decorations will not produce 'life' within.

Our task is to open the windows and doors of these castles revealing the need to accept Jesus Christ that he might instill life within. If necessary tear down the castles. It is a matter of eternal life or eternal death. This is what missions is all about and YOU are a missionary.

Scripture: 2 Chronicles 21:1-7

Jehoram *"walked in the way of the kings of Israel, just as the house of Ahab did (for Ahab's daughter was his wife) and he did evil in the sight of the Lord."* (2 Chronicles 21:6). The evil referred to here concerns the first four commandments not the last six.

You recall the last six: honor your father and mother, do not murder, do not commit adultery, do not steal, do not bear false witness, do not covet.

One may reject God, worship creation instead of the Creator, glorify his ideals, use God's Name in vain and few people get terribly upset. Yet this is the evil repeatedly referred to in the Old Testament, the evil of unfaithfulness to God.

The last six commandments must be obeyed but not to the exclusion of the first four. Think about it, if we keep the first four, the last six will take care of themselves. We can't maintain a right relationship with man if we fail in our relationship to God.

A right relationship with God begins and ends with faithfulness to Him. Some begin in faith but become obstreperous, stiff necked, and disobedient, then are disappointed in the results of their Christian lives.

First, foremost, and always we must be faithful to the Lord our God. The thing that sustained David was his total commitment to God. That is why God said, *"David is a man after my own heart,"* (Acts 13:22). What does God say about you?

Scripture: Acts 17:10-15

Auto manufacturers once recommended oil changes every 2000 miles. One oil company had a picture of a hand on its label with two fingers raised in a V indicating it was the 2000 mile motor oil. Later auto manufacturers recommended oil changes every 4000 miles; now it's every 7000 miles. Lubrication has been all but eliminated. Our souls, however, need more frequent servicing. The soul is like a rechargeable battery. The higher the charge the better the service.

What causes wear and tear on your soul? The lust of the flesh, the lust of the eyes, and the pride of life (1 John 2:16). All these drain the soul. The weaker the charge the weaker the power of resistance. A weak battery provides little service. For power one must have a fully charged battery.

The more frequently a nickel cadmium battery is charged the greater its power. This is certainly true of the soul. Daily Bible study and prayer keeps your light shining brightly (Matthew 5:14). It is when the recharging is ignored that trouble begins.

Is your recharging schedule spasmodic and capricious? Non existent?

To have the best results recharge your battery daily with the trickle charge of Bible study and prayer. Add to that the big booster charges of collective worship three times a week at church.

Treat your soul better than you treat your car. It has far greater value.

Scripture: Matthew 6:25-34

Throughout the year we rearrange our priorities. In a rural community everyone understands certain work takes precedence over other activities. Planting, cultivating, and harvesting must be done at specific times. Urban folk don't understand that. I didn't when I first pastored a rural church.

Few men maintain a 'God first' priority regardless of season, weather, or crop condition. I've known two: Otis M. and Frank K. Both men are now with the Lord; but their example survives.

In the years I knew Frank, I never saw him turn a spade of dirt on the Lord's day. If there was something on a week night at Frank's church he planned his work to participate. Once he left a couple of wind rows, rain was threatening, but Frank had a church activity so he left the hay in the field.

Otis and Frank lived by the truth of Jesus' words, *"...seek first His kingdom and His righteousness; and all these things shall be added unto you,"* (v. 33). The *these things* are what we shall eat (or feed our livestock), what we shall drink, and how we shall clothe ourselves, or pay our bills. It isn't easy learning to live that way but it becomes easier when we learn to *"seek first His kingdom"*.

You think this briar patch was written to you — well, I really wrote it to myself. I needed to be reminded of my priorities.

Scripture: Genesis 1:14-18

"*In the beginning God created the heavens and the earth...*" (Genesis 1:1). Now nobody knows exactly when that was. theologians and scientists agree that creation was a long time ago. How long? Consider this.

Astronomer Roger Lynds said two blue arcs have been discovered in the heavens. The light from them began its journey toward the earth five billion light years ago.[1] Think of it like this. If we travel at the speed of light (186,000 miles per second) it would take us five billion years to get there. Don't even ask to have that translated into miles.

Astronomer Lynds admits he and his colleagues do not know what these blue arcs are. The color suggests star formation but the arc shape is so perfect astronomers are baffled.

Isn't our God wonderful? When He created the heavens and the earth a mere 6000 years ago He put enough substance in them to keep man wondering, guessing, learning, experimenting, and changing his hypothesis for all time. To deny God's existence is to blunder into vacuous ignorance.

Yes, our God made the blue arcs. Isn't He wonderful? God in Christ created all that is. He keeps the planets from crashing together and He makes the genes function in an amoeba. Yet, He loves you so much He sacrificed Jesus on the cross to redeem you from the pit of hell. He offers His redemption to you. Will you accept it?

---

[1]New York Times Magazine, July 20, 1989, p. 70

Scripture: Matthew 16:5-12

Those who bake bread know what work yeast performs. Yeast ferments the sugar in the dough causing it to rise. What alcohol is produced is driven off by the heat in the baking process.

Jesus spoke of leaven (yeast) in two ways. First in Matthew 13:33 to represent the all pervading qualities of the kingdom of Heaven. Certainly if we allow the qualities of the kingdom of Heaven access to our lives eventually every area of our lives will be permeated with those qualities. This is the good working of leaven.

Three chapters later Jesus said, *"Watch out and beware of the leaven of the Pharisees and Sadducees,"* (v. 6). Here we have another kind of action of leaven. Leaven can work in a person as it does in bread. It has the potential of making one 'puffy'. The Pharisees and Sadducees were puffy believing they needed no repent-ance. Their headiness prevented humility. Consequently they produced the alcohol of hypocritical teaching. You can certainly become inebriated with false or hypocritical teaching.

It is interesting to note that the leaven works on the sugar not the other ingredients. It works on your sweet-ness not the rest of you. Just as the leaven's work on the sugar affects the other ingredients so leaven affects the rest of you.

Paul admonishes us, *"Clean out the old leaven, that you may be a new lump..."* (1 Corinthians 5:7). What is there in you that needs to be cleaned out before it takes over?

Scripture: Luke 7:18-23

Don't be afraid to question or doubt. To question or doubt is no indication you've lost your faith, salvation, or standing with God. Neither should you feel like a pilgrim as if you were the first person in Christian history to feel the way you do.

Before Jesus was crucified his most ardent admirer, the Elijah of the New Testament, questioned the truth about Jesus Christ. (v. 19) records, *"And summoning two of his disciples, John sent them to the Lord, saying, 'Are You the One who is coming, or do we look for someone else?'"*

To doubt and question is healthy. When you question or doubt do as Jesus told John's disciples. Look at the evidence. Verse 23 records Jesus saying, *"Go and report to John what you have seen and heard..."*

Look at the evidence. Recall your salvation experience, recall those times the Lord has worked in mysterious ways His wonders to perform in your life. Be reminded of answered prayer, even if it was for someone else.

Satan is forever busy dumping doubt on you and your experience with the Lord. If he persuaded John the Baptist to question what will he try with you? When you doubt, look at the evidence, then recall the workings of God in your life thereby adding stones to your tower of faith. Questioning should strengthen your belief so you can say with Job, *"I know that my Redeemer lives..."*

Scripture: Genesis 18:9-15

Don't be amazed when God works miracles in your life or the life of others.

Does that sound like strange advice? Did you know, "Doubt finds its roots in amazement[1]"? It's not WHEN God works a miracle that we should be amazed but when he DOESN'T.

Yet, we are no different from the disciples. They were amazed (bewildered, surprised, astonished) at the redemption of Paul (Acts 9:21), that God's Spirit was poured out on the Gentiles (Acts 10:45), that Peter had been miraculously released from prison (Acts 12:16). Did they have the background, the overwhelming evidence we have?

We have the whole biblical record, two millennia of Christian history, plus personal experience. Yet, we are *amazed* when God works. How peculiar.

We continue being amazed for two reasons. One, we forget how God worked on previous occasions and two, unbelief still holds us. Unbelief, doubt, plugs up God's channel of blessings.

What does James 1:6 say? *"But let him ask in faith without any doubting, for the one who doubts is like the surf of the sea driven and tossed by the wind."* Therefore wonder, be grateful, stand in awe of God's power but don't be amazed.

The angel asked, *"Is anything too difficult for the Lord..."* (Gen 18:14). Then in Zechariah 8:6 God reminds us that though it may be too difficult for us it is not too difficult in the sight of God. For nothing is too difficult for God—believe it!

---

[1]Avanzini, John, *WAR ON DEBT*, (Hurst, TX, HIS Publishing Company) c. 1971, p. 92

Scripture: Luke 8:26-39

Is it human nature or what? All of us are guilty of making the simple complicated while thinking the complicated is simple. How often have you heard someone say, "Awe, that's easy," because they don't know any better?

There is something that is so extremely simple, we think it's impossible. Namely, testifying of Jesus Christ.

You don't need a theological degree to give testimony about Jesus. You don't even need to know how to read and write. Often its the less learned who are the most successful in witnessing. They don't know it can't be done.

When Jesus told us to be His witnesses, he did not leave us to our own devises. In Luke 8:39 Jesus told us exactly how to perform the extremely simple task of witnessing. Jesus told the Gerasene demoniac, *"Return to your house and describe what great things God has done for you."*

Just how difficult is it to describe what great things God has done for you? That sounds like work for a four year old.

Surely we don't fail to witness because God has not done great things for us, right? Which means we do have something to describe.

The reason we fail to witness is as simple as witnessing itself. Satan has convinced us it is too difficult, too complicated, and simply impossible. Which is utter NONSENSE.

Take the challenge of proving him wrong by telling what great things God in Christ has done for you.

Scripture: Colossians 2:8-15

There is little reference in Scripture that Jesus *paid it all* as an old favorite hymn says.   There is however amble evidence of what Jesus really did on the cross. According to Isaiah he bore our sorrows and took our punishment upon Himself (Isaiah 53:4-5); and as todays reading says, He canceled the accusations against us.   We did not run up a debt on our sin credit card that had to paid. Romans 6:23 says we were the ones to be paid the *"wages of sin"*, which is death. Jesus took our wages, our punishment, our death upon Himself on the cross.

Verse 14 says, *"...having canceled out the certificate of debt consisting of decrees against us and which was hostile to us; and He has taken it out of the way, having nailed it to the cross."* Satan, the great accuser, held a long list of accusations against us. With His death on the cross Jesus told Satan, "Those charges (accusations) are cancelled.

We do suffer the consequences of sin. David suffered the consequences of his sins then begged, *"Restore to me the joy of Thy salvation,"* (Psalm 51:12).

Most people enjoy having a friend in high places who has the power and authority to cancel accusations against them. Why labor under a burden of accusations when Jesus says to sinners, *"Come to Me, all who are weary and heavy-laden, and I will give you rest,* (cancel the charges)," (Matthew 11:28).

Scripture: Colossians 2:16-23

Shadows can appear to be what they are not. The hands can make shadows of birds, dogs, mules, none of which are really casting the shadow. Likewise many things have the appearance of righteousness.

We pride ourselves on being delivered from Old Testament practices yet we practice them. Paul tells us rules regarding food and drink are a mere shadow of the reality we have in Jesus Christ (vv. 16-17). He concluded saying, *"These are matters which have, to be sure, the appearance of wisdom in self-made religion and self-abasement and severe treatment of the body..."* These are the elementary principles of the world- the way the world operates (v. 20). Paul continues, *"...but are of **no value** against fleshly indulgence,"* (v. 23).

Rules regarding food, drink, etc. are false teachings that bring us into bondage (Galatians 2:4).

How then is one to know how to live life pleasing to God? Simply by being guided by the Holy Spirit. Satan claims it can't be done, experience knows better.

To live life pleasing to God, continually thirst for Him. Be filled with His Word, invest time in daily prayer, ask the Holy Spirit to *control* your life. Then trust that He is in control.

It's when we seek to satisfy the lust of the flesh, the lust of the eyes and the pride of life that we sin (1 John 2:16). David's life long focus was on God, though he sinned, he was a man after God's own heart.

Scripture: 2 Corinthians 9:1-5

The expression "What in the world is going on?" is not as popular as it once was. So the next time someone asks say, "A whole lot is going on in the Name of Jesus all around the globe."

Missionaries are demonstrating the love of Jesus through every possible means. Including but not limited to health care, agricultural assistance, improved living conditions, water wells and waste disposal facilities and of course the building of churches. There is evangelism and education, Bible distribution, family ministry and a host of other outreach efforts in the Name of Jesus Christ.

The amazing thing is without your gifts to missions the whole structure is at risk. Paul urged giving when he wrote to the Corinthians. *"Let each of you do just as he has purposed in his heart; not grudgingly or under compulsion; for God loves a cheerful giver. And God is able to make all grace abound to you, that always having all sufficiency in everything you may have an abundance for every good deed."* (Vv 7-8).

Why does God give us an abundance? That we might perform good deeds. Those good deeds must include supporting missions thus proving our love (2 Corinthians 8:24).

"What in the world's going on?" LOTS! And all because you show your love for Jesus by giving to His work. Keep it up.

Scripture: Acts 4:8-12

Jesus said, *"The harvest truly is plentiful but the laborers are few."* (Matthew 9:37). Why are there so few laborers? Is harvesting hard work? Are we employed with other work? Do we not see the harvest?

The harvest *is* plentiful. Four out of five persons are lost. Three out of five are deceived into thinking they are saved. The church is full of folks trusting church membership, good works, baptism, and sundry other things for eternal life.

Peter said, *"There is salvation in on one else; for there is not other name under heaven that has been given among men, by which we must be saved."* (v. 12). Paul wrote, *"Believe in the Lord Jesus Christ and you shall be saved..."* (Acts 16:31).

Is the harvest plentiful because we assume that all good people are redeemed? Don't believe it. Have people tell you about their salvation experience. If their story does not match the gospel set them on the right path by showing them what the scriptures say. Do it in love and you will win a brother or sister for eternity.

If a person is truly born again there will be evidence of it in his daily life. But don't assume someone is saved because he attends church or even serves in the church. The best evidence is their testimony of what Jesus has done for them. Be sure to tell what Christ has done for you.

Scripture: Matthew 5:14-16

Is the light too bright?

Bright lights hurt our eyes. We want to dim or turn them off. That is why the world tries lowering Christians to its level, to dim their light. Jesus said, *"...men loved darkness rather than light because their deeds are evil,"* (John 3:19). He told His followers, *"You are the light of the world,"* (Matthew 5:14). Paul wrote in Philippians, *"You appear as lights in the world,"* (Philippians 2:15)

Therefore John wrote, *"Do not be surprised, my brothers, if the world hates you,"* (1 John 3:13). The light of Christ shining through the dedicated obedient believer exposes the guilt and wickedness of the world. No one likes to feel inferior, ashamed or exposed. Yet, when the light of Christ shines through you that is the effect on the world. A dedicated obedient Christian exposes the shallow inadequacy of the world. The Christian has joy; the world has sorrow. The Christian has peace the world has conflict. So the world hates you.

If the world does not hate you because you are a Christian could it be your light is hid under a bushel? Jesus admonished His followers, *"Let your light shine before men, that they may see your good deeds and praise your Father in heaven,"* (v. 16). The reason for letting your light shine before men is that God the Father may be praised. Just how brightly is your light shining in the world? Are people praising God because of you?

Scripture: Job 1:6-12

Do you ever have the opinion of Job's friends that if you're blessed you have been good and if you suffer losses of material things, or health, or position you've been bad? Satan insinuates that Job is good because God blesses him (Job 1:9-11).

There are laws of retribution. If an athlete bungles when the score is tied his team loses and the whole team suffers. If you drive too fast you deserve a speeding ticket. However if your best friend has a stroke you can't assume she's done something wicked. Even if your enemy has a car wreck and is paralyzed your shouldn't conclude that he deserved it.

Actions do have consequences but determining your level of faith by your level of success is to over shoot sound doctrine. Read again, *"I envied the arrogant when I saw the prosperity of the wicked,"* (Psalm 73:3). Not all success can be measured by material prosperity, financial wealth, etc. The righteous may be impoverished materially but be abundantly wealthy in spiritual riches. A close walk with God, a loving family, peace and joy in your heart are all riches the world longs to have.

The Bible teaches both that the wicked prosper while the righteous suffer but it also teaches that the righteous shall receive their rewards and the wicked shall be punished. Think about it and don't judge a person's goodness or wickedness by his success or failure. What if others judged you by that standard?

Scripture: Hosea 11:1-9

How do you visualize God the Father? As some ancient grandfather doting on His children? As some kindly old duffer winking at our wickedness? Or as a generous sort waiting to answer our requests. Can human language and comprehension describe God the Father? We only experience God by faith in Jesus Christ who said, *"No one comes to the Father but through me,"* (John 14:6). It's after salvation we begin understanding Who God is. Our knowledge increases by prayer, Bible study, and obedience.

When sin strains our relationship with Him, His heart aches. Though God is eager to forgive when we are resolutely obstinate, recalcitrant and rebellious He disciplines us. Many were the afflictions of Israel because they continually turned away from the Father. Discipline should result in repentance. God demonstrates infinite patience. His wrath is held in check by His love. God said, *"How can I give you up, O Ephraim? How can I surrender you, O Israel?...My heart is turned over within me; All my compassions are kindled. I will not execute My fierce anger; I will not destroy Ephraim again. For I am God and not man..."* (vv. 8-9).

The Ephraimites remained stiff necked rebellious idolaters. God called and threatened; but His compassion won over His anger.

If you feel the least bit out of fellowship with the Father run to Him now. He's looking for you. Consider your relationship to God the Father and make amends today.

Scripture: Matthew 28:16-20

If someone asked, "What is the Church's purpose?" what would you answer? Would you say that the primary concern of the church is to gather people together for worship, or that the church does a lot of good, feeding, clothing, and housing multitudes of people? Would you explain the church is the training place for Christians to be discipled? Or would you say the primary purpose of the Church is to tell the good news of Jesus Christ?

The world has many opinions about what the church should be and what it should be doing. If a church listens to the world it will be confused beyond measure and lose its sense of direction. The church's guide must be the Bible not the world. The church has received specific direction from the Lord regarding its purpose.

Of course it is commendable to aid folks with food, clothing, and housing, to gather for worship and encourage one another as Apollos wrote, "*...let us consider how to stimulate one another to love and good deeds, not forsaking our own assembling together, as is the habit of some, but encouraging one another; and all the more, as you see the day drawing near,*" (Hebrews 10:24-25).

The church's primary purpose was given by Jesus. "*Go therefore and make disciples of all the nations, baptizing them in the name of the Father and the son and the Holy Spirit, teaching them to observe all that I commanded you...*" (vv. 19-20). Is your church doing that?

Scripture: Ezekiel 18:14-18

Often the obvious is obscure. Everyone knows there are no U's in 'discipline'. Yet how often do people blame their failures on others? "You didn't tell me." "You didn't teach me." You, you, you, when in reality it should be I, I, I. The word discipline has three I's not three U's.

It is sadly possible for some folks to grow up without proper training; but even these are without excuse. The Bible teaches we can and should learn by example. *"...a son who has observed all his father's sins...and observing does not do likewise...will surely live."* (vv. 14&17). There are rewards for good behavior and retribution for bad.

After we're grown discipline is a personal thing. We call it 'self-discipline'. We discipline ourselves. So why is discipline difficult? It is difficult because it is much easier to make excuses for our own failing than it is to overlook the failing of others. Didn't Jesus say, *"You hypocrite, first take the log out of your own eye, and then you will see clearly to take the speck out of your brother's eye,"* (Matthew 7:5).

Discipline, though unpleasant, yields pleasure. *"All discipline for the moment seems not to be joyful but sorrowful; yet those who have been trained by it, afterwards it yields peaceful fruit and righteousness."* (Hebrews 12:11) Therefore give yourself the gift of peaceful fruit and righteousness; discipline yourself. You'll not regret it. One wonderful attribute to self-discipline is that everyone benefits.

Scripture: 1 Peter 2:4-10

What should we call our place of worship? Is it God's house? Is it the church? What term is really appropriate? To call our place of worship God's House is not good doctrine. You and you and I are God's house. We tend to forget that God's Holy Spirit lives within us. Paul reminded us, *"Do you not know that you are a temple of God, and that the Spirit of God dwells in you?"* (1 Corinthians 3:16) That is true of everyone who has received Jesus Christ as Savior.

It would also be technically and doctrinally incorrect to call our meeting place the church. All of us who are born again who choose to come together in a particular place for worship make up the church.

Why do we often forget that God's Spirit dwells in us and that coming together for worship we comprise the church? It is the work of Satan who causes us to forget *who* we are. When we forget we are the temple of God; that together we embody the church we are easy prey for him. We allow him to track mud into our temples. We allow him to lead us away from the body so the church is incomplete.

The meeting place of the church is cleaned regularly and afterward it sparkles. When was the last time you cleaned your temple by confession and repentance of sin? When was the last time you sparkled for Jesus? Are you a doer of the Word?

Scripture: Luke 5:27-31

Woven through denominational and non-denominational churches is a dark shadow. That shadow is called 'lack of growth'. In many churches people ask, "Why aren't we growing?" "What has happened to the fires of revival?"

One obvious answer explodes in our faces. Too often the churches demand unbelievers to clean up their act, get-right morally and socially before they attend services. The church has shut the door in the face of those whom Christ commanded us to reach with the gospel. We've become guilty of drawing rigid lines and of being judgmental.

We have forgotten the words of Jesus, *"It is not those who are well who need a physician but those who are sick,"* (v. 31). When sinners are made to feel unwelcome in Church the Church has a serious problem. Sinners are very sensitive to facial expressions, coolness, and anything that smacks of insincerity.

When sinners feel the genuine love of Christ emanating from Christians they are drawn like a magnet. When sinners see the fruits of the spirit in the lives of those who claim to be born again they are faced with an undeniable testimony.

What is the reaction sinners get in your church? Do they feel welcome even though they don't keep your rules? Do you love them the same way Jesus loved them?

For a church to grow, it must reach out to the unlovely, the unloving, the unrighteous, the unregenerate, and love them with the love of Jesus.

Scripture: Zechariah 14:4-12

In the *Wilderness* magazine there was a pictorial report about Half Dome in Yosemite Park. It was once one rock. Think of the convulsion that rent it asunder. In Zechariah God describes the rending of another mountain. *"The mount of Olives will be split in its middle from east to west by a very large valley, so that half of the mountain will move toward the north and the other half toward the south,"* (v. 4).

Why do people continue scoffing at the Word of the Lord when we have confirmation of His power extant today? The rending of the Mount of Olives will be in the last days. Also in the last days there will be a plague that atomic distruction can make a reality. *"Now this will be the plague with which the Lord will strike all the peoples who have gone to war against Jerusalem; their flesh will rot while they stand on their feet and their eyes will rot in their sockets and their tongue will rot in their mouth,"* (v. 12).

God's word speaks the truth about the past, the present and the future; but read it, believe it, hide its words in your heart. What will it take to create in your heart a hunger for the things of God? Do not let Satan defeat you, cheat you, starve your spirit. Determine to set aside everyday a time to read and be filled with God's word.

Scripture: Matthew 7:13-14

Leniency leads to the breakdown of morals, merit, and merchandise. When standards are reduced efforts are reduced. Human beings simply do not strive to accomplish more than is required.

No where in the Old Testament do we read, "The Lord probably meant..." The Word of the Lord was never a wishy-washy, do-as-you -please utterance.

Few today stand where the prophets of old stood saying, *"Thus says the Lord..."* Too many churches desire great ingatherings, popularity with the masses, and large offerings to take a firm stand on the word of God. As a result those churches are filled with weak, untaught, untrained and possibly unredeemed disciples.

The purpose of God's prophets is not to bring the word of God in line with popular belief but to bring the people in line with the word of God. Spurgeon never watered down the word yet people came for miles to hear him pronounce, "Thus saith the Lord..." Old fashioned? You bet it is and it rings true to the Word.

Let each of us adjust our lives to the Scriptures. Let us strive to live lives worthy of the gospel. Let us climb our spiritual mountains answering the upward call of God. Let us denounce sin and tradition and remove the leaven of the pharisees. Then we will see the blessing of God flow like a river. Then we will see real revival in our land.

Scripture: Jeremiah 10:10-13

Whether studying Shakespeare or science, math or moments in history the very best education anyone can get is from the Christian perspective. Many Christian young people go to state colleges only to have their faith weakened if not totally destroyed by secular and atheistic professors. Paul so aptly described the secular professor, *"always learning and never able to come to the knowledge of the truth,"* (2 Timothy 3:7).

It is so refreshing to sit in a science class and have the professor relate the wonders of creation to the God who made them. The Christian approach to science didn't diminish my appreciation of science; rather it magnified my understanding of science and my appreciation of God. It is enlightening to study history from the perspective of God dealing with man to bring about His will on the earth. I hate to think of what might have happened to my faith if it had not been for God fearing born again professors who taught me in Baptist colleges.

We should take time each day to pray especially for those men and women who have dedicated their lives to training young people according to the truth of the Bible while providing superior education. Christian schools have the added dimension providing the complete education. Pray for the men and women like Ezra, *"who set his heart to study the law of the Lord, and to practice it, and to teach His statutes and ordinances in Israel,"* (Ezra 7:10).

Scripture: 1 Peter 5:6-11

Driving to work one morning I felt severely oppressed in my spirit. Mornings are usually my best time of day. I began listening to a tape and singing praises with it. I made up my own words to the *Alleluia* chorus, "I love you, Lord," "He is my King," etc. By the time I finished singing, "He is my King," tears of joy were streaming down my cheeks. It turned out to be a super day.

Skeptics will accuse me of controlling my emotions. It was NOT positive thinking or some other psychological manipulation. Singing with the tape was an unconscious reaction to a familiar tune. Though unaware of it I had been under demon oppression. Demons can not possess a Christian but they can and do oppress us at every opportunity. Peter preaching at Cornelius' house in Caesarea said, "Jesus, ...*went about doing good and healing all who were oppressed by the devil...*" (Acts 10:38) I was casting out the demons by calling the Name of Jesus. James wrote, "...*Resist the devil and he will flee from you,*" (James 4:7)

Christ filled the vacuum of oppression with overflowing joy. The light of Christ surrounded me. Dimly in the shadows I saw hideous creatures cringing and slinking away. They couldn't bear the name of Jesus.

This was not psychological manipulation. It was the power of Jesus Christ effectively working in the spiritual realm on behalf of a believer.

Scripture: Psalm 18:20-29

How do you visualize God? As austere, kind, un-approachable, angry, loving, forgiving, fair, stern, just? People from every walk of life view God in a different way. Is it Satan that causes us to have a distorted image of our Creator? Why is it the views of God are disparate? Some see God as peering down ready to mash, even destroy anyone who does not abide by His rules. If that were the case none of us would be here.

Do you know that your image of God is a reflection from your own heart? The kind of person you are strongly influences how you see God in your mind's eye. It's true. This is not something concocted by a philosopher. Read again verses 24-26, *"With the kind Thou dost show Thyself kind; With the blameless Thou dost show Thyself blameless; with the pure Thou dost show Thy pure; And with the crooked Thou dost show Thyself astute,"* How you imagine God is a reflection of your own heart.

Those who truly know God through His Son Jesus Christ know Him to be loving, forgiving, just, kind, and the protector of us all. If you truly want to know what God is like, you must come to Him through His Son. Jesus testified in John 14:6, *"...no man comes to the Father but through Me."* When Jesus comes into your heart He changes your distorted view into a true view.

How you visualize God is up to you.

Scripture: 1 Corinthians 14:20-33

Opinions about what is appropriate in a worship service are as varied as leaves in a forest. What one feels is appropriate generally goes back to childhood experiences.

Someone raised in a very liturgical formal church may have difficulty appreciating a service in which joyful praise and hand clapping prevail. The reverse is also true, the charismatic worshiper may feel something is missing in a liturgical service.

Everyone has the right and responsibility to worship in a way that draws him closer to God. Paul encourages us to be mature, to behave as adults, not children. *"...in your thinking be mature,"* (v. 20). That means we refrain from condemning a form of worship that disagrees with you.

As long as one's mode of worship does not prevent or hinder his fellow worshipers, be tolerant. If you think someone's worship expression is unbearable, make it a matter of prayer. Pray to be filled with love for that person and pray for that person too. You can't remain unloving toward someone you regularly lift up in prayer.

A worship service should be well planned and orchestrated. Every part of it must lead each of us to worship the One True God and Father of our Lord Jesus Christ. The important thing is to follow Paul's advice, *"Let everything be done decently and in order,"* (I Corinthians 14:40). Attend the church that meets your needs, that feeds your soul, that helps you grow up in Christ Jesus.

Scripture: Ephesians 4:25-32

"HONEST adj. 1. Marked by or displaying truth-fulness and integrity; upright. 2. Not deceptive or fraudulent; genuine."[1] According to this definition are you an honest person?

Have you rationalized your pet sin yet still hide it from others? Why do we fail to be honest in these situations. Is it fear of being rejected by others; maybe even condemned? Are we deceptive because a degree of sneakiness is fun?

Habitual sin in a Christian's life is guarded at all costs. The Christian with a serious sin problem is afraid to seek help fearing condemnation. Do you know what would cure this problem? Honesty. Honesty that we are all guilty of sin. Remember what Jesus said, *"He that is without sin among you, let him be the first to cast a stone..."* (John 8:7).

Being honest with one another and getting a problem out into the open will not eliminate it. It will however open the doors of help for those who need it. They won't be afraid of condemnation by the congregation.

A good dose of honesty would certainly bolster a church's reputation. The world is looking for some honest Christians who will have the courage to admit weaknesses. There are many in this world who regard honesty very highly. When they observe that we Christians are 'sinning' on the QT it reduces the integrity of our witness. Be honest about your lifestyle in Christ. You'll be surprised how many people will note it and appreciate your candid honesty.

---

[1]The American Heritage Dictionary (Boston, Houghton Mifflin Co. 1985)

Scripture: Job 2:1-6

DON'T BLAME GOD! When illness, tragedy, strife, discomfort, and financial burdens overtake you give credit where credit is due; but don't blame God.

God's perfect creation came to a halt when Satan convinced man to sin. Plants became noxious, grew thorns, while weeds began to dominate worthy plants. Sickness, decay, and death blew across the whole earth. *"For the creation was subjected to futility, not of its own will, but because of Him Who subjected it in hope that the creation itself will be set free from its slavery to corruption into the freedom of the glory of the children of God,"* (Romans 8:20).

God is not responsible for accidents and injury. Satan IS. James wrote, *"Every good thing bestowed and every perfect gift is from above, coming down from the Father of lights, with whom there is not variation, or shifting shadow,"* (James 1:17).

There are three things to remember. First, just as Satan accused Job before God so he accuses you before the throne of grace. Second, God is the same yesterday, today, and forever. Third, when good things come to you: joy, peace, comfort, success, satisfaction, they are from God.

When calamity crosses your path don't get angry with God, instead, blame Satan, he's responsible. Then come to the Lord's house and praise His holy name. Give Him thanks for His protection and provision despite Satan's work. Paul asked, *"If God is for us, who is against us?"* Romans 8:31. The Anwer: Satan is, of course!

Scripture: Luke 14:25-35

Language is so fascinating. The vernacular often expresses ideas better than whole books of theology. A lady spoke of her minister relative who lost his life in the Gulf War as being a Christian 24-7. How jaunty. How apropos. How pleasing to the Lord.

We have a lot of Christians who are only 1-1, a few who are 2-1; but a 24-7 Christian, now that's something. Of course there are many Christians operating at various levels between 1-1 and 24-7. What is your level?

A 24-7 Christian is one who lives for the Lord 24 hours a day, 7 days a week. Just as a 1-1 Christian only lives for the Lord 1 hour a day, 1 day a week, which is usually Sunday. The blessings from the Lord increase the nearer 24-7 we get. How are your blessings? Look at your level of operation.

Samuel told Israel, "...*do not turn aside from following the Lord, but serve the Lord with all your heart. And you must not turn aside for then you will go after futile things...*" (1 Samuel 12:20-21). Is it chasing after futile things the prevents us from being 24-7 Christians? Jesus said of the faithful, "*Blessed is that slave whom his master finds so doing* (being faithful) *when he comes,*" (Matthew 24:46). When is the Master returning? What will He find you doing?

Though the Lord was addressing the church at Smyrna, His words are for all of us. "...*Be faithful until death, and I will give you the crown of life,*" (Revelation 2:10) How close are you to 24-7?

Scripture: Romans 10:13-17

In every community there are lost souls. Experience proves that lost people are not flooding the churches seeking God. God has always initiated reconciliation with man. God came seeking Adam in the Garden of Eden and still seeks sinners.

If the lost are to be won we must do the work Jesus commanded us. Jesus knows the ways of men. He knew they would not come seeking Him therefore He sent us to seek them. Jesus commanded, *"Go therefore and make disciples..."* (Matthew 28:19). He also told us where to begin, *"...you shall be My witnesses both in Jerusalem and in all Judea and Samaria..."* (Acts 1:8). This verse could read, "You shall be my witnesses in *your town* and *in your county,* and *in your state..."* Paul reminded, *"How beautiful are the feet of those who bring glad tidings of good things!"* (Romans 10:15).

Statistics say it takes an average of 13.4 visits before a prospect makes it to church. In reality then some will require more visits and some fewer visits.

Therefore let us not get discouraged if a prospect does not respond after three or four visits. After the 13th visit you may wonder; but even after the 39th visit you shouldn't be defeated. Scripture doesn't allowed us to relinquish going after the most recalcitrant, reluctant, or reticent prospect. When tempted to stop inviting remember how consistent Satan is in leading astray. Our work is cut out for us! The harvest indeed is plentiful but the laborers are few.

Scripture: Nehemiah 2:1-8

Do you live so fast that if you paused to pray it would seem a delay? If someone asked you something and you whispered a prayer before answering, would they think you were stalling?

Nehemiah must have been a reflective person. He apparently did not race through life spouting glib or speedy answers. When Artaxerxes asked, *"What would you request?"* (v. 4), Nehemiah breathed a prayer before answering. If Nehemiah had always been quick to answer Artaxerxes may have suspected deception when Nehemiah paused to pray.

Nehemiah was not alone in pausing before answering. Daniel delayed almost an hour before answering King Nebuchanezzar (Daniel 4:19). Under the circumstances and knowing Daniel we can assume that he too was praying during this delay though scripture doesn't say so.

Would we be as apt to regret our words if we followed Nehemiah's example, if we prayed for wisdom and guidance **before** speaking? Granted Nehemiah was speaking respectfully to the king. Shouldn't we speak just as respectfully to one another? Shouldn't we have enough respect for ourselves that we would guard our words? Before Eliezer accepted Rebekah's invitation he prayed (Genesis 24:25-26, 45).

Nehemiah took time to pray perhaps for wisdom, perhaps for the right words, perhaps that God would move in the heart of the king. God answered Nehemiah's prayer for Nehemiah reports, *"And the king granted them to me because the good hand of my God was on me,"* (v. 8). Would the Lord have you follow the examples of Nehemiah, Eliezer, and Daniel?

Scripture: Colossians 3:1-8

Modern idols are so deceptive we may not be aware of them in our lives. We may not know we are packing them about. Rachel carried off the household gods of her father when she left with Jacob's retinue (Genesis 31:19ff). She knew she was carrying them; but do you know what idols you carry?

The idols you carry about may not be made of wood, plaster, stone; never-the-less they are excess baggage. Scripturally anything you value more than Yehweh God is an idol. Every idol places you in danger of the wrath of God.

The dictionary defines idol: "...an object of worship; a person or thing that is excessively adored."[1] Children? Grandchildren? Spouses? Friends? Heirlooms? All can be idols if excessively adored.

Paul alerted the Colossians that such things as *"...immorality, impurity, passion, evil desire, and greed..."* were idols (v. 5). Your idol may be career, money, success, education, looks, fame, clothes; the list is infinite. Paul also lists, *"...anger, wrath, malice, slander, and abusive speech..."* (v. 8). Thus actions can be idols as well as persons or things.

Whatever the idol you have tucked away in your heart it is inviting the wrath of God. Our God is a jealous God refusing second place in your life. Is it time for some heart cleaning? Is it time to be an iconoclast? Unload your idols.

---

[1]American Heritage Dictionary, Second College Edition (Boston Houghton Mifflin Company, 1985)

Scripture: Ephesians 6:1-4

Have you ever told your children to do to something because you said so? I have. Then I learned this is not best. To insist a child do something because you said so is the old flesh raising its ugly head. Believe it or not telling a child to obey because you 'said so' puffs up your ego. It's true.

Each of us is born with the desire to control other people, situations, whatever is at hand. Parents should control their children. *"Discipline your son while there is hope..."* (Proverbs 19:18). Jesse Jackson said that discipline should begin before the child is six not wait till he's sixteen then espect someone else to straighten him out. Disobedient children are a disgrace to their parents. Solomon wrote, *"He who curses his father or mother, His lamp will go out in time of darkness,"* (Proverbs 20:20). A disobedient child in effect curses father and mother. *"A wise son accepts his father's discipline, but a scoffer does not listen to rebuke,"* (Proverbs 13:1).

The reason children should obey their parents is not because the parent says so but because GOD SAYS SO! Isn't this what Paul meant when he wrote, *"Children obey your parents in the Lord, for this is right,"* (v. 1). Paul was reminding his readers of the ten commandments. *"Honor your father and mother that your days may be prolonged in the land which your God gives you,"* (Exodus 20:12). That verse doesn't promise long life but long residency in the land which God had given to Israel.

Scripture: Psalm 55:4-11

Have you ever felt like running off and leaving it all? King David did. Yes, even kings get frustrated, find they can't cope, and suffer stress.

Many times we believe that if we were the boss instead of the employee, if we were the governor instead of the governed, "If only I was running things," life would be a lot better. Truth is regardless of your occupation or social position there are times you feel you can't cope. I've never envied my boss' responsibility.

Those times you wish to get away are natural. David wrote, *"O that I had wings like a dove! I would fly away and be at rest,"* (v. 6). He also desired to lodge in the wilderness or hide in a place of refuge.

From reading the Psalms I believe David suffered from a lot of gossips and critics seeking to dethrone him. Certainly when one feels even his friends have turned against him he does wish to get away.

Would we really be better off? Yes, for most, if it is not a permanent move. That's why we have vacations, retreats, etc. During these times of refreshment you should do something really different, something you really enjoy. For a few, a permanent change may be just the ticket for a refreshing life. It has been for my wife and I.

Whether permanent or temporary you should seek God's guidance when you want to run away. Until you can escape take time each day for prayer and Bible reading — it will refresh you.

Scripture: Jeremiah 8:13-17

Some people would rather die than repent. Sin so possesses that even life becomes unimportant. Nothing has value except satisfying the gnawing, craving, distructive desire of the flesh. The alcoholic, the drug addict, the homosexual, the prostitute are thoroughly deceived. They are convinced they can not live without satisfying the flesh. Sin is not a disease as former First Lady Betty Ford claims. Sin is willful disobedience to God.

To call alcoholism, drug addiction, or homosexuality diseases is like calling murder and robbery diseases. This kind of reasoning is additional deception from hell. One does not repent from a disease but seeks a cure.

A man robs a bank then goes to his doctor thinking he has the 'robbery' disease. The police capture a killer then call in the doctors to cure him of killing people. When will we wake up to realize that sin is sin. The only cure for sin is repentance.

Note verse 14 of our text. Instead of repenting they chose to assemble in the cities and die. Is that retarded or what? These sinners are so deceived they do not know how to blush. *"They certainly were not ashamed, And they did not know how to blush..."* (Jeremiah 8:12).

Until sinners prostrate themselves before the cross of Christ in repentance there will be no healing of the land. The Israelites waited for a time of peace, a time of healing, but it never came (v. 15). There is peace and healing only in Jesus Christ.

Scripture: Nehemiah 3:6-15

Feeling rather unimportant? Do you think your efforts don't mean much in the kingdom of God? Are others serving the Lord who seem to be more important than you?

In the kingdom of God every believer has an important role. In today's text there are government officials working along side the citizens, the skilled laboring beside the unskilled. Some are working on large projects some on small. Some perform extensive work rebuilding long stretches of the wall while others rebuild a gate, or repair a tower.

Building the Kingdom of God is similar to building a wall around a city. If there are gaps in the wall the city is as unprotected as if it had no wall at all. If there are no gates any enemy may enter at will. So with building the Kingdom of God. It must be strong in all of its parts.

How do we go about building the kingdom of God. Naturally by winning others to Jesus Christ; BUT just as importantly, is the strengthening of each one in the kingdom. You and I are strengthened by studying the word, by prayer, by encouraging others in their commitment to Jesus Christ, and by comforting one another.

Those who skip Bible study on the Lord's day contribute to their own weakness and undermine the kingdom of God. Be in Bible study, and prayer, and encourage one another. Be a builder in God's Kingdom. Your efforts are important to yourself and the kingdom.

Scripture: 1 Samuel 17:41-49

Faith is foolhardy in the eyes of the world. The heroic feats of faith in the Bible are called myths or legends. Myths and legends because the world refuses to believe in a God of miracles.

David's performance in 1 Samuel 17 teaches an important lesson. Foolhardy David acted on his faith, *"...when the Philistine rose and came and drew near to meet David,...David ran quickly toward the battle line to meet the Philistine,"* (v. 48). That was faith in action. That same act of faith is foolhardy in the eyes of the world.

We need to remember, the same God who delivered the stone slaying Goliath will strike down the giants we face, IF we believe and act to the glory of God. Believing and acting for our own benefit is foolhardy. Note David's reason for speaking and acting the way he does. *"...that all this assembly may know that the Lord does not deliver by sword or by spear..."* (v. 45). Which assembly? Both assemblies. The Philistines who rejected the God of Israel and the Israelites who rejected the power of their own God.

If you hope to slay the giants intimidating you come at them confidently in the Name of the Lord. David defeated Goliath by coming against him in the Name of the Lord. *"'You come to me* (David says to Goliath) *with a sword, a spear, and a javelin, but I come to you in the name of the Lord..."* (v. 45). It works.

Scripture: Habakkuk 3:1-6

Many churches still have 'revivals' or as they were called in the old days, 'protracted meetings'. If the series of services is to revive the church, re-ignite the backsliders for the Lord, and to get the church busy about God's work then revival is a proper term.

Why is revival needed for believers? Why is God interested in revival?

God has performed a great work in His people, cleansing them from all unrighteousness, guaranteeing them eternal life, and filling each one with His own holy and precious Spirit. Yet some slip off from their ardent devotion to the Lord. For them it is time for revival. *"O Lord, revive Thy work in the midst of the years, In the midst of the years make it known,"* (v. 2).

Whom does the Lord revive? *"I dwell on a high and holy place And also with the contrite and lowly in spirit In order to revive the spirit of the lowly And revive the heart of the contrite,"* (Isaiah 57:15). God revives all who humble themselves and return to Him. He revives all who are contrite, who repent.

God is interested in revival because God is intensely interested in our relationship to Him. When our love cools, our devotion·wanes, it impairs our relationship to the Father. God desires to revive us again. As naughty children returning ashamedly to loving parents for comfort; so we must return repenting to our heavenly Father for comfort.

Let the Lord revive you.

Scripture: Ezra 6:19-22

In 1546 John Heywood said, "Many hands make light work." That proverb later repeated by Ben Franklin is appropriate to any group of people that seek to accomplish a task. It is especially true of the church.

"Many hands make light work," means that every hand involved in the work of the church will accomplish more. When Israel rebuilt Jerusalem and the temple after the captivity everyone was involved. Even daughters worked in rebuilding (Nehemiah 3:12).

The work of the church today is not necessarily the laying of stones, or cutting and mortising timbers, yet there is much physical work to do. Small worship centers are often cleaned and maintained by the members. The grounds are mowed, snow shoveled, the building painted by the members.

One person testified she received great joy from scrubbing the rest room floor of her church. She did it to the glory of God. Are you cheating yourself out of joy by letting others do the work?

Nehemiah says the rebuilding of Jerusalem and the temple went forward because, "...*the people had a mind to work,*" (Nehemiah 4:6). When the people of God have a mind to work the work goes forward.

Afterwards, all can rejoice in what was accomplished just as Israel celebrated the Passover in Ezra's day. In every church there are the faithful hands who carry the load while the others ride along. Every one is busy and has many things to do but the Lord blesses those who put His kingdom first.

Scripture: Romans 6:15-21

"On the first day of January in the year of our Lord, one thousand eight hundred and sixty-three, all persons held as slaves within any state, or designated part of a state, the people whereof shall then be in rebellion against the United States shall be then thenceforward, and forever free." Those are Abraham Lincoln's preliminary words to the Emancipation Proclamation. With those words slaves were set free.

Though no one would want to diminish the effect of Lincoln's Emancipation Proclamation it pales next to the emancipation Christ secured for us on the cross. Before receiving Christ's redemption we were slaves to sin, (v. 17). Satan was our master. He had control of our lives. We were his puppets on a string. While slaves of Satan we were earning the wages he pays— death!

At Calvary Jesus set free everyone who would believe on Him. Just as Lincoln declared the slaves free in states that remained in rebellion so Christ set those free who met the condition. Freedom from the slavery to sin depends upon the slave believing on the Lord Jesus Christ.

Just as the freed slaves of the nineteenth century gained new life in their freedom so those set free in Jesus receive new life. *"For the law of the Spirit of life in Christ Jesus has set you free from the law of sin and death,"* (Romans 8:2). Rejoice and be glad that at Calvary Jesus set you free *if* you believe in Him.

Scripture: Isaiah 2:5-11

A woman had lived a very full life and served her government in many capacities. She was a writer and scholar. She moved among the ruling classes in America. Sadly there was no mention that she had at any time operated her life by the dictates of Scripture. She was the typical American pagan. Her biographer expressed hope at that God would be kind to this woman who had given so much to mankind. That made two people totally ignorant of the grace of God. The dead heroine and her biographer. Paul wrote, *"By grace are you saved through faith, it is a gift of God not of works..."* (Ephesians 2:8).

It's time to wake up! Christians of every creed need to be busy telling this world the good news of Jesus Christ. It is time for every Christian to realize that everyone who dies without believing on the Lord Jesus Christ as Savior and Lord has damned himself to an eternal hell. Jesus said, *"He who believes is not condemned; he who does not believe is condemned already,"* (John 3:18KJV).

What about all her wonderful deeds, her benevolent works, her gifts to mankind? Hear the word of the Lord. *"...all our righteous deeds are as a filthy garment...our iniquities like the wind take us a way,"* (Isaiah 64:6).

Those who refuse to receive the grace of God through Christ can blame no one but themselves for their eternal damnation.

WAKE UP! Tell others about Jesus before it's eternally too late.

Scripture: Deuteronomy 6:4-9

When we are 'in love' we don't care how silly we act or look. We behave like adolescents. Adolescence is the essence of being addled. We kiss in public, hold hands, our hearts throb. We shiver inside from the excitement of love. Julie de Lespinasse said, "The logic of the heart is absurd." Few will argue with her conclusion.

The world accepts silliness from those in love because practically everybody has experienced it. On the other hand, the world is convinced that our palpitating love for Jesus is absurd simply because the world has not experienced Jesus.

If you don't think the world sees our love for Jesus as absurd do what is commanded in today's reading. Constantly speak of the law of the Lord, make and wear bracelets with scripture engraved on them, write God's word on your the door posts of your house or business. The world will accuse you of carrying this religion bit too far, of being a fanatic, of being silly, and absurd.

You may be mocked and ridiculed by the world but that is incomparable to the joy of being in love with the Lord Jesus Christ. Paul wrote, *"Grace be with all those who love our Lord Jesus Christ with a love incorruptible,"* (Ephesians 6:24). Grace has been defined as unmerited favor. Isn't unmerited favor from God superior to any kind of favor from the world? Isn't the inner joy from the Lord superior to the transitory delight of the world? Be in love with Jesus.

Scripture: Philippians 4:4-8

Did you know one's life eventually reflects the thoughts of one's mind? A person who thinks about a thing will eventually act on it. This is advantageous to those seeking success. Every book on success declares what Solomon proclaimed centuries ago, *"As a man thinks in his heart, so is he,"* (Proverbs 32:7). We do become what we think about.

The mind is like a pitcher. If you fill the pitcher with polluted water you can only pour polluted water from the pitcher. If you fill the pitcher with sweet spring water you will pour sweet spring water from the pitcher. People who fill their minds with rubbish from trashy books, or trashy magazines, or trashy movies, or trashy TV, or trashy music can not help but let the trash slip out of their mouths in a weak moment. Only under extreme circumstances will people eat garbage yet many will buy garbage to fill their minds. Sin is a great deceiver.

We know that the scripture commands us to bless and give thanks. These expressions should be natural for us. But, if we have polluted our thoughts even a little the pollution will eventually surface and spill out. Pollution is never a blessing and certainly does not express thanksgiving to God.

To avoid such a pollution overflow follow Paul's advice, *"Set your mind on the things above, not on the things that are on earth,"* (Colossians 3:2). You are the sum total of your thoughts and they will betray you.

Scripture: Psalm 37:3-9

It could be when Jesus said, *"It is easier for a camel to go thorugh the eye of a needle than for a rich man to enter the kingdom of God,"* (Mark 10:25) He was speaking of more than money riches. It is often true that those rich in intellect also find it difficult to enter by faith into the kingdom of God.

God is not willing that any should perish therefore He has made entrance into the kingdom of Heaven as simple as possible. It is this simplicity that creates such great hurdles for the brilliant. Even those who do believe limit their blessings because of the simplicity of God's methods.

In our text we have four key words reducing all complex theology so children can understand. They are: *Trust* in the Lord; *delight* yourself in the Lord; *commit* you way to the Lord; then rest in the Lord and wait patiently for him. There is nothing difficult about that; yet the brilliant often muddy God's simplicity with lengthly and redundant exegesis.

Don't allow great learning or excellent intellect to impede you from gathering the promises with each of those words. *Trust* so you may dwell in the land; *delight* and receive the desires of your heart; *commit* and He will do it; rest and you will inherit the land. Wonderful promises go unrealized because we don't do the simple things God asks.

This is not to disparage learning just don't allow great learning to hinder simple faith.

Scripture: Exodus 4:1-9

When God calls us to some task do we wait for a miracle or some new ability before we begin? Do we continue making excuses waiting for God to do something great in our lives? Believe it or not, God has already equipped you to perform whatever task He assigns you. You may not recognize the equipment God has provided. You may even deny you have what it takes.

For example, if your call requires you to get training God has already given you a trainable mind. If you're to learn foreign languages God has placed in you what is needed to learn foreign languages. Yes, you will probably have to work hard and study long hours to develop what God has given you; but the raw material is there for you to develop.

Moses was making excuses to avoid doing the seemingly impossible task of facing Pharaoh to demand release for Israel. God had already equipped Moses for this task. Moses said, *"What if...?"* (v. 1). God said, *"What is that in your hand?"* (v. 2). Moses answered, *"A staff."* When David slew Goliath he did it with what he had in his hand— a sling. Nehemiah was a cup bearer not an architect or engineer yet he oversaw the rebuilding of Jerusalem and the temple.

When Moses claimed he didn't speak well God sent Aaron the brother Moses already had to be his spokesman. What is it you have in your hand?

Scripture: Revelation 20:11-15

Do you take lightly John's revelation because it seems so far off in time? In verse 12 we read, *"...and the dead were judged from the things which were written in the books, according to their deeds."* Whenever accountability is remote we tend to ignore it.

A young person seeking a scholarship may cheat on an exam. A business person may accept a small gratuity to assure a contract goes to a particular client. A lonesome wife succombs to temptation ignoring her marriage vows. Each has rationalized the correctness of their behavior. Each also forgets that God is keeping a record of the things we do in the body. Think not? *"And among the sons of the priests who had married foreign wives were found the sons of Jeshua the son of Jozadak, and his brothers..."* etc. (Ezra 10:18ff).

That's the bad news. The good news is there is forgiveness through the blood of Jesus Christ. "Oh, boy, now I can sin all I want." Not hardly! Paul wrote, *"Are we to continue in sin that grace may increase? May it never be! How shall we who died to sin still live in it?"* (Romans 5:1-2). John encourages us, *"...if anyone does sin, we have an Advocate with the Father, Jesus Christ the righteous,"* (1 John 2:1).

It's not the getting caught by our fellow man that should concern us; God already knows and has a written record. Keep your record clean by daily repenting.

Scripture: Luke 16:19-23

If you are not familiar with the Bible you will garner a lot of misinformation. The film version of a short story by John Updike was filled with outright lies portrayed as truth. The story told of teenager wanting to know where the soul goes at death. The 'preacher' supposedly quoting the Bible said the soul sleeps. The boy's parents said not to worry since he was young and strong. Most writers and most film producers can not tell the truth about the Bible or the Christian faith.

What does the Bible say about the soul's destiny at death? Jesus said, *"...it came about that the poor man died and was carried by the angels to Abraham's bosom and the rich man also died and was buried,"* (v. 22). Abraham's bosom was the Hebrew designation of heaven, the presence of God. Jesus continued, *"and in Hades he lifted up his eyes, being in torment and saw Abraham far away and Lazarus in his bosom."* No long sleep stated or implied here. Paul wrote, *"We are of good courage, I say and prefer rather to be absent from the body and to be at home with the Lord,"* (2 Corinthians 5:8). No sleep state mentioned here.

Don't trust most fiction writers or the filmmakers for Bible knowledge because if they really do quote the Bible it will be quoted out of context, and/or twisted, or grossly misapplied to the situation. If you want to now what the Bible says, READ IT!

Scripture: Judges 6:11-27

Gideon was the sixth of thirteen judges to deliver Israel after the death of Joshua. Within a generation after Joshua was buried Israel neglected the Lord's ordinances, worshipped false gods resulting in punishment. God sent one foreign army after another to punish His people for their unfaithfulness. Like us when life became too unpleasant they repented and returned to the Lord. Then the Lord called forth a leader from among the people to lead them to victory. This cycle was repeated throughout Israel's history. In Gideon's day God sent the Midianites against Israel.

What kind of man was Gideon? First, he was a man of faith, Judges 6:3 & 17-24. He was a man of humble circumstances, *"My family is the least in Manasseh, and I am the youngest in my father's house,"* (v. 15). He was a man of obedience and courage for in the night he pulled down the altar of Baal by God's command, (v. 25-27). Gideon was also a careful man in determining the Lord's will by putting out the fleece (Judges 6:32-40). He was a worshipping man (Judges 7:15). Finally, he was a man who placed full confidence in God by routing the enemy with a mere three hundred men as God had commanded.

In every age, in every nation there are Gideons pulling down the strongholds of Satan, routing the enemy, and re-establishing the Lord's people. Are you a person of faith, obedience, courage, and confidence? Is God calling you?

Scripture: Joshua 14:6-12

The ages of Bible heroes may amaze you. Abraham was 100 and Sarah a mere 90 when Isaac was born. Sarah died at 127 years of age. Afterward, at over 137, Abraham married Keturah and bore 12 more children. He lived to be 175 years old (Genesis 25:7). Caleb said, *"And now behold...I am eighty five years old today. I am still as strong today as I was in the day Moses send me; as my strength was then, so my strength is now, for war and for going out and coming in,"* (vv. 10-11). Joshua served the Lord till his dying day age 110 (Joshua 24:29). David ruled Israel for 70 years (1 Kings 2:11).

There is no age limit in the Lord's service. And retirement means going home to glory. Unless you're ready for retirement you're still on the job and under orders from the Lord.

God always strengthens for the work he has for you. Whether you're nine or ninety God has a place of service for you. At 82 my mother complained of being useless. We reminded her that it was her prayers that kept the rest of us going. Can you get so old you can't pray?

Until the Lord calls you home to retirement you need to be busy about the Father's business; busy serving Him according to the ability He gives you. "Christian's don't retire," said Charles Stanley, "they retread." It's up to you, retreading or retirement. What will it be?

Scripture: 2 Timothy 2:1-4

Writing to the captains of the Virginia regiments during the revolutionary war, George Washington said, "Discipline is the soul of an army. It makes small numbers formidable; procures success to the weak, and esteem to all." Discipline is the soul of your life in Christ.

If we expect to win spiritual battles we must be as disciplined as any army on the earth. Our Captain is Jesus Christ. If we are truly committed to Him we should discipline ourselves to be good soldiers of the cross. Not in the sense of the Crusaders but battling sin in our lives, in our communities, and in our nation.

It does not take large numbers when the soldiers are disciplined, trained, prepared for the battle. Herein lies the rub. So few believers are disciplined. Fewer still are trained or prepared to do battle with the hosts of hell. Surveys indicate most people believe the Bible; but very few are studying it.

Those attending worship on Sunday mornings far outnumber those in Bible Study. Training for the army of the Lord involves more than Bible study. It involves suffering, (v. 3). It means not getting involved with affairs that do not profit a soldier of the Lord, (v. 4).

Paul referred to Epaphroditus and Archippus as a fellow soldiers, (Philippians 2:25 and Philemon 2). The first century disciples were few in number but they turned the world upside down for Jesus sake. Begin disciplining yourself to be a good soldier for Jesus.

Scripture: Deuteronomy 31:24-29

In the days of Chaucer and even Shakespeare there were few Bibles. What Bibles there were were chained to stalls in the churches. People depended on the clergy to deliver the word. It was not all the fault of the church. Most people could not have read the word if they had it. Though by circa A.D. 1040 the Chinese were using movable earthenware type, in Chaucer's England Bibles were still being copied by hand. In 1455 Gutenberg printed the first Bible but costs were high preventing many from purchasing a Bible.

Today the story is quite different. Nearly every home in the western hemisphere has at least one Bible. Many American homes have several Bibles. In many Christian homes every family member has a Bible.

Why all these Bibles in the hands of the people? Moses said that the Law was to remain as a witness against us. The Bible is to keep us from corrupting ourselves, to guide us in right living, to lead us to salvation through Jesus Christ. God directed Jeremiah to write His words on a scroll (Jeremiah 30:8), "...*that it may serve in the time to come as a witness forever.*"

We should read it for ourselves. We should gather in Bible study groups on Sunday and at other times to discuss it. If you fail to take advantage of your freedom and opportunity to read, study, and interpret the Bible you cheat yourself out of an awesome treasure.

Scripture: Deuteronomy 8:1-9

Why does the Lord test His people? To find out about them? To learn their ways? Before we answer these questions we must decide whether God is omniscient or not. If God is not omniscient then we can answer those questions in the affirmative. Since God is omniscient we must ask again, why does God test His people?

Why was God testing Israel in the wilderness for forty years? God knew what was in their heart; but they didn't. The testing was to reveal to them their true nature. Often we think we are quite different than we really are. We have convinced ourselves that under such and such a circumstance we will do thus and so. Then a similar experience overtakes us and we fail to live up to our own expectations.

All during the testing and teaching God was taking care of Israel. Their clothes and sandals did not wear out and they never went hungry. God was preparing them for nationhood. God was preparing them to endure in the place He was establishing them.

James wrote, *"Consider it all joy, my brethren when you encounter various trials, knowing that the testing of your faith produces endurance,"* (James 1:2-3). That endurance is preparing you for a place God wants to establish you. That place may not be in a particular land but in a particular work or position. Perhaps God is strengthening you for some tough times ahead.

Testing is for your benefit.

Scripture: Psalm 41

Friendships are wonderful. A close intimate friendship is a rare treasure. A friend who loves you as a brother or sister is more precious than gold. When such relationships cease for whatever reason, the loss is great and not easily forgotten.

The closer the friendship the more painful the dissolution of that friendship. Some who have suffered the anguish of a broken friendship become gun shy. They avoid making friends reasoning that if they don't develop close relations they will be insulated from hurt.

To have a dear friend turn against you is very painful. David complained to the Lord, *"Even my close friend, in whom I trusted, Who ate my bread, Has lifted up his heel against me,"* (v. 9).

Where do you turn for comfort when someone you've loved and trusted becomes your enemy? You may be wary of other friends or relatives. You may feel they too will become an enemy.

Paul wrote, *"Blessed be the God and Father of our Lord Jesus Christ, the Father of mercies and God of all comfort; who comforts us in all our affliction,"* (2 Corinthians 1:3-4). As David turned to the Lord for comfort, and sustaining so must we.

God will soothe your broken heart. He will mend your shattered emotions. God can, if we let Him, bring beauty from the ashes of a broken relationship.

The next time you lift your heel against God remember how your friend hurt you.

Scripture: John 9:13-23

Be careful when someone says something or someone is not of God? Repeatedly the Pharasees proclaimed Jesus was not from God though Christ Himself claimed He was (John 20:21).

Jesus did not keep their rules causing the Pharasees to reject Him. This problem of keeping rules carried over into the New Testament church. Paul battled against 'church rules' (Galatians 2:4 & 14); as did Ignatius in the second century over the keeping of the Sabbath.

Fear is used to keep people in line with church rules. Being put out of the church supposedly causes folks to lose their salvation, or standing in the community, ad infinitum. The church must operate by the grace and love of God. When church rules are in conflict with God's Word it is man seeking to control. Don't be afraid of being put out a church like that; it's time to get out of that church.

The blind man's parents cheated themselves out of the blessing of knowing and following Jesus for fear they'd be put out of the synagogue (v. 22). Did they rejoice that their son could now see? Would they have stopped Jesus from making clay on the Sabbath and forfeite their son's eyesight to keep their place in the Synagogue? We may never know; but what about you?

Paul wrote, *"It was for freedom that Christ set us free; therefore keep standing firm and do not be subject again to a yoke of slavery,"* (Galatians 5:1).

Scripture: Exodus 32:7-14

We are in greater trouble today than we were a century ago. For who is standing in the breach?   A multitude of testimonies have been given about a godly parent or grandparent who stood in the breach and averted God's judgment on a loved one. Who today is standing in the breach?

Is it the lack of godly parents or grandparents? Possibly, but how do godly parents and grandparents spend their time today. We are inundated with distractions. With all our time savers we have less time than a century ago; less time for prayer, for family, for God. Is it a matter of self-discipline?

Who rises before the break of day to lift up a wayward child to the Lord?   Whose knees are callused from pleading before the throne of heaven?   Where are those who will stand in the gap not only for a wayward child but for a wayward nation?

God has not changed and neither has man. Thus the wrath of God still hangs over the head of the ungodly. God wanted to destroy Israel because they were *"obstinate"* (v. 10). God would have destroyed Israel, *"...Had not Moses His chosen one stood in the breach before Him, To turn away His wrath from destroying them,"* (Psalm 106:23).

Do you know a wayward child? Do you have a wayward friend, neighbor, spouse? You must stand in the breach. There may not be anyone else who can turn away the wrath of God.

Scripture: 1 Timothy 4:13-16

The great scripture verse for training and discipleship says, "Study to show thyself approved of God a workman that needs not be ashamed rightly dividing the Word of Truth," (2 Timothy 2:15KJV).

State law requires children to attend school hoping they will learn and become productive citizens. God has provided His word for us hoping we will learn and become productive Christians. Remember part of the great commission involves *"teaching"*. We are to go making disciples, baptizing them and, *"...teaching them to observe all things that I commanded you..."* (Matthew 28:20).

Children spend approximately six hours a day five days a week forty weeks a year learning all manner of things in order to be productive citizens. This is 1200 hours a year. If it is important for children to spend that amount of time to learn the transient things of life how important must it be for us to be learning about God's eternal things. If your Bible study is limited to an hour in Sunday School each week that's four percent of the training a child receives in secular things.

How much time should you spend each day in learninging to be a productive Christian? Busyness is a poor excuse. We manage to squeeze in our priorities. What higher priority is there than learning to be a productive child of God through studying His Word.

Take the learning challenge study your Bible atleast an hour a day. God will bless you for it.

Scripture: Isaiah 26:1-8

Some people seem to lead charmed lives. On a crowded parking lot they find a space near the door. Approaching the Interstate there is a break in the traffic at just the right moment. The rain has poured down all morning; but just as the 'charmed one' is ready to leave the rain pauses. Are these folks lucky?

No! The term luck implies chance and chaos. It proclaims that God is not in control which of course He is. These 'charmed ones' are not lucky but blessed. We know why God blesses some folks but not others. Isaiah says, *"The way of the righteous is smooth..."* (v. 7). We may argue that a certain righteous person has a rough path. We may argue our viewpoint; but God sees the heart. Jesus said some people were like white washed tombs, appearing righteous but full of rottenness within.

Have you had any of these good experiences? If so, whom or what received the credit? A Christian should never attribute anything to luck. The world does because it doesn't know any better. The child of God should praise His Name, should thank Him, for ever-thing. Paul wrote, *"in everything give thanks..."* (1 Thessalonians 5:18). Yes, in everything.

Be steadfast in mind so the Lord can keep you in perfect peace (v. 3). Trust Him at all times, in every circumstance. When God blesses you in small matters praise His Name out loud. Don't be ashamed of Jesus.

Scripture: Daniel 6:16-23

There are experiences we wish we could avoid. Painful times when we lose a job, spouse, or must face hard trials. We may face persecution because we stand firm in our faith. If we knew the future we may be tempted to do everything in our power to avoid it.

God is so gracious. He hides the future from us. Knowledge of tomorrow's sorrow would slay today's joy. In our hearts God has planted hope. It is a rare believer who gives up hope for a brighter tomorrow.

Then there are those times when we are required to take a stand fully cognizant of impending suffering. *"Now when Daniel knew that the document was signed, he entered his house (now in his roof chamber he had windows open toward Jerusalem): and he continued kneeling on his knees three times a day, praying and giving thanks before his God, as he had been doing previously,"* (Daniel 6:10). What would you have done in Daniel's circumstances? Or Shadrach's, Meshach's, or Abednego's for that matter?

We think God should detour us around the fiery furnaces and the lion pits; but He doesn't. God does not save us from these things but through them. Which is the greater testamony: avoiding calamity or surviving calamity? What do you think?

Of course no one in his right mind wishes to suffer. Yet, if our suffering brings glory to Christ we should not seek to avoid it. Who knows, God may save you through it.

Scripture: Matthew 13:53-58

Our God is able. There is nothing beyond God's ability except He cannot go against His own nature. God will not do anything that is contrary to Himself.

We humans frequently cut off our noses to spite our faces. God is wiser than that. We coerce people to decide a certain way, to behave a certain way, to obey us. Did you know God has never forced anyone to do anything?

As I often told my oldest son when he grew too big to spank, "I can't make you but I can make you wish you had. That's the way God operates. He doesn't make us. He could make us do whatever He wanted if He went against His own nature. He does make us wish we had been obedient. Surely Saul often repented of his disobedience — it cost him is kingship.

God gave us the freedom of choice at creation. He has never taken that freedom from us. Jesus did not force healing on the people of Nazareth. His desire was to heal them but they refused to believe.

God will not force even something good on those who don't want it. If He did no one would be lost. God would force redemption on everyone, they'd all be saved whether they like it or not.

Rejoice that God does not force Himself on us. Instead he woos us, calls us, invites us. How will you respond to Him?

Scripture: Jeremiah 20:7-13

Jeremiah was a fanatic. Are you one? Are your friends and acquaintances speaking about you as Jeremiah's friends and acquaintances spoke about him? They denounced him (v. 10) and sought his downfall.

The world doesn't persecute it's own fanatics. Sports fanatics are praised and encouraged. Special cause fanatics are lauded and glorified. Fanatic workers are teased but not laughed at. A fanatic for the Lord, on the other hand, is royally condemned, laughed at, and ridiculed.

You may have bumber stickers advertising every worldly thing, it's OK. Put a Jesus bumper sticker on your car and immediately you're a fanatic.

Praise the Lord for brave fanatics like Jeremiah who couldn't help but speak the word of the Lord. Jeremiah was so persecuted that he tried not to speak for the Lord. He confessed that God's word was like a fire *"shut up"* in his bones. He had to let it out.

Every believer should have the testimony of the Lord as a fire shut up in his bones. We should be that eager to tell what the Lord has done for us. You can be sure, if you lived and spoke your testimony as Jeremiah did you would be persecuted as Jeremiah was.

Try it and see. Try it at the super market, in your work place, on the street, among your neighbors. Though ridiculed Jeremiah said, *"...the Lord is with me like a dread champion..."* (v. 11). God will be with you, too.

Scripture: Luke 13:22-30

The Bible is so clear regarding God's plan of redemption yet multitudes try sundry methods that sound good to them. God's plan is so simple; but the multitudes clutter it with copious amendments. Some totally ignore God's plan convencing themselves they will be saved by osmosis, absorption, or by contact.

Jesus mentioned this latter group in verse 26 of today's reading. Just because they had been in the presence of Jesus they thought it sufficient for salvation. Since they had eaten with Jesus it was sufficient bonding for eternal life. Some had touched Jesus in the crowds thinking this would do the trick. We are not saved, redeemed, born again by any of these methods.

In both the Old and New Testaments we have the clarion call, "...*whoever calls on the name of the Lord Will be delivered,*" (Joel 2:32). And, "...*Whoever will call upon the name of the Lord will be saved,*" (Romans 10:13). It is so uncomplicated no one is excluded. The simplest mind can comprehend trusting Jesus.

To play with, adjust, amend, ignore God's simple plan of salvation is to do wickedness. Those deluding themselves with 'other' plans are called "*evildoers*" (verse 27). Why wickedly? Why called evildoers? Because they think they know more than God, that they are wiser than God, that they have a better plan. In addition, they commit the serious crime of deluding others into believing their nonsense.

Simply trust in the Lord and be saved.

Scripture: Psalm 119:9-16

What would you call a nutritious product that was totally good for you, absolutely free of calories, no salt, no sugar, yet tasty and delicious? It is consumable but you never run out of it. One purchase is all that is necessary and you may already have it on the shelf at home. The digestion of it is guaranteed satisfying. The only side affect is occasional heart ache, sometimes a bit tough to swallow, but absolutely good for you. It is guaranteed to change your life, your outlook, and you, if taken in large doses daily. Would such a product be sought by millions of people?

It may sell well but it is not consumed in large doses daily by millions of people. Many can not digest it, many claim no benefit from it, and many call it a placebo. Nevertheless, those who know the One who made it available receive great benefit from it and actually believe their lives would be impoverished without it.

Naturally it's the Bible. God's Holy Word provides all those things listed above. They are available to you absolutely without cost. An additional benefit is the more you consume it the more beneficial it becomes. Take the Bible reading challenge. Spend a minimum of 30 minutes a day reading it. Before long you'll discover thirty minutes is not enough for you'll crave more and more of the life giving nutrition. You don't starve your body why starve your soul?

Scripture: 2 Corinthians 5:11-19

The church and a bowl of popped corn are much alike. The significant similarity is the newness of each individual piece. *"Therefore if any man is in Christ, he is a new creature; the old things passed away; behold new things have come,"* (v. 17). Popped corn is not what it used to be. The Christian is not what he used to be.

Another likeness, the Christian did not become one through some long laborious process. Upon saying, 'yes', to Jesus he was saved, 'pop' in an instant. Isn't it that way with popped corn? Does the kernel slowly evolve into a popped kernel? Of course not, it explodes into its newness.

Another similarity, search all you want, no two pop corn kernels are exactly alike. There are strong resemblances but no two are exactly alike. This is also true of Christians. In some churches there are those who would press everyone into a mold. Such action anialates the freedom we have in Christ. Our similarity should be to love God and to love our neighbors. Remember what Jesus identified as the two greatest commandments.

Those pressing for conformity are the spiritually immature who have difficulty handling life without a strict code of discipline. They will never mount up with wings like eagles. They'll lay at the bottom of the bowl all hard and cold hurling accusations at those who are free in Jesus Christ. After the last saint is taken up to glory, those hard nuts may be left behind.

Scripture: 1 Timothy 2:1-8

Have you ever wondered about the sundry worship practices you encounter. In one church everything is solemn, in another there are lifted hands, even dancing in the spirit. In between are various degrees of either extreme. Each practice can be defended scripturally. The solemn service certainly follows Paul's admonition, *"...let all things be done properly and in an orderly manner,"* (1 Corinthians 14:40). In the same chapter Paul writes about praying and singing in the Spirit (vv. 14-15). In today's reading Paul writes, *"...I want the men in every place to pray, lifting up holy hands, without wrath and dissension,"* (v. 8).

Lifting hands in worship is not peculiar to Paul. The psalmist wrote, *"Lift up your holy hands to the sanctuary, And bless the Lord,"* (Psalm 134:2). David wrote, *"So I will bless Thee as long as I live; I will lift up my hands in Thy name,"* (Psalm 63:4). David was reprimanded by a jealous wife for dancing before the Lord and she had no child to the day of her death (2 Samuel 6:23).

The thorn in this briar patch is simply this: Those things the Bible portrays and does not condemn should not be forbidden by men. The scriptures say we have far greater freedom than we enjoy. Yet, congregations claiming to follow the whole Bible deny others free exercise of worship. Neither should you coerce another to worship a certain way. Attend the worship where you receive the greatest benefit.

Scripture: Colossians 3:12-17

Key words here are, "forgiving each other". Practicing forgiveness is so vital to obedient Christian living. The old song said, "Love and marriage go together like a horse and carriage". Love and forgiveness are married terms. You can't fully love without fully forgiving. The one presupposes the other. There is excellent reasoning for forgiving one another.

Lack of forgiveness gives Satan the advantage (2 Corinthians 2:10-11). How so?

When there is an unforgiving spirit the *"perfect bond of unity,"* (v. 14) is destroyed. How can there be unity when there is animosity among the members? Animosity is one of the fruits of an unforgiving spirit. Unforgiveness robs the believer of the *"peace of Christ,"* (v. 15). Unforgiveness spawns hatred in the one and dumps sorrow on the heart of the other. Where is the peace in that?

When one is filled with hatred and another with sorrow where is there room for the *"word of Christ to dwell richly?"* (v. 16). If you are holding a grudge against someone how can you be thankful to the Lord? See how Satan gains the advantage when we fail to forgive?

Why wouldn't someone want to forgive? Psychologists and counselors may provide volumes of wrong answers. We may ourselves blame numerous motives to avoid facing the truth. The simple and correct answer for not forgiving one another is pride.

Satan tempts us through our pride at every opportunity. Forgive one another and don't give Satan the advantage.

Scripture: Exodus 33:12-18

Does God have favorites? You bet; but the way is open for anyone who desires to be God's favorite. You can find favor in God's sight as did Noah and Moses. You can be a person after God's own heart just like David.

How does one go about finding favor in God's sight? The same way these three found favor in God's sight. If you examine the lives of those whom God favored in the Old and New Testaments you'll see the same qualities emerging. The qualities every believer should possess and nurture.

With Moses God spoke face to face. That is not true of any other person in scripture except Jesus who came down from the Father. Moses was very special to God.

Look at Moses's desires in today's reading. *"Now therefore, I pray Thee, if I have found favor in Thy sight, let me know Thy ways, that I may know Thee, so that I may find favor in Thy sight..."* (v. 13). Moses sought to know God, not swell his head with knowledge; but to be a better servant, a better leader, a qualified spokesman for God.

Why do you want favor with God? To satisfy your ego? To lift you up in the eyes of men? To receive many blessings?

When you desire to please the Father in everything you will find God's favor as did Noah, Moses, David, and others. That should be every believer's desire.

Scripture: Psalm 32:1-7

What is your immediate reaction to sin in your life? After the meager gratification has dispersed, after shame has set in, what do you do about sin?

Most of us do not come running to the Father for forgiveness or restoration of our relationship to Him. We are ashamed and avoid God at all costs, perhaps even staying away from church if the sin was serious enough. We behave this way because Satan has convinced us that God is angry and is going to punish us. Little children try to hide their mistakes, their disobedience to avoid punishment. So we adults trying to hide our sin also act like little kids. All the while we forget that God knew of our sin before we committed it.

What did the psalmist say happened when he tried to hide his sin? *"...my body wasted away...my vitality was drained away..."* (vv. 3-4). David did not ask for his salvation to be restored, he asked for the JOY of God's salvation to be restored (Psalm 51:12). You've experienced that, right? What's the cure?

The psalmist also gave us the cure for wasted body and wasted vitality. When he confessed his sin God forgave him of the quilt of his sin. Satan doesn't want you to experience forgiveness, he doesn't want your relationship with the Father restored.

"If anyone sins we have an advocate with the Father, Jesus Christ the righteous..." (1 John 2:1). Confess your sins and God will forgive you.

Scripture: Luke 10:1-9

One of the basic principles every disciple must learn is trust Jesus for every need you may encounter in service to the King of kings. When God calls you to go and do, He assumes the responsibility of providing the means.

God provides along the way. We were called to go on a five thousand mile journey with limited cash and no credit cards. Have you tried reserving a motel without a credit card? God provided delightfully every night for our comfort and safety. We stayed in places we would never have known about using credit cards. Each provision was made differently from the previous night's lodging. God's provision seemd capricious but was merely the fulfillment of the plans He had before we locked the door and left. Our fretting about places to stay revealed our meager faith. Looking back we see how much fun it was going God's way.

The seventy were sent out without purse or bag. This is not a beggars bag as some interpret. Neither Jesus nor His disciples were beggars. The seventy receive sufficient provision as their journey progressed (Luke 22:35). Jesus met their needs. This was not a journey to teach physical endurance but to experience the results of trusting Jesus.

The disciples believed Jesus to be the Messiah, the Son of God. Since nothing is impossible why not trust Him for their physical needs day by day? What about you?

God knows what you need before you even ask (Matthew 6:8). The truth is God has already made the provision before you realize you need it. Learn the basics, trust Jesus.

Scripture: Luke 22:35-38

These verses do NOT contradict Jesus's words in chapter 10. Jesus will soon be crucified, the situation of the disciples will drastically change. Provision will be as sufficient as when He sent out the seventy. So why does He now seem to contradict His earlier injunction.

Those making the provision are not now going to be as abundant. They will need money to pay their way when friends are not available. They will need to take traveling bags with clothes, sandals.

The first journey was through familiar territory — Galilee. Soon they will be sent throughout the world. Not only will friends be far apart they will face enemies, robbers, murderers and the like. Thus the reason for the sword. Paul testifies, *"I have been on frequent journeys, in dangers from rivers, dangers from robbers, dangers from my own countrymen, dangers from the Gentiles, dangers in the city, dangers in the wilderness..."* (2 Corinthians 11:26). Jesus warns that a sword will have greater value than a coat. It's far better to be exposed to the elements than be killed by the enemy.

This new injunction means the disciples are to use common sense, to be prudent, to be prepared as far as possible for every eventuality. Jesus will indeed be with them amid the care and prudence they themselves exercise.

No less are we expected to exercise good judgment as we go forth in service to the King. We too must go prepared.

Scripture: Ephesians 5:8-13

Jesus said, *"A lamp is not brought to be put under a peck-measure, is it, or under a bed? Is it not brought to be put on a lampstand?"* (Mark 4:21). Have you wondered what keeps Christian peck baskets from burning up? I mean all those who put their light under a basket.

I discovered a person I've known for a long time is a Christian. He has all the fine qualities of a Christian but then a lot of lost people also have those qualities. I was shocked because this person has had ample opportunity to mention it.

Why do some people witness while others seem embarrassed by their faith in Jesus Christ? Here are some possible answers.

Perhaps they've been washed by baptismal waters but never by the blood of Jesus Christ. Maybe their life style is contradictory to a life in Christ and they don't want to appear hypocritical. Perhaps some cling to a pet sin. Some are naturally shy, but this trait fits well into the principles of love and forgeiveness. Some may be self-centered instead of Christ-centered. Others may feel inadequate or insecure so they hide behind a facade of pride.

What barriers impede your testamony. The Holy Spirit will point out these barriers if you sincerely want to know. Once these barriers are identified, then you can deal with them. In most cases these barriers are only smoke screens created by Satan. Blow the smoke away and tell others what Jesus has done for you.

Scripture: 2 Chronicles 36:20-23

SOOTHSAYER: Beware the ides of March.
CAESAR: He is a dreamer, let us leave him. Pass.

So go the lines in Shakespeare's play *Julius Caesar*. On the ides (15th) of March Caesar was cut down by his friends. We accept Shakespeare's play without question. Isn't it interesting how we accept the prophecy of a fictitious soothsayer as true but ignore the fulfillment of prophecy in scripture?

Jeremiah prophecied, *"For thus says the Lord, 'When seventy years have been completed for Babylon, I will visit you and fulfill My good word to you, to bring you back to this place,'"* (Jeremiah 29:10). Daniel wrote, *"In the first year of Darius the son of Ahasuerus, of Median descent, who was made king over the kingdom of the Chaldeans— in the first year of his reign I, Daniel, observed in the books the number of years which was revealed as the word of the Lord to Jeremiah the prophet for the completion of the desolations of Jerusalem, namely, seventy years,"* (Daniel 9:1-2).

Daniel observed in the books... There is much prophecy remaining in the *book* which has not been fulfilled. Are we like Daniel reading it? Are we taking heed? Or do we treat the prophecy in God's word as Caesar treated the prophecy of the soothsayer claiming it to be merely the words of a dreamers?

A lot of Bible prophecy is in the process of ongoing fulfillment. Study the prophecies of scripture and believe them. They will be fulfilled.

Scripture: Jeremiah 13:1-11

God is not bound by human reason. His ways are higher than our's. He asks us to obey and believe. The Lord instructed Jeremiah to do what seemed unreasonable by human standards. Jeremiah was to purchase a linen waist band, wear it, then traipse two thousand miles across the fertile crescent and hide it in a rock by the Euphrates River.

Jeremiah obeyed but he surely must have wondered what God was doing. He wondered about it for the time it takes to walk two thousand miles. Was Satan on vacation all this time? No way! He nipped at Jeremiah's heels every step trying to get him to doubt the word of the Lord, trying to get him to rebel against God's direction. He does the same to us when we choose to be obedient to the Lord.

Having hid the waist band Jeremiah returned home. Can't you hear Satan objurgating Jeremiah saying, "This is dumb. You are really stupid. Of all the weird things you've done this takes the cake." Hasn't Satan spoken to you in such manner when you were being obedient to the Lord?

Jeremiah arrived home still not understanding. Then the Lord told Jeremiah to retrieve the waistband. In desperation Satan began hitting harder. Jeremiah traversed the two thousand miles and unearthed the waist band. It was ruined but Jeremiah had a message for Judah. The message for us is a clear call to obedience. There is no sin in wondering 'why'; the sin lies in doubt and disobedience.

Scripture: John 1:1-5

One atom said to the chairman of the molecular compendium, "I want to amend rule three." Another atom jiggled, "I second the amendment." The chairmolecule asked for questions; being none he announced, "All in favor of amending rule three raise an electron." Does that sound silly? Would you believe a grown educated man describing creation with such non-sense? This same scientist has received wide-spread critical acclaim. Timothy Ferris actually said, "The atoms comprising the far flung galaxies all obey the same laws because they got together at the dawn of time and worked out the rules of the game."[1]

Was he serious? His statement is as scientific as the theories of evolution. It seems scientists have more problems convincing the world of their theories than theologians have convincing the world of a God initiated, God directed creation. Evolutionists hark their theories continuously. Whom are they trying to convince? Themselves?

Evolutionists go to great lengths of complex explanation, even deny common scientific practice to avoid giving God any credit.

We know better. We have the first book of science, the Bible. Let's learn from these theorists and gather stones for our slings against the evolution Goliath. Hurl the facts of God's word against the bluster of the evolutionists. Part of Mr. Ferris' statement supports the Bible, God created it all, "in the beginning." Of course the atoms comprising the galaxies obey the same rules. **God wrote the rules.**

[1]OMNI, November 1984, p. 6

Scripture: Mark 1:32-39

Rarely a week passes but what we hear of a church about to have turmoil, in the midst of turmoil, or recovering from turmoil. In every instance blame is heaped on individuals. Sometimes long time members serve as the culprits, sometimes the leadership, even the pastor or his wife.

Church turmoil is not selective, it is not restricted to denominations, or independent churches. There is, however, a pattern regarding which churches become embroiled in controversy. Churches that are making progress in the kingdom of God are targeted.

The camouflage prevents the truth from getting out. A myriad of 'reasons' are proclaimed. The turmoil started because someone was losing their control of the congregation, or the pastor uses the 'wrong' translation, or too many changes, or, or, or. Camouflage is camouflage.

Sometimes the camouflage is a real problem but it is still camouflage to hide the real culprit. ALL church turmoil is the result of somebody listening to the Devil. They listened because they were lied to, or deceived into thinking they had the answer, or that they were right, or that somehow God had called them to be a spiritual hero.

Notice verse 39 of today's reading. There were demons in the synagogue and there are demons in the church. The demons are in the church for one purpose: to tear it up and destroy its effectiveness.

When you encounter church turmoil you'll know its source. Cast the out demons and keep the flock together following God's undershepherd— the pastor.

Scripture: Exodus 34:29-35

Those who spend time with Jesus really are radiant. When Jesus told His followers, *"Let your light shine,"* (Matthew 5:16). He was being literal.

Sadly we make too much scripture figurative, or spiritualize it then wonder where the power is. The power is impeded by our unwillingness to take God at His word, which is a lack of faith.

Those who really glow for Jesus are as unaware of their radiance as Moses was of the shekinah glory on his own face. Shekinah in rabbinic writings refers to the presence or dwelling place of the Lord. Thus we understand that God was dwelling with Moses for the glory of the Lord was on his face.

In this Christian era (since the time of Christ's ministry on earth) those who believe on the Lord Jesus Christ have the Holy Spirit dwelling in them. We should therefore glow. Some do. One person described a certain group of Christians saying, "Those people glow." Shouldn't we all?

What keeps us from glowing for the Lord? Soot keeps the light trapped in a lantern. Sin keeps the light trapped in a believer. To release the light from a lantern we must scrub the soot from the globe. Then and only then can the true brilliance escape shedding light into dark places. The same is true for the believer, daily repentance scrubs off the soot of sin so your light can shine into this dark world. Repent and let your light shine.

Scripture: Deuteronomy 8:16-20

Keep an eye on your ego. Whenever my youngest daughter would encounter someone with an enlarged ego she'd say, "They're puffy." When something is puffy it is usually full of wind. Windy folks are more tolerated than loved.

What makes us windy? The third category of sin. *"For all that is in the world, the lust of the flesh, the lust of the eyes, and the pride of life, is not from the Father, but is from the world,"* (1 John 2:16). All sin falls into one of those three categories. And Satan has been encouraging us to puff up our egos since he tempted Eve in the Garden of Eden. We like to brag even if the reason for bragging did not come by our own efforts or our imagined greatness.

Paul admonished the Romans, *"...I say to every man among you not to think more highly of himself than he ought to think; but to think so as to have sound judgment, as God has allotted to each a measure of faith,"* (Romans 12:3). The Israelites were not to get puffed up thinking God had brought them into the promised land because of their righteousness. To the contrary, God brought them in to punish the wickedness of the nations who possessed the land.

When God blesses you don't get puffy. God's blessings should engender humility not pride. Remember we are dust, we don't deserve God's blessings. So be grateful offering up prayers of thanksgiving.

Scripture: Psalm 102:23-28

Rejoice! God endures to all generations. You should remember and rest in the knowledge that God endures. He is from everlasting to everlasting. That should tell you something. God cannot cease to exist. He is eternal. He created the earth and the heavens which have endured to this day; but they too will someday perish.

Isn't our earth wearing out like a garment due to man's wastefulness and pollution? Aren't we consuming our resources faster than they can be replenished? And the heavens? What are scientists worried about in the heavens if it's not the ozone layer without which the earth will slowly heat up. Everything in which man trusts is wasting away. Many trust in science but it too is unstable often reversing opinions upon new discoveries. God endures.

Not only does God endure but He is the same day after day, decade after decade, Millennium after millennium looking after His own, controlling all that exists, and raising up some nations while punishing others.

How privileged we are to serve a God who endures. A God who is omnipotent, omnipresent, and omniscient. And notice what verse 28 says, "*The children of Thy servants will continue, And their descendants will be established before Thee.*" Since God is eternal the descendants who are established before God must also endure *through eternity* .

Rightfully does the next psalm say, "*Bless the Lord, O my soul; And all that is within me, bless His holy name. Bless the Lord, O my soul, and forget not all his benefits.*" Yes, rejoice and bless the Lord for he endures.

Scripture: Romans 12:1-8

When my oldest son was a student at SBU his classmates used to say the problem with Romans 12:1 is that the sacrifice keeps crawling off the altar. In a very real sense we've all done it. Yes, we renege on presenting our bodies as a living sacrifice. We are so sincere when we renew our commitment to the Lord. Then for whatever reason we ease back into our old ways.

We don't ease back into our old sins but we slack off in our commitment, which is breaking our promise. We ease up on reading the word as diligently as we had intended. For a while we do well rising before dawn to pray. We boldly proclaim the name of Jesus for a week or two.

The wonderful part of all this is God's patience, His grace, His desire to give us another opportunity to prove ourselves. Who else offers infinite chances to make good on a promise? Who else continually forgives failure then cheers us on in every renewed commitment?

God knows your heart, He knows the sincerity of your intention. And according to Hebrews God knows our struggles. *"For we do not have a hight priest who cannot sympathize with our weaknesses, but one who has been tempted in all things as we are yet without sin,"* (Hebrews 4:15). He knows and understands how difficult commitment can be. He was commited to the cross. Thank Him today for bearing with you all these years.

Scripture: James 1:21-27

Words must be understood in context. For example on my old membership card for the National Education Association is the word 'active'. What does the word mean there? Did I run for office, did I campaign for issues, did I participate in the meetings? No! Since the signer of the card didn't know my involvement the word 'active' simply meant I had paid my dues. Paying dues made me an active member whether I participated or not.

Many church members understand 'active' in the same way. Giving an offering once or twice a year they believe they've paid their dues calling themselves 'active' members. Ask them the pastor's name; better yet what did he preach on last Sunday.

The dictionary defines ACTIVE; "participating, not passive or quiescent; functioning, characterized by energetic action."[1] The word energetic also means enthusiastic.

Are you energetic, enthusiastic, excited about your church? James wrote, *"...prove yourselves doers..."* (v. 22). A doer is one who accomplishes, gets things done. A doer is a worker, a servant, causing things to happen. A doer, an active member is a builder. He is excited, enthusiastic, sold on his church. He constantly tries to attract others to it.

Are you a 'dues payer', a 'once a week attender to appease God so you can be a *get on with your on life* kind of active member? Or are you a functioning, participating, energetic, enthusiastic member getting things done in service to the Lord? How do you define the word active?

---

[1]*The American Heritage Dictionary* (Boston, Houghton Mifflin Co., 1985)

Scripture: Daniel 3:13-18

Where are real life heroes to inspire our children? Today's youth are given magical heroes to emulate. Supernatural characters which are impossible to imitate cannot serve as true heroes.

The Bible is full of real heroes from Noah to the Apostle Paul. Very human yet very great. Our nation as all others have had human heroes to emulate, praise, and appreciate. Russia has its Alexander Nevskis, England has its Winston Churchills, and we our Frederick Douglasses and George Washingtons. With a plethora of real heroes why should we cajole our children with fantasy?

Parents should emphasize that these cartoon characters are make believe but Abe Lincoln, G. W. Carver, and Albert Einstein are real flesh and blood heroes.

Every child should have a father or mother for his hero or heroine. In my hero list I must include my father and mother peremptorily. They raised me and that was heroic in itself. How often I exasperated them and thwarted their efforts to guide me in the right directon. Finally, I succombed. This was not accomplished except by a whole hearted cooperative effort on their part.

You can be a hero, a heroine by putting your whole heart into it. Scripture says, *"Train up a child in the way he should go..."* (Proverbs 22:6). Guide your children in their choice of heroes. Make Biblical heroes live by reading about them to your children. You'll never regret turning your children away from fantasy heroes to real flesh and blood heroes.

Scripture: Acts 5:26-32

Do you know who John Leland was? He was the one man most responsible for the First Amendment to the Constitution guaranteeing freedom of religion. In March 1788 he led the Virginia Baptist General Committee to press for 'guarantees' of separation of church and state. He proclaimed that the Constitution did not provide enough protection.

On July 4, 1768 five Baptist ministers had been arrested for preaching without authority of the local magistrates, compare Acts 5:28. Bail was set at £1000 each in addition to a 45 day confincement. This was one of the many atrocities driving Leland forward. Leland's friend James Madison strove to differentiate between 'toleration' and complete 'religious freedom' at the constitutional convention. Yet the guarantee was absent.

Pastor Leland preached religious liberty at every opportunity. He led Baptists to press for absolute religious freedom. Leland wrote a pamphlet with 10 objections to the Constitution foremost was the lack of a guarantee of religious liberty.

James Madison needed Baptist votes to be elected from Virginia. Baptists elected him because he already was a fiery advocate of religious liberty and had been since his student days at Princeton. Madison was in charge of formulating the Bill of Rights. He consulted men of all walks including his dear friend John Leland who said, "Let freedom of religion lead all the rest in the Bill of Rights." It does. Freedom of religion and freedom of conscience are still enjoyed by us today. May we never let these freedoms go.

Scripture: 1 Peter 3:13-17

A massive effort to discredit the Bible, Jesus, and all that we Christians believe is becoming more blatant. Not only have books been written and published but popular magazines have joined the crusade to ridicule and even reduce Christ to a mere human. Others vociferously proclaim the Bible can not be believed, that it is full of contradictions and errors.

It's nothing new. The Ebionites in the first century and the Unitarians today claim Jesus was all human and not divine and that "we'll all be saved in the end". In contrast the first century Docetics claimed Jesus to be all divine and not human, that his crucifixion was only an illusion. John wrote, *"And the Word became flesh and dwelt among us..."* (John 1:14). And, *"What was from the beginning...our hands handled..."* (1 John 1:1).

Paul warned Timothy, *"...have nothing to do with worldly fables fit only for old women..."* (1 Timothy 4:7). Peter said the untaught and unstable distort the scriptures (2 Peter 3:16).

Those claiming the Bible contradicts itself and cannot be believed cannot prove their position based on scholarly investigation. Every implied contradiction is based on incomplete knowledge and limited understanding.

You need to know what you believe, why you believe it and then take your stand. Peter wrote, *"You therefore, beloved, knowing this beforehand, be on you guard lest, being carried away by the error of unprincipled men, you fall from your own steadfastness,"* (2 Peter 3:17) Needless to say we who believe in the Lord Jesus Christ are quickly becoming a minority.

Scripture: Malachi 3:8-15

No one would deliberately toss money into a trash basket but poor stewardship is the same. We all waste dollars weekly. The biggest waste is not tithing. God challenges us to trust him saying, *"Bring the whole tithe into the storehouse...and test me now in this...if I won't...pour out for you a blessing until there is no more room,"* (v. 10).

Let's do a little math. Is nine tenths greater than seven tenths? The tither has nine tenths of his income left. The non-tither only has seven tenths left. The non-tither holds back his tenth leaving seven tenths. How so? *"If...a man wishes to redeem part of his tithe, he shall add to it one fifth,"* (Leviticus 27:31). One fifth is twenty percent added to tithe makes thirty percent. The non-tither only has seventy percent remaining.

You say, "If the non-tither won't pay the tenth he surely won't pay the fine. Yes he will. If we don't pay the tithe God collects it plus the interest. It goes for unexpected break downs, medical or legal bills; but it goes. We forget that God doesn't always harvest in the fall. A person may live well withholding the tithe; but a day of reckoning is coming.

What was God's promise? *"Test me and see if I won't bless until there is no more need."* Can your seventy percent reach till there is no more need? NO! Your ninety percent can.

Scripture: 2 Kings 13:20-21

The Bible often refers to the spring of the year. It was in the spring of the year David got in trouble with his neighbor's wife (2 Samuel 11:1ff). The king's favor is like the spring rains (Proverbs 16:15). As far as I can tell the spring of the year in scripture nearly always refers to a time of refreshing.

It was in the spring of the year the man whose body touched the bones of Elisha arose to life again. Spring is the time we think about resurrection, about new life. The deadness of winter loses its grip. Buds burst forth at the tops of the trees. The greening continues groundward until the tree has all new foliage.

Spring should remind us of the beautiful life we have in Christ after receiving Him as Lord and Savior. When you look across the hills spangled with blossoms and bright green leaves be reminded of the resurrection to new life we have in Jesus Remember how you began to blossom and bear fruit for the Savior.

Just as the man buried in Elisha's grave sprung to life when his dead body touched Elisha's bones so we too were dead in trespasses and in sins. When we were touched by the blood of Jesus in the washing and renewing of regeneration He gave us life (Titus 3:5). Thanks be to God, our bodies may experience autumn and winter but our souls have eternal spring— eternal life.

Scripture: Psalm 139:13-18

David praised God for making him as he was. He gave God glory for being aware of the formation of his bones and inward parts. He thanked God for taking so much interest in him before he was fully made. Was David special?

Yes and no. David was special in that he never turned away from God becoming a man after God's own heart. Yet, David was not special because God is aware of the formation of every bone of every creature ever conceived. He knew you before you were born and he loved you before you were conceived.

Perhaps you are not satisfied with the way God made you. Many people would change something about themselves if they could. Would you? The desire to be whole is understandable yet some of the most beautiful people are confined to a wheel chair or have other impairments. And there are some truly handsome whole people complaining about how God made them. It is not how God made you but your attitude that makes the difference.

Instead of complaining because your nose is too big, your eyes to small, your hair too thin, or something else; begin thanking the Lord for how you are made. We are all *"fearfully and wonderfully made,"* (v. 14). And God loves you despite how you feel about yourself.

The saying is trite but makes the point, "I complained because I had not shoes until I met a man who had no feet."

Scripture: Ezekiel 8:16-18

Daily sinners turn their back on God, ignoring His warnings and His promises. Yet, millions of times a day they cry, "Oh, my God!" or mention His name in some other way. The world mentions God's name but refuses to honor or serve Him.

What sinners should be saying is, "Oh, my Satan!" He is the one they serve, honor, and seek to please. Why should they call on Him in whom they do not believe? If they do believe in God they are no better than the demons (James 2:19). It is not belief in God that makes the difference but acceptance of the Lord Jesus Christ.

In the same way unbelievers should not say, "For heaven's sake". They should instead say, "For hell's sake," since it is where they're headed.

In today's text the people turned their backs on God and His temple then prostrated themselves toward 'Mecca', toward Satan, toward Baal. They filled the land with violence, committed abominations, and provoked God.

The time will come when they will seek God, call upon Him, desperately need Him. Does the world really believe that God is some great cosmic utility that it can plug into when it needs a bit of fixing, or a smidgen of power, or perhaps a miracle? Then when all is well pull the plug and go its marry way.

God says, "...*though they cry in my ears with a loud voice, yet I shall not listen to them.*"

Scripture: John 5:1-9

Understanding character is one of the things I emphasized during two decades of teaching English and American literature. My students taught me there is more than one way to understand a character's words, motives, predicament. So you may not agree with my understanding of the man by the pool of Bethesda. I offer it as only one point of view.

He was the typical excuse maker. He's the fellow who never takes responsibility for himself. He wimpers and whines over his predicament making only unsuccessful efforts to resolve his difficulty. It seems in thirty-eight years he could have been cured of his ailments. "Oh, woe is me!" is his constant cry.

There are those today who wring every milligram of sympathy from any listener they can snag. When one listener leaves they tug the sleeve of another. We meet them at the market, in church, at work. Nothing is ever their fault. The reasons for their condition range from the ridiculous to the sublime.

Jesus asked him, *"Do you wish to get well?"* Does he say, "Yes"? Does he really want to be healed? Look at his answer. Excuses, excuses, excuses. How shocked he was when Jesus overruled him saying, *"Arise, take up your pallet and walk."* He was so shocked, he did so.

Poor man, now he must be a productive citizen. When you meet excuse makers tell them you'll pray for them to become whole productive people. Maybe they'll start avoiding you.

Scripture: 1 Samuel 25:9-17

On this first day of April pranksters enjoy playing tricks on others. Children especially delight in 'getting one over' on a friend or playmate. Usually these pranks are harmless. The term fool however has an entirely different connotation in scripture.

The word for fool in Hebrew is nabal and denotes a wicked person rather than one who merely lacks sense. Nabal's wife Abigail described her husband as, *"this worthless man,"* (1 Samuel 25:25). His actions prove his name.

In the wisdom literature the word fool takes on a different sense. Here it is contrasted with wisdom which comes from God. Thus in the wisdom literature 'fool' means someone who is incogitant, careless, arrogant, self-sufficient, and indifferent to God and His purposes. These are the scoffers of wisdom, instruction, and faith. The Proverbs warn against associating with a fool. There are different words for those lacking common sense, who are ignorant, or who engage in silliness.

In the Greek one of the words translated 'fool' is moros from which we get our word moron. This word denotes a lack of sense or intellect. After reading the full report of David, Nabal and Abigail we might attach the term moron to Abigail's husband.

The real fool or moron anytime of year is the one rejecting God's wisdom, instruction, and redemption. Do you know any fools, those admitting they need to accept Jesus but refusing to do so? Don't give up trying to give them wisdom.

Scripture: Nehemiah 2:9-10,19-20

Have you noticed whenever someone begins a project the detractors are right at hand to discourage the work. Before a stone was laid in rebuilding Jerusalem Sanballat and Tobiah began opposing the work. Initially they opposed the work because it displeased them because someone came to seek the welfare of the Jews.

There opposition is understandable since they hated the Jews. Jesus' disciples didn't hate Him yet they opposed honor being poured out on their Lord. *"The disciples were indignant...'What is this waste? For this perfume might have been sold for a high price and the money given to the poor,'"* (Matthew 26:8-9).

In verse 19 Sanballat accused Nehemiah of rebelling against the king. If one tactic doesn't work discouragers will try another. They'll resort to ridicule when other tactics fail (Nehemiah 4:3).

In the church we hear such discouraging words as, "We've never done it that way before." "We've gotten along just fine till now." "We can't afford it." "We don't need it." "Who's going to pay for it, drive it, teach it, administer it, etc. etc."

Discouragers all work for the same person. God loved the Jews so who would be opposed to helping them? Jesus is Lord of all, who would oppose Him? The work of the church is inspired by the Holy Spirit, who opposes the Holy Spirit?

Nehemiah knew he was performing the work God had set before him. Therefore he assured his enemies that his work would succeed.

Scripture: John 1:14-17

While taking an evening course in Drama Interpretation at Webster University with other teachers working on Masters Degrees, a black sister in the Lord and I began talking about our favorite hymns during the break. We decided to sing Amazing Grace. With great beauty and volume she began singing, I harmonized singing the bass. When we began there was much chatter. Before we finished there was silence.

I've forgotten the lady's name but I can still see her singing that grand old hymn. Our hearts were knit together as we sang. Though many years have passed I clearly remember the exhilaration, the sheer pleasure of singing that testimony in a class whose professor was an agnostic.

John wrote, *"For of His fulness we have all received, and grace upon grace,"* (v. 16). Truly, without Jesus there is no grace, no favor, no joy, no forgiveness of sins, no eternal life. For of His fulness we have received all these things.

Consider that while we were rebelling, each going his own way, seeking to satisfy the lust of the flesh, the lust of the eyes, and the pride of life: Jesus died for us. THAT is amazing grace! That is unmerited favor.

Someone said, "Justice is getting what we deserve. Mercy is not getting what we deserve; but Grace, Grace is getting what we don't deserve." "Amazing grace how sweet the sound that saved a wretch like me." By grace we have been saved. Proclaim it! Rejoice in it!

Scripture: Exodus 3:13-18

Our largest problem is 'I'. Paul had the difficulty. Abraham, Jacob, Samson, Saul, David, Jonah are all prime examples of the I AM rebellion. When Moses inquired at the burning bush, *"Whom should I say sent me?"*, God said His Name was *"I AM WHO I AM."* Therefore God must be the I AM in our lives.

God must be the One who runs our lives. We find it difficult to be totally committed to the Lord, to let Him run our lives. Jesus took your punishment for sin upon himself. Doing your own thing demonstrates ungratefulness. Pray God will establish His desires in your heart so you won't be ungrateful.

We keep injecting our little 'i' into God's running of our lives which hinders successful Christian living. And what happens— disaster. God desires good for us (Jeremiah 29:11) but we spoil it. We spoil it by inserting our little 'i'. Do you see what happens? God says, "I want to run your life." We rebel, insert our 'i', and RUiN God's plans for us.

Not only do we do this with our own lives but we do it with the church and with the lives of others. What buttinskies we are. It's bad enough to RUiN our own lives without RUiNNING someone else's. If you are committed to Him you'll keep your little 'i' out of God's business and let Him RUN you not the other way around. Put your 'i' in and you RUiN it every time.

Scripture: 2 Peter 1:12-14;3:1-2

How soon we forget. Unless we make a conscious effort to remember, scripture and God's spoken word to us it slips into oblivion. Larry Lea in his book *The Hearing Ear* recommends keeping a prayer journal.

Peter wrote to those of the dispersion so they would have his reminder after he died. God instructed Jeremiah, *"Now go, write it on a tablet before them And inscribe it on a scroll, That it may serve in time to come As a witness forever,"* (Jeremiah 30:8).

What are some of the things you might write in a prayer journal. Naturally we can record the things we request from God then mark when He has answered. While that is good, there is something better to record. Write down those things God tells you in your prayer time, *lest you forget them.*

In June of '89 I began keeping a prayer journal. It has served often as a witness, and a reminder of *what God said.*

When Satan aims his favorite weapon I can look up in my prayer journal what God really said. Remember, Satan's favorite tool is doubt. Didn't he plant doubt in Eve's mind saying in essence, "Did God really mean...?"

Don't pit your memory against the mind boggling moves of Satan. Begin to keep a journal today of what God tells you. OH, YES, God does speak to us today if we will but listen. He speaks to us through His written word but also in our spirits. Listen for Him.

Scripture: Psalm 100

Recently we celebrated the tercentennial of the birth of Johann Sabastian Bach and George Frederick Handel. Both contributed greatly to our world of music and to the music of our hymn books. Handel is known for his oratorio *The Messiah* while Bach is known for his *Mass in B.*

What would a worship service be without the singing of praises to God? One whole book in the Bible is dedicated to songs.

The very word *psalm* means twanging of a harp; to play a stringed instrument. Since the twelfth century however the word psalm has meant a sacred song or poem used in worship. Notice how many of the psalms are "to the choir master with stringed instruments".

Here are a few psalms telling us to make a joyful noise. *"Shout joyfully to God, all the earth; sing the glory of His name,"* (Psalm 66:1). *"sing for joy to God our strength; shout joyfully to the god of Jacob,"* (Psalm 81:1). *"O sing to the Lord a new song, for He has done wonderful things..."* (Psalm 98:1. Scripture counsels us to sing praises and give thanks. *"It is good to give thanks to the Lord and to sing praises to Thy Name, O Most High,"* (Psalm 92:1). *"I will sing of lovingkindness and justice,"* (Psalm 101:1).

Sing to the Lord each day. Let hymns of praise be on your lips all day long. Humming, or whistling hymns in public is a great testimony.

Scripture: Song of Solomon 7:10-13

The themes of love and youth are eternal. In today's text we have two young people doing the things young people enjoy doing: being together, looking at things, sharing, giving gifts, and in general enjoying themselves. Edna St. Vincent Millay wrote *Recuerdo* (Spanish for *I remember*). It's a poem about two young people like those in our text.

It begins: "We were very tired, we were very merry—/We had gone back and forth all night on the ferry." In the second verse we read, "And you ate an apple, and I ate a pear,/From a dozen of each we had bought somewhere;/And the sky went wan, and the wind came cold,/And the sun rose dripping, a bucketful of gold." Millay was remembering her youth.

In our text the young people go to the country, villages, and vineyards to see the blossoms and smell the fragrances. The speaker talks about fruit *"I have saved up for you..."* (v. 13). People do not change from century to century, nor by geography.

What hinders us in later years from the carefree escapades of youth? Is it self-consciousness, cares, profession, what? Most people would like to occasionally experience such release and they can if they will.

Love doesn't change. Look around at older folks holding hands, kissing in public, kicking up their heels unrestrained, unafraid, uninhibited. Take time occasionally to let yourself be young again. You'll feel the stress drain away and be renewed.

Scripture: Psalm 33:6-12

Counseling is big business in America. Offices are opened in shopping centers, office buildings, churches. You can find counseling offices most anywhere. Why is there such a felt need for counseling? Simply this: people are not listening to the counsel of the Lord.

Folks mess up their lives then trot off to some counselor to straighten out the mess, salve their wounds, and make it all better. They mess up their lives because they ignore God's instructions for living. They were never taught to *follow directions*. My students were required to follow directions. No employer will keep help that can't follow directions. We understand that but don't carry the reasoning into daily living. What a strange breed we are.

God's directions for life are clear, direct, comprehensible, and so very practical. Who knows more about life than the One who created it? The counsel of the nations (world) is nullified by God's counsel (v. 10-11).

One pastor tells people seeking counseling, "Attend our services Sunday morning, Sunday evening, and Wednesday evening for a month, if you still need counseling I'll consider it." What this pastor was saying is simply this: when you expose yourself to biblical preaching, apply the counsel from the Bible and pulpit to your life your need for counseling greatly diminishes.

This pastor reported that most of those who attend services for a month and apply the teaching to their lives for a month discover they don't need counseling after all.

Scripture: 2 John 7-13

John states his purpose in writing this letter *"For many deceivers have gone out into the world..."* (v. 7). Those who deny Jesus Christ is Lord and that He has come in the flesh are the anti-Christ. We have them knocking on our doors, decivering pamphlets, seeking to lead the weak away from the teaching of scripture. Some twist scripture claiming only a certain number will go to heaven. Others claim visions from angels and visions emanating from a fleshly mind (Colossians 2:18). Paul warned, *"But even though we, or an angel from heaven, should preach to you a gospel contrary to that which we have preached to you, let him be accursed,"* (Galatians 1:8)

Indeed they have gone out, two by two. They claim to believe in God. Wonderful, *"the demons also believe and shudder,"* (James 2:19). They quote scripture adding and taking away as it pleases them. The antichrists knocking on your door are not limited to Mormons and Jehovah's Witnesses. *ANYONE* who denies Jesus Christ is the Son of God and Lord of all serves the antichrist.

John warns, *"Any one who goes too far and **does not abide in the teaching of Christ**..."* (v. 9). Those requiring adherence to laws are among those who *"go too far"*.

John simply commands they be left standing outside (v. 10). Neither are we to greet them or offer aid of any sort. Does that sound harsh? Would you help a snake that was trying to kill you? Read the text again and pray for understanding and application of John's words.

Scripture: Psalm 119:49-56

Geoffrey Chaucer wrote, "Whan that Aprill with his shoures soote/The droghte of March hath perced to the roote,/...(So priketh hem nature in hir corages);/Thanne longen folk to goon on pilgrimages..." *Trans*: When in April his showers shoot,/the drought of March has pierced to the root/...so pricks them nature in their courages,/then folks long to go on pilgrimages.

Along the way to Canterberry Chaucer's pilgrims told tales. Chaucer intended to write 120 tales but completed only 24, known as *The Canterberry Tales*.

Pilgrimages to shrines is still made by some folks. The journey to some holy place supposedly provides healing, or sanctification, or some other benefit. Not denying these benefits remember each of us is on a pilgrimage through life.

The psalmist writes, *"Thy statutes are my songs In the house of my pilgrimage,"* (v. 54). The house of his pilgrimage is his body in which he is traveling. During his pilgrimage he receives hope and comfort from the Lord while suffering derision and indignation. He declares God's word has revived him. The songs he sings are the statutes of the Lord.

On your pilgrimage do you experience hope and comfort in the midst of derision and indignation? Does the word of the Lord revive you from day to day? Do you sing songs of God's statutes as you travel? What tales are you leaving along the way as you live your life before others? Your life reveals what you are.

Scripture: Mark 6:21-26

Watch your words, your pride may break your heart. Vocal commitment trips all of us once in a while. Usually the results are no more than embarrassing, or we find ourselves doing something we wish we could escape. Some have sold property or heirlooms before realizing how incautious they were. Who would relish Herod's place in our text? Yet, by our own audacity we could position ourselves in such a predicament.

Herod cornered himself first by double intoxication. He was intoxicated with the wine and with his step-daughter's dancing (vv. 22-23). In like circumstances many have cornered themselves with rash words. When the offer is accepted and the terms stated the one making the commitment often regrets his brash boasting.

The second thing that cornered Herod was his pride (v. 26). Herod respected John, believed him to be a holy and righteous man, and had protected him from Herodias, his murderous wife (John 6:19-20). Regardless, Herod thought more of his image, his position, his pride than he thought of or feared John the Baptizer (v. 26).

A boastful tongue and pride crush the heart beyond mending. Herod was sorry at the moment and I believe he was sorry ever afterwards. Letitia Elizabeth Landon said, "Were it not better to forget/Than but remember and regret?"

In the first century B.C. Publilius Syrus said, "I have often regretted my speech, never my silence." Keep Herod's experience in mind when you've a mind to boast and make audacious commitments.

Scripture: 2 Kings 22:14-20

A few decades ago a car full of young people had a tragic accident on a bridge near Keokuk, Iowa. Of the several young people only one professed faith in Jesus Christ, he was the only one killed. Satan would have you believe it doesn't pay to follow the Lord Jesus Christ. Not long past a dear friend retired from his business leaving it in the hands of able sons. Within months of his retirement the Lord took him home. He had served the Lord faithfully all the years I knew him. We wonder and question the death of the righteous.

Isaiah wrote, *"The righteous man perishes, and no one takes it to heart; And devout men are taken away, while no one understands. For the righteous man is taken away from evil, He enters into peace; They rest in their beds, Each one who walked in his upright way,"* (Isaiah 57:1-2). We do not always see the evil from which these righteous ones were rescued. In our text Josiah the king is promised death before his nation is punished by the Lord. The destruction did not follow on the heels of Josiah's death; but came later.

Is death of the body really a tragedy? Not for the followers of Jesus Christ. For them it's going home after a long journey. Many saints look forward to their dying day. Rejoice, God cares enough to deliver us from evil by taking us home to glory.

Scripture: Psalm 121

This psalm is less emotional, less ecstatic in its expression of faith than others expressing the same ideas. This psalm expresses quiet faith in the Lord who is our guardian.

The hills mentioned in verse 1 are not just any hills but the hills upon which Jerusalem is built. Solomon's prayer of dedication advises Israel to turn to the temple when troubles arise (1 Kings 8:33-35). The psalmist reminds us that prayers offered toward Jerusalem are heard and answered. There is nothing magical about geography; the help does not come from the hills but from the Lord.

The word translated *keeps* means *guards*. The Lord guards your foot so it does not slip, He Who guards you does not sleep. What value is there in a sleeping guard? Not only is God guarding the individual, He is guarding the nation.

God is also our protection (v. 7). In the desert climate shade is protection from the consuming sun. Thus the Lord not only guards He protects. From what are we protected? We are protected from the smiting of the sun and moon. Sun strokes are common in hot climates. The Shunnamite's son probably died of a sun stroke (2 Kings 4:18-20). But moon stroke? Not hardly. These references point to being guarded by the Lord day and night, being guarded against unnamed, undefined dangers over which the Lord has total control.

What good news to those who love the Lord: we are guarded and kept by God Himself— all day and all night.

Scripture: Mark 16:1-9

Sometime around this day much of the world celebrates Easter. As a special day Easter was not established until the first Council of Nicaea in A.D. 325. The impetus behind this council was Constantine's desire for closer relations between church and state. It was a political move.

When should the resurrection of Jesus be celebrated? Until A.D. 325 Christians celebrated the resurrection of Jesus *every* first day of the week. On two occasions it was on the *first day* of the week when Jesus appeared to the disciples (John 20:19 & 26). Paul commands offerings be set aside on the *first day of the week* (1 Corinthians 16:2). Should we not follow the example of the New Testament instead of the political move of a dead monarch?

Of course it would mean the pseudo-righteous must attend worship more than once or twice a year. Scripturally attendance on Easter Sunday is absolutely worthless for impressing God. It has as much redemption value as wearing Easter bonnets or hunting for colored eggs. If you only favor God with your presence on Easter Sunday, stay home and watch TV. God wants you to draw near to Him with your heart not your appearance in church once a year.

HOWEVER, if on that once a year visit you come under the conviction of the Holy Spirit and are born again, making Jesus Lord of your life Easter will benefit you. You shouldn't miss that opportunity for anything.

Scripture: Luke 20:19-25

This is an onerous day for Americans. Today, income taxes must be paid, at least the tax forms must be post marked by midnight tonight. Margaret Mitchell said, "Death and taxes and childbirth! There's never any convenient time for any of them."

Taxes have been resisted and hated since they originated sometime before the days of Solomon. The American revolution was fought over taxes. Henry David Thoreau willingly went to jail protesting the use of his tax money. Some tax proposals are put to the vote of the people which makes accountability of how the money is spent more likely.

Since there is great waste in every tax supported agency should we resist and go to jail as Thoreau? That's not what Jesus taught.

If there was ever the wasting of tax moneys consider the opulence provided the Caesars by taxes. The taxes extracted from the Jews paid the army that oppressed them. Did they have reason to resist taxation? You bet they did.

What did Jesus teach the conniving religious rulers about taxes? *"...render to Caesar the things that are Caesar's, and to God the things that are God's,"* (v. 25).

Yes, the tithe is the Lord's whether you are taxed or not. If you wish to reduce your taxes, tithe. Tithes and offerings to your church are deductible. Rejoice and pay taxes gladly. Your responsibility is to pay taxes; the politicians must account to God how they spend your tax money.

Scripture: Genesis 3:20-24

When Apollos wrote the letter to the Hebrews he reiterated what God did in the Garden of Eden. Adam and Eve sinned, realized they were naked and hid from God. When God came seeking them (as He seeks sinners today not the other way around) they heard the consequences for sin. Then God did something wonderful setting the example for all of Hebrew history and preparing for the sacrifice of Jesus on Calvary.

In verse 21 we read, *"And the Lord God made garments of skin for Adam and his wife, and clothed them."* There is a lot of teaching in that verse. What we need to notice is that God shed blood to cover their nakedness, their sin. Blood was required for the covering of the first sin, the sacrifices of the Old Testament further establish this teaching, then Jesus shed His own blood on Calvary providing forgiveness of sin for all time; past present and future.

There is no other cleansing from sin. *"'Although you wash yourself with lye/And use much soap, The stain of your iniquity is before me," declares the Lord God,'"* (Jeremiah 2:22). As it says in Hebrews, *"...without the shedding of blood there is no forgiveness of sins,"* (Hebrews 9:22).

So what are you using to cleanse your iniquity away and make you presentable to God? Have you been washed by the blood of Jesus? If not isn't it time you place yourself under the cleansing power of the blood of Jesus?

Scripture: Leviticus 10:1-8

There are three ways to understand why Nadab and Abihu brought on their own deaths. Some suggest the sheer enthusiasm of the moment impelled them to offer strange fire before the Lord. Consider what has just happened. *"Then fire came out from before the Lord and consumed the burnt offering and the portions of fat on the altar; and when all the people saw it, they shouted and fell on their faces,"* (Leviticus 9:24). They may have been caught up in the excitement of the moment.

A second view portrays them desiring to share in the glory their father just experienced. This couches their actions in jealousy. Aaron was big stuff in the eyes of the people. If you remember, the Israelites tended to pay more attention to Aaron than to Moses.

Finally, there is the simple fact of outright disobedience. In chapters 1-7 of Leviticus we learn what specific directions regarding sacrifices were given by Moses to Aaron. Nadab and Abihu heard these directions with their father.

The point is simple. God is holy and He will be respected. When Uzzah steadied the Ark so it wouldn't fall in the mud he was struck down for the sin of disobedience. Uzzah was a Kohathite he knew *how* the ark was to be moved. Had David moved the Ark by God's direction instead of on an ox cart, Uzzah would not have reached out to steady it. These were hard lessons; but have we yet learned how holy God is?

Scripture: Exodus 20:1-17

This is Constitution Day in Canada. The constitution of 1982 provided new fundamental laws and civil rights for all Canadians. Queen Elizabeth II signed the document at Parliament Hill, in Ottawa, in April of that year.

Constitutions are wonderful documents specifying how a nation should conduct itself and govern itself. Most school children are required to study the constitution of their country. That's good, don't you think?

There is an interesting thing about laws and constitutions that never ceases to amaze us. God provided all the law we need in the ten commandments. Yet, from the Exodus until today we have been explaining and interpreting these ten laws until whole libraries are devoted to housing our commentary on them.

Do we need all these volumes of explanation and application because we humans are always trying to figure some way to justify getting around the law? Perhaps. It is really impossible for man to keep laws. Adam only had one restriction, can you believe it, and he couldn't abide by it. How can we expect the keeping of volumes of laws?

Part of the problem lies in the difference between the letter and the spirit of the law. If we earnestly sought to keep the spirit of the law there would be little need for all this interpretation of it.

Jesus reduced the 10 Commandments to two. *"You shall love the Lord your God with all your hear...soul...and strenth and your neighbor as yourself."* (Luke 10:27). Can we do it?

Scripture: Revelation 2:1-7

Do you know what the three R's to successful living are? Immediately you think of the three R's applied to secular education: readin', writin' and 'rithmatic. Those three R's are needed in the physical world in which we live. Everyone should get a good grasp of them; but there are three other R's that each of us must apply throughout life.

The first R is for Remember. We must daily remember the rock from which we have been hewn. As Isaiah wrote, *"Listen to me, you who pursue righteousness,/Who seek the Lord:/Look to the rock from which you were hewn,/And to the quarry from which you were dug,"* (Isaiah 51:1). The rock Isaiah mentions is the rock of faith from which Abraham was hewn. We must remember we are a people of faith.

The second R is for Repent. *"In repentance and rest you shall be saved..."* (Isaiah 30:15). How many days do you live free from sin? If you say, "None" you are honest. Since we sin everyday we must repent everyday.

The third R is for Return. After remembering we are a people of faith, after repenting of both sins of commission and sins of omission we must return to our commitment to the Lord.

That's what Revelation 2:5 says, *"Remember therefore from where you have fallen, and repent and do the deeds you did at first..."* These are three R's that give success in life. Apply them.

Scripture: Genesis 11:1-9

In preparing to teach the history of the English language I did considerable research. More than one linguistic scholar testified that all languages can be traced to three roots which *seem* to have developed from one single language. Isn't that what Genesis tells us? *"And the whole world used the same language and the same words,"* (v. 1).

Noah had three sons from which the whole world was populated. Sociologists recognize three basic *race* strains. All other variations are combinations of the three. The similarities between the three basic races, they say, suggests all came from a single source.

Isn't it amazing, language and anthropological researchers strain their brains figuring out what Moses wrote in Genesis. It's to our advantage. These scientists prove time and time again the accuracy and truth of the Bible. The more information scientists and historians and scholars in other disciplines extract from the past the more the Bible is confirmed as absolute truth.

To be persuaded to disregard scripture is Satan's deception. "Surely those ancient words can't be reliable," says Satan. So a whole society is reconstructed on a few bones and a broken pot. What wonderful imaginations some scholars have. Even when the evidence supports the Bible most scholars refuse to admit the Bible is right.

If you have a copy of the Bible you have the greatest most accurate, most reliable text available to man. God's word can be trusted. Read it, believe, depend on it, hide its words in your heart.

Scripture: 1 Peter 1:10-12

Open your Bible and put your finger between Malachi and Matthew. If you have additional material in the back separate it with another finger. Now look and see how much is Old Testament and how much is New Testament. In most Bibles there are four times as many pages in the Old Testament as in the New Testament. Does that tell you anything?

It is very sad so many Christians ignore the Old Testament. God has preserved the Old Testament along with the New for your edification and understanding.

In order to understand the New Testament thoroughly it is necessary to have knowledge of the Old. Peter reminded us, *"It was revealed to them* (the old prophets) *that they were not serving themselves but you..."* (v. 12). If your Bible has cross references notice how often you are referred to the Old Testament in support of the New.

Peter writes, *"The prophets who prophesied of the grace to come..."* (v. 10). Surely what they said has great significance for us. A lot of what those old prophets foretold has not yet come to pass. We cannot afford to ignore it.

As Jesus walked with two disciples to Emmaus He revealed something wonderful. Luke records, *"And beginning with Moses and with all the prophets, He explained to them the things concerning Himself in all the Scriptures,"* (Luke 24:27). Since the New Testament had not been written Jesus was revealing the importance of the Old Testament.

Scripture: Genesis 7:1-12

Comedians have provided a wrong impression of how Noah got the animals on the ark. The truth is Noah did not get the animals on the ark. Noah did not spend one minute ranging about gathering the animals male and female, clean and unclean. Can't you see Noah with his walking stick driving a pair of brontosaurs to the ark, or a pair of bear?

The Hebrew says, "the animals came two and two" to the ark. The animals came of their own accord. Does it seem strange to you? Consider the migration of Monarch Butterflies, or geese, or whales in the sea migrating thousands of miles. Who drives them? Who guides them to their new destinations? Cattle alert the farmer of a change in the weather. So what is strange about the animals coming to Noah to enter the ark?

The NIV says it best, *"male and female, came to Noah and entered the ark, as God had commanded Noah,"* (Genesis 7:9). "The animals collected about Noah and were taken into the ark" (Keil & Delitzsch). The Septuagint says, "Pairs went in to Noe into the ark." Genesis has the facts.

Faith in the veracity of scripture goes back to Genesis 1:1. Right there you either believe or you don't believe. Either God created everything or He didn't. If you can't trust Genesis how can you trust John 3:16? Our thinking and understanding my be in error; but God's word is without error.

Scripture: Job 40:15-25

It's St. George's Day in England. St. George died April 23, A.D. 303. Legend says his faith helped him slay a dragon that demanded daily sacrifice. When the king's daughter became the intended victim he killed it. Were there such things as dragons? Let's look at scripture.

"Can you draw out Leviathan with a fish hook?" (Job 21:1). Leviathan was not an elephant or hippo as some believe. Leviathan was more likely a sea inhabiting dinosaur. NOPE, dinosaurs didn't live millions of years ago as the religion of evolution claims. There have been too many reports hushed up by evolutionists to prove their notions are incorrect. One need merely compare the **facts** of scripture to the **theories** of the God deniers.

Reread today's text carefully. Does that sound like an elephant to you? It is an excellent description of a dinosaur. Have you seen an elephant with a tail like a cedar? Neither has any one else.

Consider these *facts*. Beowulf (written about A.D. 600) slays three monsters whose descriptions match those of dinosaurs and compare well with Job 41. In the 15th century the Sioux Indians saw a Pteranodon get struck by lightening— they called it "Thunderbird". The description of it's remains matched those of the Pteranodon. Over four hundred species have become extinct in the last three hundred years. At that extinction rate we could lose all the dinosaurs in five hundred to a thousand years. Space does not allow further rebuttal.

One final word, God is talking in Job 40 and 41. Surely He knows an elephant from a dinosaur. Believe Him, He created them.

Scripture: 2 Samuel 18:28-33

One of the saddest verses in the Old Testament is 2 Samuel 18:33. Being a father of sons and daughters I can imagine how David felt. Had someone physically deracinated David's heart it could not have hurt more.

True, Absolom was in rebellion against his father. He had murdered his brother Amnon for what Amnon did to Tamar. Absolom was no angel of a son. Yet his father loved him.

When we look at David's family and personal life we see a great deal of heart ache. Granted, David brought it upon himself. Though we may be forgiven, the consequences of sin in this life often remain. Nathan delivered God's word to David saying, "...*the sword shall never depart from your house...I will raise up evil against you from your own house hold..*" (2 Samuel 12:10-11). David repented then Nathan said, "*The Lord also has taken away your sin, you shall not die,*" (2 Samuel 12:13). Yes, the Lord took away his sin but he still suffered the physical consequences. The Lord will forgive someone for smoking but it doesn't inoculate against emphysema.

The Lord did not deliver the man after His own heart from the consequences of sin so why should He deliver us? And though we rebel against God and rise up against Him; though we are guilty of (murder) hating our brother GOD LOVES US. Just as David's heart ached over Absolom, just so God's heart aches over us. God does love you.

Scripture: Jeremiah 10:1-5

In our county there are many icons in yards. Some with shelters over them, some must withstand the elements. All have some religious significance. Human beings are prone to make statues and honor that which their eyes can see. Yet, throughout the Old Testament the word of the Lord speaks against honoring images.

Pagan peoples lived all around Israel. Each nation had its own gods, its own form of worship, its own temples, and high places. Any Bible reader is familiar with such names as Dagon, Baal, Molech and Asherah. Sacrifices were made to these gods, sometimes human sacrifices were offered up. Israel was fascinated by these practices, even joining in human sacrifices.

Today's scripture describes these icons, these false gods. It tells how they are made, then ridicules them. God says these man made objects of veneration have the redeeming value of a scarecrow in a cucumber field (v. 5).

The tragedy is the veneration and hope afforded Christian icons in many places on the globe. In one country a particular statue was carried from village to village in the hopes of better crop production, better living conditions; in hopes of appeasing God. How sad to be so misdirected. The last two phrases of verse 5 say, "*For they can do no harm, Nor can they do any good.*"

The sin is not in having a statue of a saint. The sin is placing faith and confidence in a material object expecting an answer.

Scripture: 1 Chronicles 29:1-9

In 1710 Christopher Wren completed St. Paul's Cathedral. In my home town, St. Louis, are several cathedrals: The Old Cathedral on the river front, the St. Louis Cathedral, Christ Church Cathedral, etc. These are all magnificent buildings erected at great expense. Other houses of worship also inspire people to *"be still and know that I am God,"* (Psalm 46:10[KJV]).

So often when a congregation is planning a building program or in the midst of one, some wonder, "Is this to the glory of God or the glory of man?" There are critics of beautiful worship centers claiming the money should be invested in missions, helping the poor, the sick, the homeless.

Let's look at two examples in scripture. First, this example in 1 Chronicles. To date there has not been anywhere in the world a temple with greater beauty, surpassing opulence, richer accoutrements, nor absolute perfection than Solomon's temple. The second example is the anointing of Jesus' feet with the expensive perfume. What was Jesus' repsonse to the critical disciples? *"...the poor you have with you always, you do not always have Me,"* (Matthew 26:11).

The briar here is why shouldn't we honor our God with awe inspiring places of worship. It's not the building, not the cost, but our attitude. An open air hut is a fabulous temple when your heart is right. Can we apply Jesus' words, *"...these things your should have done without neglecting the others,"* (Matthew 23:23)? You must decide.

Scripture: 2 Corinthians 11:1-4

Poet William Blake 1757-1827 wrote a poem about Jesus the *Lamb* and another about Satan whom he called *Tiger*. Willam Blake was a man led astray by the spurious teaching of Jakob Boehme. Blake's early poems appear to be on target. In his poem *The Lamb* he attributes creation to Christ exactly as John (John 1:3). In *The Tiger* we begin to see doubt creeping in. He asks, "Did he smile his work to see?/Did he who made the Lamb make thee?"

Blake was a genius in many respects having earned his living by engraving for book publishers. As his poems were published he acquired a small follwoing but when he died at 70 his poetry was practically unknown.

His brilliance led him to follow Jakob Boehme. Boehme used abstruse terminology, incorporated ideas from astology, the mystics, and in general was deceived into believing he had been called to reveal the secrets of God's nature. Of course in doing so he denied what scripture declares about God's nature.

Paul's fears expressed in our text are well founded. Because Satan leads astray Paul advised Timothy, "...*guard what has been entrusted to you, avoiding worldly and empty chatter and the opposing arguments of what is falsely called 'knowledge' — which some have professed and thus gone astray from the faith...*" (1 Timothy 6:20-21).

Satan still leads astray. Stick to God's written word and reject everything contrary to it.

Scripture: Psalm 50:16-23

Sweet sounding phrases do God no justice. All is not sweetness and kindness with Him. Those ignorant of spiritual things, of the Bible, and lacking a real experience with Jesus Christ have a very twisted concept of God and life.

For God to be meaningful He must be the center of life, not a peripheral personality whom we salute, half heartedly when we remember how good life is. Life is not always good. Anna Quindlen brings this out in an article she wrote for the New York Times (November 25, 1987). Her point is that of giving thanks, but her article does not say God must be the center of life. She wrote, "...it's right and proper to stop every once in a while and say, 'Life is good, and we're thankful for that'". That sounds good, but she admitted she'd have difficulty explaining, "Who is this God anyway?"

It's forgetting WHO God is that perpetrates our downfall. We forget God is absolute holiness, perfection, truth. He IS still in control. He is totally aware of everything including the thoughts of the wicked and the works of him who *"orders his way aright"*. We honor Him when we offering thanksgiving. Are you thankful?

We must have God in Christ at the center of every area of our lives. Is God the center of your life? Do you know Who He is?

Scripture: Romans 11:1-5

Aren't our favorite heroes Abraham, Isaac, Jacob, Joseph, Moses, Joshua, David, Elijah, Isaiah, Jeremiah, Amos, Paul, Peter, and our Savior Jesus Christ? All Jews. The same people the Nazi's classified inferior.

Hitler, an evolutionist[1], proclaimed superiority to a certain race namely his own. All race prejudice is the result of believing in evolution. To justify his evolutionary theory of superiority yet include Christ, a very twisted theology emerged. A story was fabricated saying Mary had relations with a German soldier who really fathered Christ. This lie allowed for acceptance of Jesus into the "superior" race. Only the deceived, duped, and disgruntled every believed this nonsense. Now a half century later there are still some believing it. Satan's lies die hard.

Israel has always been God's chosen people. In the first nine chapters of Exodus God calls the Jews *"My people"* at least fourteen times. Paul wrote, *"God has not rejected His people whom He foreknew,"* (v. 2). The Jews are God's chosen people; but as Paul writes in Romans 9, not all Israel is physically descended from Abraham. Remember what John the Baptist told his listeners, *"...God is able from these stones to raise up children to Abraham,"* (Luke 3:8).

"It is not the children of the flesh who are children of God, but the children of the promise are regarded as descendants," (Romans 9:8). Therefore it is those who have believed on the Lord Jesus Christ who are the true Israel. Are you born by faith into Israel?

---

[1]According to some biographies Hitler was an admirer of Darwin.

Scripture: Amos 2:6-12

We relax when calamity is proclaimed against our enemies thinking they deserve it. Truth is, we may even cheer a little bit. Amos begins proclaiming, *"For three transgressions and for four..."* against Damascus, Gaza, Tyre, Edom, Ammon, Moab, and Judah. Can't you see the people cheering because God is going to punish their enemy-neighbors for their iniquities?

The expression *"for three transgressions and for four"* does not mean three or four transgressions. Three may indicate completeness or fullness and the four might then mean full to overflowing. The hearers understood this and did not dispute it. Surely the enemies transgressions are full to overflowing. Aren't the atrocities of our enemies greater than our own.

During the Gulf War many cried out against Iraq for murdering children; yet many of these same people approve of abortion. As Amos proclaimed the sins and punishments on Israel's neighbors, the people applauded. Then Amos stopped preaching and went to meddling for he said, *"For three transgressions of Israel and for four..."* (v. 6). When the message came home Israel no longer wanted to listen.

In Amos 7:12-13 King Amaziah tells Amos to go home and there eat bread and prophecy. Have you noticed we never condemn the things we do. Just like Israel when the finger is pointed at someone else we approve. When the finger of indictment is pointed at us we don't want to hear it. Are we any better than Israel? Try to prove it.

Scripture: Genesis 8:13-22

Cultures the world over celebrate the planting season, or as Genesis says, *"seedtime"* (v.22). The pagans of ancient England celebrated by crowning the May-queen. Tennyson wrote, "You must wake and call me early, call me early, mother dear;/Tomorrow'll be the happiest time of all the glad New Year;/Of all the glad New Year, mother, the maddest, merriest day;/For I'm to be Queen o' the May, mother, I'm to be Queen o' the May."[1]

The male counterpart to the May Queen was Jack-in-the-Green. The May Pole dance originally was a "seedtime" celebration. In the modern world we rush to the markets to buy our seed, and potting plants.

We should be reminded of God's promise, *"While the earth remains, Seedtime and harvest, And cold and heat, And summer and winter, And day and night Shall not cease,"* (v. 22). We are reminded when we see a rainbow. Shouldn't we also be reminded when it's cold or hot, when it's summer or winter, when it's day or night? The psalmist wrote, *"He has made His wonders to be remembered..."* (Psalm 111:4).

God says, *"While the earth remains..."* The earth shall not always remain. Peter tells us, *"...the heavens will pass away with a roar...and the earth and its works will be burned up,"* (2 Peter 3:10). Until then be reminded these things shall not pass, so give thanks.

The Big Bang theorists have it wrong. The *big bang* is at the beginning but at the end not .

1Tennyson's *The May Queen* (1832)

Scripture: Joshua 10:38-43

Throughout the Old Testament we read how the "Lord fought for Israel". The Israelites never once gained a victory by their own strength, cunning, military strategy, or overwhelming numbers. They won impossible battles because God did their fighting for them. David gave this wonderful testimony, "...*that all this assembly may know that the Lord does not deliver by sword or by spear; for the battle is the Lord's...*" (1 Samuel 17:47).

The battle is the Lord's yet we have folks believing the Lord can't handle situations. They take control as if the Lord is unable to care for His church. They elect themselves to fight the Lord's battles; to deal with every situation in the church. In reality it is supposed to be the other way around. No where in scripture will you find the Lord needed anybody to fight for Him, or defend Him, or protect His honor, or His glory, or His church, or His Word.

On the other hand there are many many examples of the Lord defending His people, caring for His flock, and providing grace sufficient for any burden they might need to bear. Believe it or not God is at your side to fight your battles *if you'll let him.*

What do you think victory in Jesus means? Yes, it means victory over sin but also victory in life's daily battles. The battle is the Lord's. Turn your weakness into strength but giving your battles into the Lord's hands.

Scripture: James 4:13-17

Planned your summer vacation yet? If not consider praying about it. Some may object, "What if that's not how God wants me to spend my vacation?" Then it's time to make the discovery before being making a mistake.

Have you considered God's plans are better, more exciting, than your own? God's plans never ever carry the risk of regret. God has good things planned for you. *"'For I know that plans that I have for you'. declares the Lord, 'plans for welfare and not for calamity to give you a future and a hope,'"* (Jeremiah 29:11).

Have you considered volunteering as a missionary this summer? Most pastors can tell you whom to contact for just such an exhilarating experience. From my resources there are openings both at home and abroad for volunteers.

Of course you'll pay your own expences; but who was going to pay for your vacation anyway? Volunteering for summer missions is a double investment. You get to do something really neat and you make an investment in the kingdom of God.

Of course some won't even volunteer to help at the church on their day off. When it comes time to enjoy their investment in the kingdom of God there'll be little treasure to draw from in eternity.

Don't be guilty of the sin of presumption; presuming upon God that what you plan meets His approval or is anything near the wonderful plans He has just for you. Reread verse 17.

Scripture: Titus 1:5-9

In the margin of my Bible (Oh, yes, I make notes in the margin of my Bible) I've written next to this text, "Forget not the rest of the qualifications." Some folks hold tenatiously to some of these qualities and let the rest slide. They do it to all scripture.

Some would restrict divorced persons or one who drinks wine from even standing in the pulpit but a pugnaciouis evangelist, or a minister who doesn't control his children is A-OK. What about the pastor who's wife is inhospitable? How can he rule the church when he can't rule his spouse? Are there quick tempered ministers? Yep. Is anyone refusing to let them preach to the people?

Let's apply the *whole* scripture not just those parts that suit us. If you find I'm guilty of that in this book please write and tell me. There are, indeed, things said in God's word that don't suit me. Which means, I must change not God's word. Should I just leave it out? Hardly.

As you study God's word keep your mind and heart open to what God is saying to *YOU*. His word was written to YOU, and me, and everyone who'll read it and take it to heart. This is not an easy task but wonderfully rewarding.

It is no easy task because God's word requires changes we don't want to make. It's kind of like having to grow up; but after your grown you like it.

Scripture: Amos 4:1-5

Knowing scripture can be entertaining at times. Often some experience or something you see brings to mind things in the Bible. We meet Bible characters everyday. There are times the reverse is true when scripture brings to mind an experience.

Today's text reminds me of a PTA* meeting in a town I lived in long ago. A well padded woman there, was dressed in a tight black dress. She bore the image of a sophisticated lady until she whipped out a nail file and began cleaning her nails. I chuckled, saying to myself, "One of the cows of Bashan".

The cattle of Bashan graze everywhere. All are hollow pretending to be more than they are, demanding service, expecting favors. T. S. Eliot described them, "We are the hollow men/We are the stuffed men/Leaning together/Headpiece filled with straw. Alas!" (from *The Hollow Men*).

God is not pleased with such. The days are coming when retribution will fall upon them. Some Bashan cattle may indeed be rich, educated, hold high positions, have their pictures on magazine covers; but none of it has value before God.

What makes them hollow and displeasing to the Lord? God has called, cajoled, given hardship (Amos 4:6ff) and blessing to bring them to Himself. God has already said, *"What more was there to do for My vineyard that I have not done in it?"* (Isaiah 5:4). They are hollow because they do not possess the Holy Spirit by faith in Jesus Christ. Do you?

---
*PTA, Parent-Teachers Association

Scripture: Jeremiah 32:6-15

Our heavenly Father takes more interest in our spiritual and physical development than any earthly father. We tend to forget that. In today's text we see God taking a personal interest in Jeremiah's spiritual as well as physical well being. God works concurrently to develop both.

God informed Jeremiah that his cousin Hanamel was coming to sell his field to Jeremiah. When the cousin arrived Jeremiah confesses, *"Then I knew that this was the word of the Lord,"* (v. 8). This small fulfillment encouraged Jeremiah to make the greater commitment of purchasing the land. This may seem like a small thing in our eyes until we look at the whole picture.

The Babylonian anialation of Judah was imminent. What God asks Jeremiah to do seems impractical, even foolish. Who wants to buy land when an enemy is about to take over the country and the deed will become worthless? Jeremiah ingored the impracticality and bought the land.

Jeremiah's faith in God's promises grew, he has increased his property, and has an object lesson for the Jews. The Lord had been telling Jeremiah that He would restore the nation after seventy years (Jeremiah 25:11ff). Though the future was bleak, though the promise of restoration appeared impossible Jeremiah says in verse 17, *"Nothing is too difficult for Thee."* See the increase of Jeremiah's faith?

God is no less interested in your spiritual and physical development. What steps of faith is He asking you to take?

Scripture: Judges 3:7-14

Othniel was the first of thirteen judges to judge Israel after the death of Joshua. Thirteen times Israel "...*did what was evil in the sight of the Lord...*" (v. 7). Thirteen times God allowed an enemy to conquor and oppress His people to bring them to repentence. Thirteen times in the book of Judges the people repented and called upon the Lord. Thirteen times God raised up from among the people a deliverer to deliver His people from bondage.

Who then is to say God is impatient, unmerciful, and unforgiving? God's grace exceeds our comprehension. It overwhelms us. Yet some would take advantage as Paul wrote in Romans 6:1-2.

God still deals with us as He did with those ancient Jews. He allows various degrees of distress, discomfort, and discouragment to permeate our lives. When life becomes too unpleasant we begin to examine what's out of kilter. We discover our relationship to the Father is out of kilter and we repent. God then restores the *joy* of our salvation.

God does eventually runs out of patience. He told Jeremiah, "*Do not pray for the welfare of this people,*" (Jeremiah 14:11). There was a wicked man who brazenly opposed the church. I began praying for him. One day the Lord said, "Do not pray from him anymore." It hurt my heart for I knew God was through trying to bring him to repentence. In two weeks this man was dead.

Don't presume upon the grace of God.

Scripture: Ephesians 6:10-17

Did you go out in public naked yesterday? Don't get angry finish reading. You should have discovered by now that God is more interested in your spiritual self than your physical self. To rephrase the question: Did you go out spiritually naked yesterday? Is that better?

The Celts fought naked. Their ferocity conquered the Romans in the last two centuries B.C. The armor of a Roman soldier was designed both for protection and defense as a result of the Celtic attacks. No doubt Paul was looking at a Roman soldier when he wrote these verses.

Note there is no armor for the back. The Roman soldier was not to turn tail and run. Neither is the Christian. The helmet of salvation is to protect our thinking from Satan's influences. The spiritual battle-ground is not in the heart but the head. The breastplate of righteousness is to protect our emotions. The shield is to quench the flaming darts from hell. The sword to ward off blows from the enemy. You must be girded with truth (sincerity), and wearing the shoes of the gospel.

Being thus prepared Paul says, *"...having done everything, stand firm,"* (v. 13). It is difficult to stand firm but it corresponds with James 4:7, *"Resist the devil and he will flee..."*

You wouldn't think of going out physically naked; so don't go out spiritually naked. Before your feet touch the floor in the morning put on the full armor of God. Play it safe.

Scripture: Leviticus 3:1-6

As you read about the animals for sacrifice the words *"without defect"* are repeated. Have you considered what those words mean to a herdsman or shepherd? To the herdsman or shepherd God is making a very tough requirement.

If you have attended a county or state fair and observed the care show animals receive it will help your understanding. God asked for the blue ribbon animals to be offered. He wants nothing but the best.

A family depending on livestock for their livelihood value their animals highly. The best are used for breeding to improve the herd or flock. Breeding stock is chosen very carefully for sturdiness, specific musculo-skeletal development, weight gain, etc. To lose a prize animal is a great loss. For God to require it to be sacrificed is a large request in the eyes of the family.

Offering their prize bull or ram can mean a decrease in herd production. It can mean long term economic shortage. Yet, God required the best they had. Did Israel starve for giving their best to the Lord? Did families suffer great loss for meeting God's requirement? No. They suffered loss for unfaithfulness, spiritual adultery; but not for obedience.

God demands *your* best. Your best talent, your best effort, your best skills. Whatever God asks from you He wants your best. And why not, He gave nothing less than His best on Calvary for you. To offer less than your best is to insult God to His face. It's not advised.

Scripture: John 8:1-11

Adultry does not require physical contact between persons. Too often those pointing the finger at divorced and/or remarried people are equally guilty. Jesus said, *"...but I say to you everyone who looks on a woman* (or man) *to lust...has committed adultery already..."* (Matthew 5:28). Their accusations prove Jesus' words in Matthew 5:32 which should read, *"...stigmatized as adulterous..."* (Lenski p. 230ff).

Certainly this is true. Many divorced persons are accused of having commited adultery whether they have or not. The adultry is not the issue but the rending of *"...what God has joined together..."* (Matthew 19:6). God hates divorce (Malachi 2:16) yet He divorced Israel (Jeremiah 3:8).

This briar patch is *not* in defence of divorce but in defence of *the divorced* whether or not they remarry. The attitude of the church must be to make every effort to preserve a marriage. However, if it fails, and marriages will fail because we live in the flesh, the church must have the attitude of Christ in John 8.

Divorced persons do not need to be kicked by Christians; they hurt enough already. It hurts having your life torn up. Give comfort not accusation. Demonstrate love not segregation. Above all don't treat the divorced as dirt the way many church members do.

God loves those who have suffered divorce and God forgives the sin of divorce upon repentence! God will also make something beautiful out of the single life or a second marriage *if the divorced person will let Him.*

Scripture: Isaiah 47:12-15

Have your read your Horror-scope* today? DON'T!
Satan has convinced many Christians to believe
there is some truth in the horoscopes, in astrology. There is
enough coincidence to make astrology believable. However, if you read a sun signs book straight through you'll
discover all the signs say the same thing in different words
and in a different order. It's one of the best deceptions
going because most people only read their own sign.

To say there is some good in astrology is to put
sugar in rat poison then eat it because it has come good in
it. No rational person would agree to eat sweetened rat
poison but many swallow the poison of astrology.

You rarely hear someone protest that the horoscope
was *wrong*. When it misses (which is most of the time)
people make excuses instead of throwing it all out as
Satanic nonsense. God classifies astrology with witchcraft
(v. 12). God mocks the mediums and astrologers saying
they *"chirp and mutter"* (Isaiah 8:19Leupold) indicating how
trivial their words are. They are worthless. They cannot
rescue. They are themselves condemned to the fire.

God goes on in Isaiah 8:19 to ask, *"...should not a
people consult their God? Should they consult the dead on behalf
of the living?"*

If you've been a horoscope reader it will take a
conscious effort to stop. To read them for fun opens the
door to demonic influence. Read your Bible instead.

---

*Yes, horror-scope! If you saw it through God's eyes that's how
you'd spell it too.

Scripture: Psalm 27:1-6

Whether it's a garage sale or some kind of entertainment people arrive early. To get good seats people will spend the night on the side walk then pay an outrageous price. What is the lasting benefit of being first at the garage sale or having the best seats? These are temporal things providing only momentary satisfaction. What great effort and expense is wasted on that which will not last.

Have you seen people arriving early for church services eager to get in and receive the benefits? Do they spend the night sleeping at the doors so they can get a good seat? I've never seen it and I doubt you have. That day may come when it's too late for the church to benefit any of them. Ironically but true, people arrive early for church to get a seat in the back.

Note what the psalmist declares the benefits of being in the Lord's house are, "*...in the day of trouble He will conceal me...my head will be lifted up above my enemies...I will offer sacrifices with shouts of joy...*" Though his father and mother forsake him God will take him up (v. 10).

Getting to church early and staying late with God's people ought to be the desire of your heart. If you can't stand church how will you enjoy heaven?

The next time you see people arriving early for the worlds pitiful offerings remember where the true values are. Then get yourself to church early to get a good seat down at the front.

Scripture: John 19:23-27

Americans celebrate Mother's Day the second Sunday this month. Florists provide special bouquets, ministers often prepare special messages. Resturants enjoy excellent business. All manner of economic benefit spills from this special day.

How much of it is truly in honor of motherhood and how much is a hollow display. My mother always appreciated a hand made card more than a store bought variety. Most mothers would rather have something you spent time on than something you spent money on. Truth is most mom's in their latter years would prefer you spent time *with them* instead of money on them.

Mother's need to be loved, honored, and appreciated more than just one day a year. My heart aches for those mothers whose children will ignore them on Mother's Day. It's a cruel and vicious thing to do.

We must follow the example of Jesus. Though His pain was excruciating He took care of His mother. He provided a home and someone to look after her in her old age. No doubt in His suffering Jesus remembered the care and devotion Mary poured into His life. He knew she was growing older and would need care.

This Mother's Day make a point to spent time with your mother, put your own needs and interests in the closet and please your mom. **Make** her a card. You're not too big or too old for that. It'll give her great memories. It'll be a Mother's Day for you to remember too.

Scripture: 2 Peter 3:14-18

There has been a long quiet controversy about whether or not a spokesperson for the Lord needs formal training. Both sides point to those who have been successful to prove their point. Even in scripture we have men who were educated and men who had no formal training.

Moses, Samuel, and Ezra were highly educated. Moses received the training of a prince of Egypt. He had been prepared from babyhood to be a ruler. To my knowledge no one in the Old Testament was better trained. Samuel was raised from childhood to be a servant of the Lord. Ezra, too, was well educated and a teacher of the law.

On the other hand there's Amos. What he lacked in formal schooling he made up for in commitment. And David had no special training. Neither did Joshua or Nehemiah.

In the New Testament we know Mark, John, and Peter had no university degrees. Paul and Dr. Luke however were well educated.

Peter is warning against those who are ignorant and proud of it. You've met them, heard them preach, and wondered how they got so far in the ministry. You can detect them because they are unstable and distort those things which are hard to understand. However, I've heard supposedly educated preachers distort what is hard to understand. So the debate continues.

It's always best to check what you hear from the pulpit against the Bible. The educated speaker may be wrong and the other one right.

Scripture: Mark 11:20-26

There's the old story about taking a bucket of mud to the top of a certain hill and stirring it until it becomes gold. The secret? You are not to think of a white horse. Well, that settles that.

Faith is different. When Jesus cursed the tree He immediately saw it as already withered. The disciples did not. Here in is part of the secret of moving mountains. *"Now faith is the assurance of things hoped for, the conviction of things not seen,"* (Hebrews 11:1).

Does it help if we are desperate? Or have an undeniable desire? It may. Jairus was told, *"Do not be afraid any longer, only believe,"* (Mark 5:36). His daughter was resurrected. Which raises the question, "Are we serious enough in our requests to God?" These questions can't be answered here; so look at another part of receiving what we ask from God.

We can not expect God to answer our requests when we harbor resentment (that is unforgiveness) in our hearts. Does a disobedient child get favors from mom and dad? Hardly. Jesus commanded, *"And when you stand praying, forgive..."* (v. 25).

Faith is part of getting answers to prayer; equally important is being on good terms with the Father. We must grow in both areas: learning to believe without doubt, AND in developing a forgiving spirit. God is eager to help you achieve both. He desires to give you good things, to answer your prayers. He also wants you to be forgiving.

Scripture: Ezekiel 36:22-27

Do you ever feel rather special because God blessed you when you knew you needed discipline instead? Do you feel rather proud of yourself thinking, "Maybe I'm not so bad after all." Most of us have had that experience.

Perhaps we need to look deeper, examine the circumstances, consider how the blessings we received reflect upon the God Who gave them. Am I trying to deflate your ego? Yes.

The Jews no doubt were bad mouthing God because of their circumstances. They had only been complainers since they left Egypt. Here they are scattered from the land God had promised them, they are being persecuted, so they complain. God accuses them of *"profaning His name."*

To complain against the Lord is not a sin if you complain *to Him.* Many of the Psalms express complaint against God. Jeremiah complained to the Lord. Elijah complained claiming to be the only one left who had not bowed his knee to Baal. What would you think if a wife complained about her husband to all she met? The Jews were complaining to everybody about God.

For the sake of His holy name God restored the Jews to their homeland. For the sake of His holy name God often blesses us.

Just as the ancient world watched to see how God treated the Jews; so the modern world watches to see how God treats His own. The next time you're blessed, repent and thank Him with all your heart.

Scripture: Romans 8:1-4

My favorite verse is Romans 8:1. It tells the whole story of salvation and how those who are washed by the blood of Jesus ought to treat one another.

First, it tells the story of salvation through Jesus Christ. Before being born again we have an infinite list of accusations against us. Every sin we have committed accuses us. We stand condemned. Jesus told Nicodemus, *"He who believeth on Him is not condemned: but he that believeth not is condemned already, because he hath not believed in the name of the only begotten Son of God,"* (John 3:18KJV). So, those who are in Christ, who have believed on Him are no longer condemned.

Second, *"no condemnation"* reveals how believers should treat each other. Sad to say but there is a spirit of condemnation in many believers. They condemn everyone who does not live the Christian life as they do. Some are bound up in "church rules" so they condemn those who live free in Christ. *Please note: there is a difference between church rules and scripture.* Some are just plain gossips. Others have difficulty living freely in Christ so try to prevent others from doing so.

"There is therefore now no condemnation for those who are in Christ Jesus" means no condemnation before God AND **no condemnation from fellow believers**. If your brother or sister in Christ annoys you, pray for them, encourage them in the word, love them, and discuss your problem with them. Maybe it's you who needs to change.

Scripture: 1 Corinthians 4:6-13

Sarcasm gets the job done when other forms of expression fail. In today's reading Paul is being sarcastic. When dealing with prideful folks it takes strong words to knock the wind out of them. One of the main problems in the church at Corinth was *pride*.

What is at issue here is the judging of God's anointed by the congregation. This remains an issue in churches today. Congregations fire, dismiss, or run off the pastor when they have no business doing so. You can't honestly support congregational church government with scripture. It has caused more problems than any other form of church government. When the congregation is in *one accord* as in Acts it works great, but how often is that true?

"Big-shot-itus" had the Corinthian church split four ways (1 Corinthians 1:12-13). The Corinthian church was *"already filled, already rich, had already become kings, were prudent, strong, distinguished"* ONLY IN THEIR OWN EYES. Those who raise their hand or voice against God's anointed today have the same opinion of themselves smothered in false humility. They forget Who the Head of the church is so make themselves the head of the church.

Study your Bible, examine church history, look at the lives of those who've "run off the preacher". You will see there is no blessing in raising your hand against the Lord's anointed. Better to pray for, love, encourage, bear with the man of God than work against him. The pastor serves the Lord; but he shepherds the congregation.

Scripture: Hosea 7:8-16

When I was a child my grandmother lived upstairs. She loved to bake but her oven did not heat evenly so she had to occasionally turn whatever she was baking. Ephraim was a "...*cake not turned...* " (v. 8), meaning he was burnt on one side and raw on the other. He was half-baked, lopsided, not evenly developed. Ephraim had made himself unfit.

Israel mixed itself with the pagan nations when God intended for Israel to dwell alone (Numbers 23:9). God was to be Israel's sole provider, protection, helper. Ephraim was sprinkled with gray hair and didn't know it. Meaning Israel's strength was ebbing away as in old age. Loss of the knowledge of God deprives a person or nation. They can't read the handwriting on the wall, they can't see their true nature. When you turn away from God and His gospel you cut off the fountain of life.

No longer looking to God for guidance Ephraim like a *"silly dove"* fluttered between Egypt and Assyria. Cooing first to one then the other. Neither was able to satisfy Ephraim's desires.

How like so many Christians who have turned aside from following the Lord to seek satisfaction in the world. Instead of turning to God for their needs they turn to the pitiful offerings of the world.

Don't be a cake not turned. Become all you can be by trusting fully daily always in the Lord Jesus Christ. He and He alone is the satisfaction of the soul.

Scripture: Genesis 2:10-17

This is the time of year gardeners get busy tilling, planting, and looking forward to a bountiful harvest. Whether or not one enjoys gardening; it is hard work. For those with lethargic desks jobs gardening rediscovers forgotten muscles. The sore muscles are worth the transport gardening provides.

To believe work is punishment for Adam's sin is to have misread the Bible. God created man then put him in the garden to take care of it. Just what Adam's work entailed we don't know, he got himself kicked out before we could find out. But work was instituted *before* sin entered the picture.

Your work will be enjoyable if you are doing what God wants you to. In my own life teaching was enjoyable right up to the time God had other work for me to do. I still enjoy substituting occasionally but I don't want to return permanently to the classroom. Life all around is so much better when we are doing our best being busy with what God has for us to do.

In the Garden of Eden everything was perfect: no thorns, no weeds, no plant destroying bugs, no drought or flood. Can you imagine gardening under those circumstances?

There's good news. God is going to restore the primeval pristine perfection of His original creation (Romans 8:19-22). Then we will experience the work Adam had been given to do before he sinned. Meanwhile, what work has God given you to do? Are you doing it with joy?

Scripture: Acts 2:1-13

Pentecost in the New Testament is the birthday of the church. Just as there were scoffers then (v. 13), there are some today who deny the coming of the Holy Spirit in power and the speaking in tongues that resulted. To argue that Luke's report is a theological construction is to deny the facts.

The 120 who gathered in the upper room were looking for Jesus to return in power and glory. What came upon them was totally unexpected (v. 12). The fact that the listeners from many languages heard testimony in his own tongue substantiates glossolalia (speaking in tongues).

What would be interesting to find out is what happened to the 380 who were *not* in the upper room. Paul tells us Jesus appeared to more than 500 disciples at one time (1 Corinthians 15:6). Acts 1:15 says there were about 120 persons in the upper room waiting as Jesus had commanded. 500 minus 120 leaves 380.

Did the 380 get tired of waiting? Did they have more important things to do? Did they not believe anything special was going to happen? Why weren't they with the apostles? Did they receive the baptism of the Holy Spirit at a different time and place? No one knows.

What we do know is that having been filled *to satisfaction* with the Holy Spirit the disciples went forth with power, conviction, enthusiasm, and authority. When a Christian lacks those qualities, has he been filled with the Holy Spirit? You decide.

Scripture: Leviticus 23:15-21

Whitmonday (the Monday following Pentecost Sunday) is celebrated in a special way at All Saints Church in St. Ives, Huntingtonshire, England. The event is called *Dicing for Bibles Day.*

A bequest (in 1675) with the intent of providing Bibles for poor children of the parish required them to win a Bible at a dice game. The tradition has lasted to this day when each year six Bibles are given away. Whitmonday means White-Monday just as Whitsunday means White-Sunday, that is, Pentecost.

Pentecost was inaugurated in the Law. In Old Testament times it was an agrarian festival embodying great celebration and thanksgiving. Also called the Feast of Weeks it was a time of covenant renewal. How apropos to give Bibles in remembrance of Pentecost.

Many churches provide Bibles to children or teens at specific times in their growth. Some receive a Bible at Confirmation, some when they enter their teen years, many others receive a Bible when they are water baptized. When did you receive your first Bible?

An organization that distributes Bibles around the world is the Gideons. Their work gets Bibles into countries where missionaries are restricted from entering. They place Bibles in prisons, motels, hospitals, and distribute them outside public school buildings.

There are many glowing reports of lives changed because someone gave a Bible away. The Bible is a valuable treasure. Like food it must be consumed to be beneficial. What affect has the Bible had upon you? How has it changed your life?

Scripture: Isaiah 3:16-24

Sin destroys in more ways than the death of the soul. It kills youth, beauty, opportunity, joy, peace, good health, ad infinitum. You've seen it happen time and again. A young person has everything going for him or her but sin destroys it.

Years ago there was a beautiful blonde girl in my class. She had everything a person could desire until she started doing drugs, sleeping around, and ignoring the principles her parents taught her. Our paths crossed a decade after she graduated. She was as Isaiah describes in today's reading. She had aged terribly. Instead of looking 28 she looked 58. Instead of beautiful blonde hair her hair was crisp, brittle, and falling out. Instead of the peaches and cream complexion her face was mottled. Instead of smooth skin she was withered. Sin had destroyed her it wasn't something listed in medical books.

There were two close friends in my classes. One born again the other not. I saw them again years later. The Christian was still vigorous, young, attractive. He had a fine family. The other had become an alcoholic. He looked drawn, tired. His eyes were sunk in. His family life was in turmoil because of his drinking. His health was shot.

Isaiah tells it as it is. Reject the Lord and take the consequences. OR serve the Lord and enjoy the consequences. Your daily choices determine how your life will develop. In light of these things, how are you deciding? It's up to you.

Scripture: 1 Kings 2:1-11

Queen Victoria was born May 24, 1819. The Monday preceding May 24 Canadians celebrate Victoria Day. When William IV died, Victoria was 18. She was awakened in the middle of the night to be made Queen. She reigned until her death 64 years later. Victoria married her cousin Prince Albert in 1840. They had four sons and five daughters.

During her reign the sun never set on the British Empire. Dickens lived and wrote; Sherlock Holmes became popular; Tennyson wrote *The Idylls of the King* and *Crossing the Bar*. Lewis Carroll wrote *Alice in Wonderland*. Stevenson wrote, *Treasure Island*. In France artists Monet, Renoir, and Rodin began their work.

Queen Victoria influenced styles from architecture to clothing and furniture. She influenced the thought of the nation. Victorian principles are *honesty*, *morality*, and *propriety*. Only Elizabeth I has had as much influence on every area of life in British history.

King David reigned seven years at Hebron and thirty-three at Jerusalem. Second Samuel recounts David's reign. During David's reign Ussah dies moving the ark, Philistia, Assyria, Ammon are defeated. From David's sin with Bathsheba the joy and victory began to drain from his life. Incest, murder, and rebellion are in his own house. David died an old and broken man. Yet, David is called a man after God's own heart.

David never turned aside to worship other gods. Both David and Victoria demonstrated a fidelity to the Lord God. What's good for rulers is good for us.

Scripture: Habakkuk 3:16-19

Have you ever received news so terrible it drained your strength and will? How did you react to it? Did you cry out to God? Did you curse and swear because tragedy had crashed into your life?

Habakkuk heard from the Lord news that literally sapped his strength. He wrote, *"I heard and my heart pounded, my lips quivered at the sound; decay crept into my bones, and my legs trembled,"* (v. 16NIV). What Habakkuk heard was the total destruction and annihilation that was coming upon his people. God was bringing the Chaldeans against His people to punish them for their sins. The wicked swallow up the righteous. The rich oppressed the poor, the haughty trampled down the humble. God had had enough.

Following his expression of distress and devastation Habakkuk makes an awesome affirmation. He sets the stage painting as bleak a picture as he can imagine. Verse 17 describes no less than a devouring famine. Habakkuk declares though such devastation come, *"I will exalt in the Lord, I will rejoice in the God of my salvation,"* (v. 18).

Is it possible to exalt in the Lord and rejoice in the God of your salvation when tragedy deracinates your heart? Yes! but only when you have grown up in your faith. Begin today declaring your joy in the Lord when little aggravations make your path bumpy. Then when severe tribulations come you'll be firmly rooted in your faith. You'll be unshaken, declaring as Habakkuk your confidence in the Lord.

Scripture: John 7:37-43

We like to think that we would not have disputed about Jesus had we heard Him preach. Yet, we have debates over translations of the Bible.

There can be errors in translation. These mistranslations prove it. In a Copenhagen airport, "We take your bags and send them in all directions." A detour sign in Japan, "Stop: drive sideways." In a Swiss menu, "Our wines leave you nothing to hope for." In a Soviet weekly, "See exhibition of 15,000 artists executed over the past two years." Some errors in translation are not humorous. Errors in scripture translation would be tragic.

Unless you are a Hebrew and Greek scholar you must depend upon a translation. Every English version is just that, a translation. There were English translations before King James paid scholars who depended heavily upon Jerome's Latin Vulgate to make a *new* English translation. The KJV published in 1611 is in Shakespearean English.

It's curious how the KJV became known as the *"Authorized"* version when King James never authorized (affixed his seal) to it. Had he affixed his seal all other English translations would have become illegal.

As language changed up to date translations were made. Some may be better than others. All are accurate. Some Bibles are not a translation at all. The *Living Bible* is a paraphrase, expressing the essence but not necessarily the precision of the original. The translation you prefer is the best one for you. A better approach is to study from several translations.

Scripture: Psalm 139:17-24

Do you hate those who despise the Lord or do you have pity on them? Does the psalmist really have the right attitude? Should we agree with the psalmist hating those who hate the Lord?

Consider what happened to those nations and peoples who despised the Lord in the Old Testament. Were they not destroyed from the earth? Was not their punishment complete destruction?

Many people refuse to believe a loving God would destroy thousands of people. It's not the love *of* God that is in question here but our love *for* God.

When someone deliberately insults your mother, father, wife, husband, child, or best friend doesn't it make you angry? When someone speaks evil about someone you cherish and honor don't you want to strike back? Your love and devotion for God are on the line here. Shouldn't your love and devotion for God be superior to love and devotion to others? It's a simple matter, do you honor and love God or not?

There are expressions of devotion, love, honor, and commitment to the Lord throughout the psalms. If you pity those who hate the Lord how can you agree with verse 17, *"How precious also are Thy thoughts to me..."*

The psalmist wants nothing coming between God and himself (vv. 23-24). These verses do not contradict verses 21-22; but support them.

Perhaps each of us needs to acquire a better understanding of Who God is. Then we'll be more devoted to Him hating those who despise our precious Lord.

Scripture: Psalm 141:1-4

A friend was on a mission trip in Africa when he became exceedingly ill. As Paul says of Epaphroditus, *"...he was sick to the point of death..."* (Philippians 2:27). As he lay on his cot thinking he would soon be meeting Jesus, the Lord gave him a vision. In the spirit he was projected above the earth. All across the American continent were fires and smoke rising to heaven. A voice said, "These are the prayers of the saints being offered up for missionaries." After the vision he got well and returned home.

The psalmist writes, *"May my prayer be counted as incense before Thee;"* (v. 2). In a famous cathedral the custodian listened to tourists touring the building. Some sparrows had entered an open window and were circling in the sanctuary. A tourist mentioned them. The custodian thought, "They ain't sparrows, they're some o' Sunday's prayers that ain't got out yet."

How high do our prayers rise? Are they like flames of fire giving off an odor of incense before the Lord?

The psalmist added, *"Set a guard, O Lord, over my mouth; Keep watch over the door of my lips,"* (v. 3).

Perhaps we should commence our prayer time asking the Lord to set a guard over our mouths. *"...God is in heaven and you are on the earth; therefore let your words be few,"* (Ecclesiastes 5:2). Don't be a prayer babbler. Make your requests known to God with thanksgiving. Be quiet also and listen for God to speak.

Scripture: 2 Samuel 19:11-15

Today is Oak Leaf Day in Britain in honor of Charles II. In September 1651, after his defeat in the battle by the English Parliamentarians, Charles hid in Boscobel's famous oak. Thus he escaped his pursuers and was able to regain his throne in September 1660. NO, he didn't hide in the oak for nine years.

Charles II was one of England's most popular monarchs. When he regained his throne there was great celebration. He is still remembered for many good deeds. In his honor it is customary to wear an oak leaf on May 29 in remembrance of his oak tree rescue. The day is also called *Royal Oak Day.* Children forgetting to wear an oak leaf are reminded of their omission by being pushed into a bed of nettles or similarly punished.

David, too, lost and regained his throne after the rebellion of his own son Absalom. The defeat he suffered at first, being forced to flee Jerusalem, and relying upon old friends was doubly difficult because his own son was rising up against him. Upon Absalom's death David wept bitterly. Then God restored David to his throne and his kingdom.

When he regained his throne there was jubilation by some and repentance by those who were either acquiescent or supportive of the revolt. Throughout Israel's history there was loss and restoration. That is true of us also. God is faithful to restore His own who seek His will and are obedient to it.

Scripture: 1 Samuel 7:1-14

This is the traditional Memorial Day for Americans. Today the war dead are remembered. Many small towns have erected monuments honoring those who died in the wars. There will be parades, flags placed on the graves of service men, etc.

Monuments are erected as reminders of great moments in our history. They range from small plaques to large structures such as the arch at St. Louis.

Robert Robinson wrote, "Here I raise mine Ebenezer;/Hither by Thy help I'm come;/And I hope by Thy good pleasure,/Safely to arrive at home:/Jesus sought me when a stranger,/Wandering from the fold of God;/He to rescue me from danger,/Interposed His precious blood."[1]

What is that monument Robinson raised? I believe he meant the monument of living his life in Christ. Your life in Christ is a testimony, a monument to Jesus Christ's work in you. Does your "monument" honor your Lord?

Coinciding with honoring the war dead, Memorial Day is a traditional time for family reunions. There is usually someone present at these gatherings who will ask a child, "Whose child are you?" This person may notice certain similarities with one or another branch of the family.

As you think about your *Ebenezer* think also about what similarities you have with Christ. Does the world have to ask, "Whose child are you?" Can they tell you don't belong to the world's family? What characteristics set you apart, make you different, show you're part of God's family?

---

[1]*Baptist Hymnal*, (Convention Press: Nashville, TN, 1956) p. 313

Scripture: Daniel 2:14:23

Daniel, Hananiah, Mishael, and Azariah were men of prayer. They did not live in the vacuum of a prayerless life. To seek the Lord's help was not something new but something ordinary. Granted their present situation was desperate, they were about to be slain.

How different from those who try existing in the vacuum of a prayerless life. Every area of their lives is in rags and pieces but they don't know it. Then when dire circumstances drive them to the wall they remember to look up. Do they even consider whether or not God will hear them?

Every year there is a day set aside for prayer. Is that what the nation really needs, a day of prayer? Is this how we salve our wounds? Is God going to suddenly forget the wickedness we have been heaping up?

For an individual or a nation that's been creaking by ignoring God, refusing to speak to Him, forgetting to thank Him, what's needed is a day of repentance. Just as a parent does not grant requests to the disobedient child so why should God grant requests to those who ignore him until they are in trouble?

These four men in our text had the habit of daily prayer. When tragedy came rushing at them, they prayed and God answered. Just like that. Then notice something we often forget-- Daniel praised and thanked the Lord *before* he went to the king.

Is there a lesson here for you and me? A lesson to be remembered and practiced?

Scripture: 2 Corinthians 1:2-4

What human being is better qualified to reveal God than a father? A father who is loving, kind, thoughtful, generous, strict, fair, and sincere provides his son or daughter with images of what God the Father is like. Children will transfer what they see in their earthly father to God the Father. That is why a brash, unloving, undisciplined, unjust father gives a child a distorted picture of God.

Of course no earthly father can fully portray God; but he can start a child's thinking in the right direction. It is important for fathers to heed the words of Paul, *"Father's do not exasperate your children..."*NIV (Ephesians 6:4). A father exasperates his children by constantly and severely restricting their freedom to be children. Too often fathers expect their little ones to think, talk, and behave like adults. This exasperates a child. Children must have room to grow.

That does not mean that children should be allowed to do whatever they please - that too is exasperating for a child. Read the rest of Paul's advice , *"...instead bring them up in the training and instruction of the Lord."* (Ephesians 6:4)NIV

Since children learn best by example father's abide by your own expectations. Do as you want them to do.

On *FATHER'S DAY* this year let each father decide to be the best father he can be by God's grace and with God's help. Instead of expecting something from your children in your honor, give
them a reason to honor you.

Scripture: Luke 13:10-17

No wonder they crucified Jesus, He bucked the establishment. This woman had been bound by Satan in a stooped position but the religious leaders had been bound by Satan in a stupid position. When Jesus pointed this out they got bent out of shape, (*No pun intended*).

Isn't it amazing how tradition can get in the way of doing good deeds. Isn't it amazing how animals are valued above people. As Jesus reminded them, they loosed their animals on the Sabbath; but they would keep a human being bound in sickness when she could be made well. That is stupid thinking.

Isn't it also amazing that the general populace had more sense than their rulers. Luke records, "...*and the entire multitude was rejoicing over all the glorious things being done by Him*," (v. 17). They were glad to see this dear woman healed, so what if it was the Sabbath.

Do our traditions ever get in our way of doing the *right thing*? Sure they do. Traditions are too numerous for me to give an appropriate example so look honestly at your own traditions. Do they hinder, help, or are they totally innocuous.

Do you know if you exercise your freedom in Christ you will be "crucified" by wagging tongues? Jesus asked his opponents, "...*why do you yourselves transgress the commandment of God for the sake of your tradition?*" (Matthew 15:3). Nothing's changed. We still transgress the commandment of God for the sake of tradition. What shall we do about it?

Scripture: Romans 10:1-11

When discussing the condition of lost people invariably someone will defend them saying, "Oh, but they are very sincere." From the human point of view that's very commendable. The problem is one can be as sincere as sincere can be and still go to hell. Sincerity is not where it's at.

Paul writing to the Romans explains, *"For I bear them witness, they have a zeal for God..."* (v. 2). Many people have a zeal for God, for good works, for being honest, for going to church. All these things are commendable, honorable, should be encouraged; BUT none of them bring salvation to the zealot.

Paul continues, *"...but not in accordance with knowledge. For not knowing about God's righteousness, and seeking to establish their own, they did not subject themselves to the righteousness of God,"* (vv. 2-3). All those sincere folks have established what they believe to be righteousness. They have mapped out their own plan of salvation. And their map will lead them to hell.

The righteousness of God can only be known, acquired, made efficacious through Jesus Christ. *"For Christ is the end of the law for righteousness to everyone who believes,* (v. 4). All the sincerity you can muster in anything else is worthless until you come first to Jesus for forgiveness and eternal life.

Yes, you can be sincere and be sincerely wrong. Many are. In verses 9-10 Paul tells you exactly how to be saved. Until you do that, nothing, but nothing else matters.

Scripture: Isaiah 30:13-18

Do you tap your foot waiting for the microwave? Are you impatient at traffic signals? Are you that harried and hurried? Did you know it is sinful to be pressured to that extent (v. 15)?

Verses 13-14 describe very well what can happen to those living high pressure lives. Christians are not immune to stroke, heart failure, and stress depression. Often the destruction to health is total, *"like the smashing of a potter's jar..."* (v. 14).

Jesus set for us the perfect example. We would do well to emulate it. If anyone had a high pressure ministry, if anyone had an important work to do, Jesus did. Yet, he did not ignore Himself to get the job done. Reread the life of Christ at your leisure not as though cramming for final exams. Jesus took time for quietness with the Father. *"And in the early morning while it was still dark, He arose and went out and departed to a lonely place and was praying there,* (Mark 1:35). To slip off for time with the Father was regular practice for Jesus. *"But He Himself would often slip away to the wilderness to pray,"* (Luke 5:16). He also instructed His disciples to *"come away"* from the crowds (Mark 6:31-32).

If the Son of God needed time alone with the Father what do we need? Jesus separated Himself from ministry to be refreshed, revived, revitalised by time alone with God. Then we too must separate ourselves from our responsibilities for time with God. Start today.

Scripture: Matthew 23:29-36

There was a great diplomat in Europe. He encouraged his people to work and make something of their country. He wooed the neighboring nations into cooperating with him. He convinced church leaders he was a nice guy. He was photographed reaching out to the old, the poor, the children. From all appearances he was the greatest humanitarian Europe had known. He had opposition to be sure but he was such a good diplomat he won most hearts to support his cause. His name? Adolph Hitler.

You see, in essence, diplomacy is a lie. One dictionary defines diplomacy: adroitness or artfulness in securing advantages without arousing hostilities.

Jesus was no diplomat! He wasn't interested in popularity, or being accepted by the "in" crowd. Speaking to the hierarchy of the church He said, *"You serpents, you brood of vipers, how shall you escape the sentence of hell?"* (v. 33). It takes strong measures to pull down a righteous facade.

We were blessed to know a dear old lady who spoke the truth. One Sunday evening I lamented, "apparently no one needed to make a decision in the morning service." Mary said, "Oh, yes they did." Those needing to make a decision knew she spoke of them. She was painfully honest and we all benefitted from it. Sometimes her words cut me to the quick but I loved her for she was right.

Let's stop being diplomatic about sin, backsliding, and spiritual whoredom. Tell the truth in love even if it hurts. Jesus did.

Scripture: Jonah 4:1-9

How grown up are you? Don't count your chronological years; look at your attitude when things don't suit you. Do you pout when God acts contrary to your wishes. Are you disturbed when God forgives and blesses your antagonist, your enemy?

Jonah was angry because the great city repented and God spared it. Ninevah was the capital of Assyria one of the arch enemies of Israel. Apparently he didn't believe God would *actually* spare it. Didn't he remove himself to a safe distance then wait for it's destruction (v. 5)?

Jonah is pouting. God has done exactly what He said He would. Jonah preached repentance (after being disciplined) and the people of Ninevah listened and repented, so God spared them. This was not Jonah's idea of dealing with an enemy. Do we ever feel we have a better idea than God does?

Even though Jonah pouts God watches out over His servant. He provided shade; then took it away to teach Jonah a lesson. God allowed discomfort for Jonah's benefit; to teach him a lesson (vv. 7-8). God uses our discomfort to get our attention and teach us.

Not only was Jonah a pouter he was very obstinate. He said, *"I have good reason to be angry even unto death,"* (v. 9). Then God told Jonah "what for".

We don't know if there was a change in Jonah's heart. What's important is this: when God deals with you is there a change in your heart? How grown up are you?

Scripture: 2 Corinthians 9:6-12

Would you rather groaning or gracious? For some to be gracious makes them groan. The gracious person is a generous person. Let's look at some qualities of a gracious person.

First, notice they are happy most of the time. No one is happy 100% of the time; but a gracious person has a positive happy outlook. Naturally this kind of person is fun to be around. So second, a gracious person draws others to themselves. They are fun to be around because, three and four, they are genuine and sensitive to others. No one likes a fraud especially those suffering from big-shot-itus.

What really sets the gracious person apart is, five, they see needs as an opportunity instead of a threat. Six, they see how much they can give instead of how little. Oh, Oh, we just lost a bunch who thought themselves gracious. A gracious person, seven, finds joy in giving (oops, just lost a few more). They find joy in giving because, eight, they are other-person centered.

Of coarse this all rests on a foundation of faith in God and His promises. The gracious person, nine, has learned he can't outgive God. He knows this because he's tried. And finally the gracious person, ten, is fulfilled, because he has contributed to meeting the needs of others.

No, it's not easy becoming a gracious person. Nothing worth while is easy. By the grace of God we can all be gracious persons. Let the Lord help you.

Scripture: Galatians 4:21-31

Do you have the *Little Red Hen* attitude about salvation? The idea that you can do it yourself. Or worse that you are responsible for your eternal security?

God promised Abraham he would become the father of a multitude (Genesis 17:1-5). Since the possibility of the promise was growing more remote Abraham said in his heart, "Then I'll do it myself". Every Bible reader knows the awful results from which the world still suffers today.

Paul is not writing about "do it yourself families". He is writing about "do it yourself salvation". Legalism in all forms is the adultery of doing it ourselves instead of trusting and waiting on the Lord.

The Lord provided Isaac through Sarah though she was past the age to bear children. Just so, God provides our salvation we being incapable of providing it for ourselves. God also keeps us secure in Him for the same reason. We can't do it ourselves.

The legalists (v. 29) persecute those who live by the Spirit to this day. We are children by grace not by keeping legal regulations. Those trusting keeping the law will not inherit the kingdom of God (v. 30).

The Galatians reverted to legalism so have many churches today. Legalism results from *"false teachers who...sneaked in to spy out our liberty which we have in Christ Jesus in order to bring us into bondage"* (Galatians 2:4). We must guard the freedom we have in Christ. Avoid those who would bind you with legalism.

Scripture: Hebrews 3:7-11

Have you been to a stage play lately? One of the main persons in a stage production is very rarely recognized. They remain out of sight and sound of the audience. This person is especially important in an amateur production. It is the prompter.

Those who have been born again by the blood of Jesus Christ have a prompter who is never seen or heard by the world. As you and I go about on the stage of life we are being prompted by the Holy Spirit.

He has a key role as we play our many parts as parent, child, neighbor, boss, student, teacher, employee, spouse. Just as an actor on stage may become unsure of the lines so we often become unsure of our lines as Christians. Therefore, we must have our ear cocked to hear our spiritual Prompter.

"Today if you hear His voice, do not harden your hearts as when they provoked Me, As in the day of trial in the wilderness," (v. 7). Do not harden your heart means choosing what you want in opposition to what God wants. That's your trial, your test. Mordecai warned Esther to do what was right even though it could cost her her life (Esther 4:13-16).

What is the Holy Spirit prompting you to do that is not exactly to your liking? What is God's voice saying to you by way of direction for your life? Do not harden you heart in rebellion. Do not go astray in your heart.

Scripture: 1 Samuel 4:19-22

Luther nailed his 95 theses on the church door thus beginning a new direction for the church. His paper was visible to all. Today, God has nailed something else over the doors of many churches. Throughout the world there are churches with the word *Ichabod* over the door. Those with spiritual discernment see it, recognize it, know what it means.

Just as the Lord warned the church at Ephesus, *"I am coming to you, and will remove your lampstand out of its place- unless your repent,"* (Revelation 2:5). From the world's perspective these churches appear healthy, strong, doing a good business. Inside they are dead for the glory of the Lord has departed. The church may be very socially active. It may operate many humanitarian ministries. The services may attract great multitudes; but are people being born again? Are lives being changed?

The only times Israel was defeated in battle was when there was sin in the camp. The Ark had been captured by the Philistines. When Eli heard it, he fell over, broke his neck and died. Are there people that concerned about having *Ichabod* over the church door? So concerned it knocks them over? Does anyone care God has removed His lampstand?

Dear people of God examine your church to see if *Ichabod* is written over the door. Pray for God to reveal it to you. And ask what you should do about it. *"Who knows whether or not"* you came to your church for just such a time as this (Esther 4:14).

Scripture: John 9:1-12

Trials and tribulations are not always the result of sin. Jesus correcting the disciples' thinking said, *"it was neither that this man sinned, nor his parents..."* (v. 3). Granted, we create our own trails and tribulations. We disobey God, get into difficulties, then cry for Him. We disobey because with our finite minds we think obedience is foolishness.

What Jesus did to the blind man made no sense to anyone. The man was blind and Jesus sticks mud in his eyes. Can't you see the foolishness of that? Sure you can if you pretend you don't know the end of the story. Had the disciples also forgotten what Jesus just said about the man being blind to bring glory to God? How often we gripe and grumble about our situation instead of seeing how it can bring glory to God.

After putting mud in his eyes Jesus commands him to go wash it out. Notice something, Jesus never commands us to do something without also encouraging us to do it. Sometimes things get worse before getting better. The mud in the man's eyes encouraged him to wash it out. He does and gains his sight. The miracle resulted from obedience not the mud.

Obedience to God brings redemption and restoration from calamity, hardship, and times of privation. God does this through our obedience to bring glory to Himself and benefit to us. Which do you want; glory or benefit? Who cares about the glory as long as you enjoy the benefits.

Scripture: Exodus 32:30-35

There was a wealthy southern farmer who made it a practice to work on the Lord's day. He prospered and enjoyed his wealth. One afternoon he hailed the local pastor who was driving by. "Look," he told the pastor, "how excellent my crops are." He went on bragging about how he had expanded his operations then added, "I always work on Sunday. What do you think about that preacher?" The Holy Spirit gave the pastor wisdom for he said, "God doesn't always harvest in the fall."

Moses had great love for the people of Israel. He interceded for them after the golden calf incident. He chose to have his name blotted from God's book if God refused to forgive the people (v. 32). Paul wrote, *"For I could wish that I myself were accursed, separated from Christ for the sake of my brethren..."* (Romans 9:3). God does not accept the exchange of one human for another for salvation. Only Jesus could atone for our sins. God told Moses, *"Whoever has sinned against me I will blot him out of my book,"* (v. 33).

Then God revealed that retribution for sin is not immediate. *"...nevertheless **in the day when** I punish, I will punish them for their sin,"* (v. 34).

Harvest time is coming for every person. There is a day of evening coming, a day when God will balance the books. The wicked shall receive that which they have chosen and the redeemed shall receive eternal life. Are you ready for the harvest?

Scripture: Zephaniah 1:7-13

Three things we need to note about our seriousness toward God. First, we are to keep silent before Him. The Lord is King of kings and Lord of Lords. As such He has absolute authority. This call to be silent is for us to cease every manner of opposition and argument to His will. It calls for complete submissive obedience to Him Who can enforce His will. The call to be silent also calls the hearers to stop babbling before their idols.

The second thing regards our manner of dress. Many clothes are imported today; that's not the problem. The problem was the people of God did not want to be recognized as the people of God by their manner of dress. Don't we find the same rebellion today? Fashion and style often over rule decency and propriety. God had given regulations regarding their clothes (Numbers 15:38f and Deuteronomy 22:11f). With the specifications God also gave a reasons.

Finally, this business of jumping over the threshold, refers to a Philistine custom inaugurated at the down fall of Dagon (1 Samuel 5:1-5). Applied to the Jews and us means to get rid of silly superstitions in worship. Pseudo-piety is a silly superstition; thinking certain body posture or motions have significance with God. Religion had degenerated to "external, sanctimonious piety," (Laetsch) and meticulous ritual with no inner devotion to God.

We would do well to examine our manner of dress and worship. Are we guilty of Judah's sins? Do we take God seriously?

Scripture: Micah 5:1-4

Have you ever had to back track on your opinion or words? Some folks won't back track when faced with opposing evidence. Often we make rash statements without full knowledge. It's nothing new. Those who heard Jesus preach and witnessed the miracles were divided in their opinion.

"'Surely the Christ is not going to come from Galilee, is He?'" (John 7:41). They disputed because they only had partial knowledge. They were familiar with Micah 5:2, and Isaiah 11:1. Everyone from the least to the greatest looked for the Consolation of Israel to come from Bethlehem. Even when Philip called Nathaniel, Nathaniel queried, *"Can anything good come out of Nazareth?"* (John 1:46). That the Christ was to come from Bethlehem the city of David was ingrained in their thinking. They had confidence in the words of the prophets. We know that Christ came from Bethlehem because the gospels say so.

When we don't have full knowledge as those listening to Jesus where can we place our reliance? We should always place our reliance on the Bible. If some one comes to you with a *new revelation* compare it to the printed word of God.

The people most easily led astray by spurious doctrines and false religions are those who are ignorant of the Bible. They are like a wave of the sea tossed about by every wind.

What is the devotee of Jesus to do? He must study the Bible until he knows it better than anything else. Start today.

Scripture: John 21:1-11

According to our obedience God provides. Can you say Amen to that?

After the resurrection Peter and the other fishermen returned to the work they knew to do. They were not the kind to sit and wait for God to fill their mouths. Their life long profession seemed so natural so they continued followed it. Had they forgotten Jesus said He would make them fishers of men?

Let's bring it home. Do you know believers who have returned to their old manner of life? Perhaps they had been called to special service which they performed for a while but then went back to the old occupation?

For these disciples there efforts proved worthless. They fished all night and caught nothing (vv. 3-5). Do you ever wonder why you're not making any progress? These professional fishermen did. Their labors were fruitless as our's often are because they were not directed by the Lord.

Then when their labors were directed by the Lord the catch was so great their nets were about to tear (vv. 6-11). After this Jesus again commissioned the disciples telling Peter, *"Tend my lambs,"* (v. 15).

If your labors seem futile it's time to examine them. Are they directed by the Lord? It's easy to be doing a good work and fail because it is not what God has for you to do.

It's as true as true can be; according to our obedience, God provides. It requires faith and trust but it works. I know from experience.

Scripture: Hebrews 6:1-8

Many will argue that one can *lose* his salvation. The problem is that of understanding of terms. People speak of "falling from grace". Falling from grace is not the same as losing your salvation. My children fall from my good grace and pleasure in them but they're still my children. One is born into the family of God (John 3). Can one be unborn from the family of God? Regardless of what my children do or even if they deny I'm their father it doesn't change their relationship. They are still my kids.

One of the references used to "prove" one can lose his salvation is verse 6 of today's reading. The Greek word here is *parapipto*. The word does not mean to fall *away* but "to offend", "to sin" (Kittel, VI:171). The writer is speaking of deliberate sin which does indeed hold Jesus up to open shame.

The following verses do not prove the incorrect understanding that one loses his salvation. The ground drinks the rain as we receive the Holy Spirit. It then produces vegetation just as we should be producing fruits meet for repentance and glory to God. If the ground produces weeds just as we may produce wood, hay, stubble, **its the vegetation** that gets burned up not the ground. It is our works that get burned up (1 Corinthians 3:15).

The works can not be redeemed just as weeds are not miraculously changed into vegetables. I'm confident many will dispute this briar patch. That's OK.

Scripture: Mark 12:41-44

"All they do is beg for money", is the excuse many people give for not going to church. In reality very few messages are preached about money contrary to scripture. Ask these people how many sermons they've heard about money or who preached them and they probably can't tell you.

In the Bible there are 500 verses about prayer; 500 about faith; but 2000 about money. Of Jesus' 38 parables 16 were about money. One in ten verses deals with money.

These same folks who gripe about money should avoid watching PBS television because they beg for money weeks on end several times a year. What about not giving to the United Way because they beg for money along with the bundles of requests that come in each week's mail. Though most of these mendicants do some good none compare to the benevolent work of the church.

In addition, ask any of these secular beggars for a financial report and see if you get one. Your church publishes a financial report on a regular basis. You see where the money goes, how it's spent, what benevolent work it's doing.

Those who attend church but don't pay their way have a different problem. They soak up the heat and air conditioning, are ministered to by the pastor and staff, have their children taught the word at no expense to them. Only the church and PBS are free to non-payers. Pay your way, you'll be glad you did.

Scripture: 1 Thessalonians 5:12-22

The children's saying, "Sticks and stone will break my bones but words will never hurt me" is simply a lie. Words are very powerful. Words can build up or tear down more quickly than anything else. Words carry more weight between friends and relatives than between enemies.

Your enemy can say terrible things to you and "so what". Let a friend, spouse, or someone else you love say something in a harsh tone and it hurts. It cuts right down to the heart. James warns us of the terrible destruction of words, "...*how great a forest is set aflame by such a small fire! And the tongue is a fire...*" (James 2:4-5). You and I have said some pretty burning things in the past for which we should seek forgiveness.

In today's text Paul urges us to use our words constructively. How do you show appreciation? By expressing it in words, by telling someone what a fine job they did. How do you esteem someone? In the same way to their face and to others. Brag on those you love and esteem. Satan would have you criticize and all of us are guilty of being critical as if *we ourselves were perfect.*

Give flowers to the living. Don't stand by the casket telling others what a grand ol' soul she was. As you esteem, admonish, encourage, do it patiently with love and sincerity. Never forget words are powerful, sharp, soothing, constructive and destructive. Choose your words wisely.

Scripture: Psalm 38:1-8

American author Christopher Morely said this generation has two main problems, namely: the past and how to escape it; the future and how to avoid it. We've made great advances in science, we've forged ahead in psychology, we excel all others in curing social ills; yet none of these has eased the burden of life, the burden of guilt.

Regardless of our efforts man continues to sin, continues to feel guilty about his sins, therefore bearing a tremendous burden. He may admit his oppression is the result of sin. He may not recognize why he is restless and dissatisfied. Modern man feels imprisoned, incomplete but doesn't know why.

Evolutionary theory has eliminated absolutes in morals, authority, and human worth. Why shouldn't you do what feels good *if* you are only glorified swamp matter. The psalmist recognized that sin removed the health from his bones (v. 3). The condition of the soul has a direct and proportional effect upon the body.

Human efforts at best put a band aid on cancer. Psychologist, counselors, and others advise us to prune the tree of dissipation and willful disobedience. We need to cut it down, better yet deracinate it. In Psalm 39 the psalmist claims though he guarded his mouth his condition grew worse.

There is only one answer to Morely's dilemma--repentance of sin and faith in Jesus Christ. All other efforts are pitiful, paltry, and piecemeal. *"Many are the sorrows of the wicked...he who trusts in the Lord, lovingkindness shall surround him,"* (Psalm 32:10).

Scripture: Hebrews 11:32-40

I remember an old song, "This world is not my home/I'm just a passin' through/if heaven's not my home/then Lord what will I do/the angels beckon me/from heaven's open door/and I can't feel at home/in this world anymore". That's something we should remember. This world is not our home. In fact and reality it's a pretty shabby place.

We can't imagine better because this is as good as we've known. We can't imagine what the world God created was like before man sinned and all nature fell. We can't imagine perfection.

Satan likes deceiving us into thinking that life here is superlative, wonderful, and can be made better. He likes to make us think we don't deserve this wonderful planet. Quite the contrary is true.

Did you notice one pointed phrase in today's text? Did it jump out at you?

Remember everything must take a back seat to the Bible's authority. When the Bible says something not agreeing with us or our understanding it's we who are in error *not the Bible*.

Therefore accept and believe a very neat thing revealed here. The writer writes, "...*men of whom the world was not worthy...*" (v. 38). Truth is, the world is never worthy of God's children. If you are born again, the world is not worthy of you. You are a prince or princess of the eternal heavens, a child of the King of kings. This world is not your home, you **are** just passing through. Believe it! Live it!

Scripture: Zechariah 8:13-18

God is sovereign. He can do as He pleases for He gives account to no one. In one instance He promises harm for those who provoke Him to anger. In another instance He forgives the provocation (always upon repentance). God destroys and redeems.

We easily understand punishment for sin. Understanding God's grace and salvation is difficult. Just what is God's purpose for redeeming those who repent and believe? Zechariah quotes God saying, *"I will save you that you may become a blessing..."* (v. 13). Are you meeting God's purpose?

This world is blessed to have the children of God residing here if only temporarily. If it weren't for us, God would have no reason to preserve it further. So we are a blessing in that sense but there's more.

We are to speak the truth, judge with truth and judgment for peace with our communities (v. 16). Would that be a blessing to everyone? Absolutely.

Why does the Lord comfort and encourage by repeating *"Do not fear"* (vv. 13 & 15). God knows that Satan will deceive us to fear being a blessing. What's there to fear except what people will think because we are a royal priesthood, a peculiar people (1 Peter 2:9). Many in this world are skeptical of kindness from strangers, so we withhold kindness fearing their skepticism or reprisal.

Nevertheless, there is nothing to fear while we are fulfilling our purpose of being a blessing. What we should fear is failing our Lord, failing in our purpose.

Scripture: Jeremiah 28:9-14

A remarkable sequence of events continues in the world. The false teachers and false prophets of Jeremiah's day are with us still. They prophecy man and the world are evolving into a better existence. According to these false teachers who deny the God of creation, we are steadily, if slowly, moving upward toward our own perfection.

Crime and violence statistics do not confirm their prophecy but they remain undaunted. Those proclaiming the *theory* of evolution as fact are deluding the world with a false hope.

The big bang theory is backwards; that's how the world ends not how it began. Why not evolution in reverse? If bestiality were not a thing practiced God would not have restricted it (Exodus 22:19; Leviticus 18:23 and 20:16). Was the evolutionary ape-man the result of bestiality? Who knows?

The evolutionist can't fit God into their theory. *"And God created man in His own image, in the image of God he created him; male and female He created them,"* (Genesis 1:27). The Bible is truth, evolution is imagination run amuck.

The false prophets around Jeremiah proclaimed peace was imminent. Instead Israel spent seventy years of captivity in Babylon just as God said. What will you believe today, evolutionary *theory*, or the perfect word of God? Don't be deluded the world is not getting better. Read your newspaper.

For Israel there was hope of restoration after seventy years. When the evolutionist see Christ coming in all His glory they will cry for the rocks to hide them. Read your Bible.

Scripture: Matthew 4:1-11

We have an adversary who does not quit. He never tires, he never takes a day off, he is constantly at us. It's remarkable he does not change his tactics and needn't because they still work. He hit upon a plan in the Garden of Eden and he's stuck to it.

Notice how he approaches the Son of God. Satan says to Jesus, *"If you are the Son of God..."* (v. 3). Satan comes at us and often persuades us with the same ploy he used on Jesus, Eve, and every other person who ever lived. The ploy is *doubt.*

It is doubt that dismantles faith. It is doubt that reduces our effectiveness as witnesses for Jesus. Doubt is one of the things that keeps our prayers from being answered. Remember Jesus said, *"...if you have faith and do not doubt,"* (Matthew 21:21).

Satan came at Jesus with the same time worn tactics he used on Eve; the lust of the flesh, the lust of the eyes, and the pride of life. Lust of the eyes, *"...command these stone to be made bread,"* (v. 3). Pride of life, *"...throw yourself down;"* (v. 6) which would have gained Jesus an immediate following. And the lust of the eyes, *"All these things I will give you..."* (v. 9). At Calvary Satan tried again through a human mouth (Matthew 27:40). He *never* quits.

Though Satan's tactics are ancient; we are just as naive as Eve, which doesn't say much for our progress does it?

Scripture: Acts 13:1-4

In many churches nominating committees begin their work. The electing of deacons, teachers, and other workers takes place during the summer getting ready for the a new church year. All year pulpit commitess seek ministers to fill the pulpit. Other churches may be involved in ordaining men and women for various ministries. How much care is taken to determine the will of God?

Too often, unqualified, uncalled, un-anointed people are stuck in jobs because somebody has to do it. Wouldn't it be better if the job went undone until the Lord called a person to serve in the position? Do our methods agree with scripture?

The church, meeting at Antioch, was not specifically considering sending out missionaries. They had not planned a world wide outreach program and then sought somebody to do it. *"...while they were minstering to the Lord and fasting, the Holy Spirit said..."* (v. 2).

How many ordaining councils, how many nominating committees **wait** for the Holy Spirit to designate those He has chosen to serve? Ah, but we are on a schedule, we have so many things to do, we are all very busy, so we forge ahead without God.

Barnabas and Saul were elected by the Holy Spirit for service. They were sent out by the Holy Spirit (v. 4). There ministry was successful because of the impetus and empowering of the Holy Spirit.

If we claim the Bible to be our guide in faith and practice, perhaps we need more emphasis on the latter.

Scripture: Joel 2:21-27

Whatever your circumstances, wherever you are, regardless of how bleak the future looks, your hope is in the Lord. *"The Lord longs to be gracious to you, And therefore He waits on high to have compassion on you. For the Lord is a God of justice; How blessed are those who long for Him,"* (Isaiah 30:18).

The first verse of today's text contains a beautiful phrase: *"Do not fear...rejoice and be glad."* Those are comforting words when we are facing depressing days. Those are strengthening words when we feel we can't go on. Those are encouraging words when we have suffered reversal after reversal.

God promises to provide for His own because He loves them so much. It is because He loves us that He demands repentance before blessing (Joel 2:13-14). God knows unrepented sin eats away at us, destroying us. He wants the best for us. His promises are good. His blessings are only blocked by our stubborn hearts.

God has already begun the blessings of those who long for Him. He has sent the early and latter rains. He promises full threshing floors, wine vats overflowing, plenty to eat and be satisfied.

Do you long for these blessings of the Lord? Is that what we're to long for? Isn't our longing supposed to be for the Lord?

It requires discipline on our part to cast aside the physical to yearn for the spiritual. However, that's what is required. As we seek Him He provides for all our needs.

Scripture: Isaiah 44:9-17

Every where on earth human beings worship something. If it is not some natural part of creation it is something man himself creates. Often man worships what seems beyond his understanding: the sun, moon, fire, etc. Others in their deception and imagination invest man made forms with supernatural powers.

The interesting thing to note is the dichotomy between pagans (those worshipping anything except the Lord God) and Christians. In verses 12 and 13 we see two qualities that are lacking in many Christians. As the man shapes the idol he, *"gets hungry and his strength fails; he drinks no water and becomes weary,"* (v. 12). We see here sacrificial dedication to his work, to his god which his hands created. In his devotion he avoids eating and drinking to finish his *important* work.

In the next verse we see what great care is taken in measuring, shaping, finishing. This pagan gives his best effort to make a god for himself. The idol is in the form of a man to set in the house. It can not move but must be carried about.

Praise the Lord, we have followers of Jesus making the same sacrifices of the first man. We have Christian workers as meticulous and devoted as the second man. Both are in the minority.

The Christian should be the best he possibly can be. God deserves sacrificial devotion and our best efforts. Let me challenge you to avoid mediocrity, half hearted effort, and the "this'll do" attitude. Give your best, always.

Scripture: Judges 13:1-7

Have you ever skipped those passages in the Old Testament that just were not all that fascinating? For example, the lists of "begats", or the ordinances of the Tabernacle, how about most of the book of Numbers. There are so many other chapters in the Old Testament packed with action, heroes, miracles, and neat stuff.

However, we cheat ourselves of greater understanding when we skip those less interesting portions of scripture. As you read the life of Samson, Israel's thirteenth judge, you see in some respects he is a rascal. His riddle for instance (Judges 14:12ff). His admiration of beautiful women is another trait to make some frown. Did you notice in today's reading a special designation for Samson?

He was to be a Nazirite to the Lord. Don't confuse Nazirite with Nazarene. In Numbers 6 you can read the very specific restrictions a Nazirite accepts for the duration of his being set apart to the Lord. As you read Samson's biography about the only restrictions of the Nazirite he observed were letting his hair grow and not drinking wine or anything from the grape vine. How would we know this without reading Numbers 6?

Samson was a rapscallion. Nevertheless, God used him. His strength was *not* in his hair. Reading carefully you'll see the Spirit of the Lord came upon him when he needed strength. In his heart he remained a Nazirite. Compare the regulations of a Nazirite with the life of Samson. You'll have a better understanding of him.

Scripture: Joshua 9:3-15

Con artists have been around for a long time. Some popular scams against old people in rural areas are offers to paint the roof, or pave the drive, or repair lightening rods. The first rain washes the paint off, the paving costs many times more, copper lightening rods are replaced with aluminum. People get bilked, and milked all the time.

There is a way to avoid being taken never mentioned in the public media. The lesson is taught so well in today's reading.

Joshua stood by Moses many years. He had been well trained to lead the people. What happened that he was taken in by these crafty deceitful Gibeonites?

The Israelites had been under a lot of stress. They were busy conquoring the land God had promised. They had experienced miracles; eg. the wall of Jericho. They had experienced defeat because of Achan's sin. They were tired. In that frame they let their guard down.

Did you know Satan waits just out of sight for you to let your guard down. He's very patient because he knows you will eventually let your guard down. When you do, he moves in and you're defeated.

The secret to avoid being taken is verse 14. The men depended on their own insight, their own wisdom, and were taken in. It's what they did NOT do that beat them. Don't you fall into the same trap. Always take time to seek counsel from the Lord. Tell the person making the offer you'll have to pray about it.

Scripture: Jeremiah 5:1-9

Years ago one only heard turpiloquence when men were by themselves, no ladies present. Today even women folk us foul language. Foul language comes from a fowl mind. It only takes a chicken brain to use filthy language. Jesus said, *"Not what enters into the mouth defiles the man, but what proceeds out of the mouth, this defiles the man,"* (Matthew 15:11). Men and women who use dirty language either don't know they are defiling themselves, or they don't care. Dirty Language disturbs most of us.

There is language that does not offend us but offends the Lord. It breaks one of the ten commandments. It is using God's name in frivolous speech, taking His name in vain. All around people speak of God or Christ with flippancy and disrespect. This should disturb everyone who loves Jesus Christ. Does it?

There is another area in which the tongue is derelict. The Lord accuses the Jews, *"Although they say 'As the Lord lives,' Surely they swear falsely,"* (v. 2). The phrase "As the Lord lives" had no more meaning to them than a sneeze.

These nine verses reveal the life style of those who glibly said, "As the Lord lives". They refused to repent, they didn't keep God's ordinances, they forsook the Lord, and they committed adultery with their neighbors. Their reference to "the Lord" was a hollow facade.

Does your speech defile you? When you say the Lord's name, what does it mean to you? Does your lifestyle match your words?

Scripture: 2 Thessalonians 3:1-5

Don't be discouraged. Don't be down hearted. You do not know how your life would be if God were not protecting you. DON'T SCOFF! Satan is a ready and able enemy seeking to make your life as miserable as hell itself. Though you may have hardships and difficulty, trials and tribulations, pains and sickness unto death *it could be worse.*

Satan can do no more to you than what God will allow. Believe it or not Satan is under the authority of God. For a season God has allowed Satan *limited* freedom to work his way in the world and test the faith of men. Look how Job was tested; yet Satan's freedom was restricted. He could not take Job's life.

"In this you greatly rejoice, even though now for a little while, if necessary, you have been distressed by various trials, that the proof of your faith...may be found to result in praise..." (1 Peter 1:6-7). Those who are suffering usually do not understand nor are willing to accept what they are experiencing with a great deal of grace. Too often the pain just plain hurts so much little matters except relief.

God protects us from Satan. If you are nearing the end of your endurance reach out with strength to the Lord. He *"is faithful, and He will strengthen and protect your from the evil one,"* (v. 3). That is a promise. Trust the Lord to be loyal to His word. Despite your circumstances God does love you.

Scripture: Luke 10:29-37

Two nations sharing a long border have maintained "good neighbor" relations for many decades. They are Canada and the United States. Today is Canada Day or Dominion Day depending on the person speaking. Today Canadians commemorate the confederation of Upper and Lower Canada and some of the Maritime Provinces into the Dominion of Canada which occurred July 1, 1867.

Good neighbors are better than close relatives in most any crisis. Neighbors will often do more for you than your own kin. This was the case in the parable Jesus told the weaseling lawyer.

Seeking to justify his actions he asked, *"And who is my neighbor?"* (v. 29). Then Jesus told the story about the Samaritan who helped a neighbor when the neighbor's own people refused to get involved. The victim's own people were pretty high class too: a priest and a Levite. Have you noticed those whom you expect to help often excuse themselves? Just as often, true assistance comes from strangers.

It bothers me to call this Samaritan the *good* Samaritan because it implies all the other Samaritans were bad. Jesus does not designate *goodness* or *badness*, why should we? Samaritans were not pure blood Jews so the Jews hated them. Jesus was tearing down walls of prejudice.

The Samaritan met all the victim's needs. Binding up his wounds and later paying for his recovery. He proved to be a good neighbor.

Are there walls of prejudice between you and your neighbors? Isn't it time they came down?

Scripture: 1 John 2:18-24

There are three things the Lord created, established, and made which together create an enigma. God created summertime and sunflowers. Summertime and sunflowers go well together. Sunflowers flourish in the summer, grow tall, and produce much fruit (many seeds).

The Lord also established summertime and the church. Here is the enigma: few churches flourish in the summertime. Few churches produce much fruit in the summertime. Granted people go on vacations; but don't they attend church while on vacation? If they did the churches, though lacking their regular members should be filled with visitors, right? Tain't generally so.

Why is that? Do we take a vacation from God too? What if God took a vacation from you? As a parent there were times I wanted to take a vacation from the kids; but I didn't. I rejoice that God has never taken a vacation to get away from me— though I'm sure (speaking in human terms) He deserves it.

Surely John's indictment in verse 19 does not explain the summer slump in church attendance, or does it? What do you think?

As you make vacation plans, as you travel plan on attending church. Robyn and I had a delightful time with the folks at University Baptist Church in Laramie, Wyoming. They invited us to join them for a picnic in the mountains. Had we been on vacation from God we'd have missed that good fellowship.

Attend church while on vacation. You'll meet more of God's family, find inspiration and refreshment, and please the Lord.

Scripture: Acts 19:23-29

Money rules the world. Those with money have the power and those without don't. It's that simple.

As a disciple of Jesus Christ you can boldly advance the kingdom in many ways with little opposition from the world. You can have evangelistic campaigns. Distribute literature. Hold services in public places. Witness door to door. Advertise. UNTIL what you do for the Lord affects the pocket book of the world, the world doesn't care.

Most of Paul's opposition had been from loyal Jews. The world thought him rather curious, interesting maybe; but no real threat— UNTIL the pocket book of the world was touched.

When converts rejected Artemis and stopped buying silver shrines it affected the pocket book of the world and immediate reprisal was in order. When the craftsmen heard what Paul and *these Christians* were doing *"...they were filled with rage..."* (v. 28). *"And the city was filled with confusion..."* (v. 29).

You can tell where their devotion was. It wasn't really Artemis they loved, it was the money they made off her (v. 25). It was a business for them, not a religion. Sadly, there are Christians just like these silver smiths.

Before we condemn them as stupid pagans examine some of the trinkets and "treasures" advertised in religious magazines. Are these advertisers really interested in your spiritual growth and your commitment to Jesus Christ? I'm not saying they aren't. That's for you to decide; but you should always question the motives of anyone who is charging for the gospel.

Scripture: Psalm 144:12-15

Today is the birthday of the United States of America. In 1776 the American colonies declared their independence from King George, unfair taxation, and military abuse. The focus of the nascent nation was on freedom of conscience, freedom of worship, etc. Many but not all of the founding fathers believed in God. Some like Thomas Jefferson did not believe in the God of the Bible but in some central controlling force. Later Emerson, Thoreau and others rejected the God of the Bible.

The number of Americans rejecting God increased. The first public school was established to teach children how to read the Bible. Today the Bible is outlawed in many public schools. Though Congress opens with prayer few public school children enjoy the privilege.

What nation doesn't desire to enjoy the benefits listed in today's reading? The people of the United States have enjoyed these things; but their blessings have caused them to forget God.

Laws protecting the "day of rest" have been stricken from the books. New laws are being proposed to encourage social decay and degeneration by opening the flood gates of wickedness.

If the United States or any nation hopes to enjoy beautiful sons and daughters, abundance, and freedom then that nation **must** have the God of the Bible as their God. *"How blessed are the people whose God is the Lord!"* (v. 15). Making God central in any nation begins by making God central in the hearts of the people one by one. Who is central in your heart?

Scripture: Nehemiah 8:1-8

On the Isle of Man the parliament and the people assemble at Tynwald Hill on Old Mid-Summer Day to announce the laws enacted during the past year. This is the ancient meeting place of the Vikings. The word Tynwald means *thing*, or *field*, here it means parliament.

It was late September or early October in the days of Ezra and Nehemiah when the people gathered to hear the reading of the Law. Tisri (October) was the festival month. Three major celebrations were observed: *The Feast of Trumpets, The Day of Atonement,* and *The Feast of Tabernacles.* The people gathered in Jerusalem from the villages and farms for the celebrations.

The people asked to have the law read to them (v. 1). A special podium had been constructed just for this purpose (v. 4). Ezra opened the book in the sight of all the people and all the people stood up (v. 5). Before reading, Ezra blessed the Lord (v. 6).

The reading of the law had a wonderful impact on the people for they were all weeping. Probably the portion read "consisted of certain sections of Deuteronomy...and ...the Torah which were adapted to convict the people of their transgressions"[1] Hearing the Law the people realized how they had exposed themselves to the wrath of God.

How are people affected today by hearing the Bible read? Do they stand in honor of God's word? Are they convicted of their transgressions? What impact does scripture have on your life?

---

[1]Keil, C. F. and Delitzsch, F. *Commentary on the Old Testament,* (Peabody, MA, Hendrickson Publishers) 1989, 3:231.

Scripture: Genesis 1:27-31

An early Inca god was Veracocha, whom, they were told, had created the world and taught goodness and virtue. He also created men and women in his own image. The ancient Peruvians rejected this god because they did not have beards but Veracocha did. He left, supposedly walking across the water promising to return in a time of crises.

See how the story of creation though distorted had passed from generation to generation from the beginning. The ancient Peruvians, descendents of Shem, traversed the bearing straights migrated through the western United States and settled along the western coast of South America. Over the centuries the original story of creation became mixed with pagan concepts, neutralized, and finally rejected. Paul wrote, *"For even though they knew God, they did not honor Him as God or give thanks; but they became futile in their speculations, and their foolish heart was darkened,"* (Romans 1:21).

The myths about a bearded god proved to be the Incas' undoing. When the Spanish came wearing beards there was no resistance. The Incas believed Veracocha had created them and was returning. Of course the coming of the Spanish proved disastrous. The Incan culture was wiped out.

We are only one generation from having such myths propagated in our own society. If we fail to instill the Bible in our children they too will fall victim to mythical nonsense. Begin today to teach your children the word of God. Keep the Bible before your children any way you can. For suggestions see Deuteronomy 6:6-9.

Scripture: 1 Corinthians 15:12-19

So often what we understand and practice and have reasons for doing are misunderstood by other people. Missionaries discover this when they try explaining the Christian faith to peoples of other cultures. Those who translate the Bible discover there may not be words to express such things a *reconciliation* and *resurrection*.

One translator was stuck trying to find a word for *faith* the natives would understand. A runner entered, handed the translator a letter, then collapsed on the floor, exhausted. The translator asked, "What do you call what you just did?" The runner told him. The translator had a word for faith, fulling relying upon, trusting.

When the Spanish faced the Peruvian King Atahualpa they tried converting him and showed him a crucifix. He struck it from their hands and pointing to the sun proclaimed, "My god lives." The massacre which followed could have been avoided had the Spanish seen the crucifix with Atahualpa's understanding.

Before denigrating people for rejecting Jesus try to find out what their understanding of Him is. Just as Atahualpa didn't understand the crucifix people don't understand Jesus because they lack knowledge. Had the Spanish explained the sacrifice Jesus made on the cross, that He arose from the dead and lives and reigns Atahualpa may have believed. Instead they killed him because they misunderstood Atahualpa's actions. They thought he insulted their Lord.

The best testimony is telling how Jesus loved you when you were lost in your sins. How he loves and wants to redeem others also.

Scripture: 1 Samuel 26:1-5

Do you ever waste time pursuing something you know is destined to failure? Perhaps not, perhaps you're wiser; but some people do.

King Saul pursued David for years yet he knew David was to be the next king. Saul speaking to David after one of their close encounters said, *"And now, behold, I know that you shall be king, and that the kingdom of Israel shall be established in your hand,* (1 Samuel 24:20). Then Saul begged a promise from David. *"So now swear to me by the Lord that you will not cut off my descendants after me, and that you will not destroy my name from my father's household,"* (2 Samuel 24:21).

It seems strange that King Saul would make such a request from the man he was seeking to destroy. It is unusual but not unheard of. Decades ago a student threatened to meet me after school and beat me up. He met me after school but did nothing. He pursued what he knew could not succeed. Then a year or so later I received a letter from a military attorney. This same student had given me as a character reference. I did not mention the after school incident but provided an honest and good reference for him.

Getting angry at God is pursuing what can't succeed. Then a time comes when we need Him. Isn't it good to know God doesn't hold a grudge. When you come to Him in repentance He responds. Praise His name!

Scripture: Luke 24:13-27

When I was a student at Hannibal-La Grange College we were required to bring our Bible to certain classes along with the text book. Whenever someone brought only a New Testament we said all they brought was a pocket knife instead of a whole sword. No disrespect for the New Testament was intended.

The writer of Hebrews said, *"For the word of God is living and active and sharper than any two edged sword..."* (Hebrews 4:12). Most swords have two edges just as your Bible has two parts: Old Testament and New Testament.

A two edged sword is much more effective in battle than a single edged sword. Paul tells us in Ephesians to take *"the sword of Spirit which is the word of God,"* (Ephesians 6:17). We need the sword of the Spirit for our constant battle with Satan. What weapon did Jesus use when attacked by the Devil? Repeatedly Jesus said, *"It is written..."* and then He quoted scripture. Jesus and Paul did not have the New Testament at their disposal; but we do. Let's try it.

We would do well to acquaint ourselves with the *whole* Bible. We will multiply our understanding by comparing the two testaments. *"And beginning with Moses and with all the prophets, He explained to them the things concerning Himself in all the Scriptures,"* (v. 27).

Challenge yourself to find all the Old Testament references to Jesus Christ. It will be an enlightening study revealing all that Christ did was foreordained by God. And you will sharpen your sword skills.

Scripture: Matthew 5:17-20

Some of you have been raised in churches that had services three times a week. I was raised that way and don't question whether to attend on Sunday evening or Wednesday evening. It is just something expected. Recently the Holy Spirit had me examine my motives for faithfully attending all the services.

When we do our duty simply because it is our duty we are guilty of "works righteousness". This was the fault of the scribes and Pharisees. Theirs was works righteousness. They kept the law but for the wrong reasons. Jesus said, "*...unless your righteousness surpasses that of the scribes and Pharisees, you shall not enter the kingdom of God,*" (v. 27). The scribes and Pharisees depended solely on their own efforts for acceptance with God.

In the rest of His sermon on the mount Jesus revealed the kind of oppressive righteousness the scribes and Pharisees maintained. They held to the letter of the law but denied the spirit of the law. Didn't they oppose healing on the Sabbath thereby honoring the letter of the law above human beings?

The same principles apply to us. Do we attend church out of duty, to appease God, to earn points, to fellowship with the saints, or to worship the Lord and be touched by Him?

Maybe it's time you examine your motives for going to church. This is not to encourage you to stop going to church but to start going for the right reasons.

Scripture: 2 Thessalonians 3:10-16

We have whole families enjoying living off the fat of the land. Most government assistance programs engender laziness and reward it. How we got into this mess is a long story but can be told in few words. The government provided for the needy because the church couldn't do it. The church couldn't because the people of God were unfaithful in their giving. If the local churches provided for their neighbors Paul's exhortation could be administered with equity and integrity.

What he writes in verse 10 is not harsh— it's reality. *"...if anyone will not work, neither let him eat."* A hungry person will work if there's no other way. The government has provided "another way" so many choose not to work. They expect God or somebody to put food in their mouths.

God feeds the birds of the air but they have to get out and scratch and peck and look for their food. Have you seen the earth worm crawling up a tree looking for someway to get into a bird's beak? No, that's ludicrous. It's just as ludicrous for human beings to expect to be fed without putting forth some effort in return.

Praise the Lord there are poor people who work when they can, who would rather pay their own way, who are a real contribution to society. Let us help them any way we can. These folks should be encouraged not penalized for trying to support themselves. What can you do to help them support themselves?

Scripture: Isaiah 41:10-16

There is no comparison between the Christian faith and all other religions. Every cult controls its constituents with fear. Don't the Mormons threaten severe retribution if one converts to Christianity or breaks their rules in other ways? Don't Jehovah's Witnesses keep their adherents on a guilt trip? These things are contrary to the word of God.

Three times in today's reading God says, *"Do not fear,"* (vv. 10, 13, 14). God loves you. God says, *"Since you are precious in My sight, Since you are honored and I love you..."* (Isaiah 43:4). Repeatedly God tells His people, "Do not fear! Do not be afraid! Do not be anxious!"

God promises success and victory to those who love and serve Him. Listing the references would fill pages in this book. Read your Bible discovering the promises of God for yourself.

Yes, scripture says we are to fear the Lord our God. We should love Him so much we fear we'll disappoint Him. And, yes, those who reject the all powerful, all sufficient, all atoning work of God must fear eternal damnation. God is STILL in control. He has made every provision for your redemption. To reject His provision is to choose death.

Why do people flock to cults? Pride. They are too proud to accept what God has done for them at Calvary. They insist on doing *something* for their salvation. The only thing they can do is believe on the Lord Jesus Christ. It's up to you, a life of fear or a life of peace.

Scripture: Matthew 15:1-12

The truth is often offensive. People prefer delusion and deception to declaration. Our society has dug itself into a real chasm trying to avoid offending anyone. As a result ab-solutes are nebulous. Everything has become shades of gray.

Kurt Vonnegut wrote a story about a society in which every one was made equal. The strong wore weights so they could do no more than the weak. The brilliant wore hearing aids that blasted shrill sounds to keep them from thinking better than the dolts. Is his story prophetic? It seems so.

The danger is not in making the strong weak or the brilliant dumb. The danger lies in obliterating the absolutes of scripture. *"The person who sins will die,"* (Ezekiel 18:20). *"The wages of sin is death..."* (Romans 6:23). These are absolutes. Whether they become hazy or ignored doesn't matter.

The disciples told Jesus He had offended the scribes and Pharisees (v. 12) because He told them the truth. Jesus offended a lot of people, perhaps that's why many proponents of "Non-offensiveness" reject Him.

An administrator corrected me for telling a student he couldn't become a brain surgeon because he wasn't smart enough. His IQ was 69. Should I have perpetrated the student's delusion?

Christians must proclaim the truth regardless of how offensive it may be. We must declare the absolutes of the Bible. Sin is sin and results in death whether the world likes it or not. And faith in Christ results in eternal life whether the world believes it or not.

Scripture: 1 Samuel 23:1-14

David lived a very successful life because of one thing. Whether tending his father's flocks, running from King Saul or ruling the nation of Israel David did so successfully. Why? How? What was the secret of his constant success?

The answer: David inquired of the Lord then believed and acted. So we have a three fold answer. First he asked God what to do. Second, when God told him he trusted the word of the Lord. Third, we know he trusted because he obeyed the Lord.

Now review your own life. Are you successful in the things you try to accomplish? Are you having victories in your life? Do you really believe God and then by faith do what He tells you to do? Be honest with yourself.

David must have learned as a young man tending his father's flocks to inquire of the Lord. While alone with the sheep he learned to *listen* to God's voice. Then as he trusted and obeyed he learned God's way was always best.

In order for you to accomplish as David did you too must acquire these skills. Here's how: Remember to seek God's direction in ALL decisions. Then *wait* for His answer, His directions. And finally act by faith knowing God will bring it to pass.

It won't be easy because we desire to go our own direction and do things our own way. That's chancy at best. Follow David's example to develop a life of victory and success.

Scripture: Zephaniah 2:8-11

God is aware of your sufferings. He is aware of your aspirations. He knows how you feel. He knows how you hurt. He is keeping a record of those who taunt, ridicule, and mock you for your faith. The problem is we forget that God is that concerned about each one of us.

Some may think, "Surely God is not that particular." Consider what Jesus said regarding how particular God is about you. *"Indeed the very hairs of your head are all numbered..."* (Luke 12:7). That's more particular than you are about yourself, right?

Therefore, when mocked, ridiculed, persecuted for your faith— relax. God already knows about it. He is keeping score and at the right time He will pass judgment on your enemies. In today's text God indicates He will utterly destroy the enemies of His people.

Our responsibility is not to seek revenge, fight back, or even talk back. Our responsibility is to remain devotees of Jesus Christ. We are to be faithful to Him regardless of what others say or do. We are not at this time facing lions as did Christians in earlier times.

What was their attitude? They cheerfully accepted the plunder of their houses for the sake of Jesus Christ (Hebrews 10:34). They bravely went to their deaths trusting Jesus for their eternity.

Never forget God cares about you. Jesus said we are more valuable than many sparrows and God cares about sparrows (Luke 12:6f). Don't let Satan deceive you into thinking God doesn't care. The Bible says otherwise.

Scripture: Nehemiah 4:15-23

At times each of us becomes discouraged. Fatigue settles in, our progress seems slow, we lack a sense of accomplishment, success keeps slipping behind the horizon. In times like these we must cry out to the Lord to lift our spirits and to give us encouragement.

While the Israelites rebuilt the walls of Jerusalem they were under constant threat of attack by their enemies. As Nehemiah reports they worked with one hand while carrying a weapon in the other. This slowed the progress. Two hands working together accomplishes more than three working separately. The hours were long. They worked from dawn until *"...the stars appeared..."* (v. 21).

These Israelites needed encouragement, they needed affirmation that God was with them, that they were doing the right thing. Nehemiah provided encouragement saying, *"At whatever place you hear the sound of the trumpet, rally to us there. Our God will fight for us,"* (v. 20).

Satan enjoys keeping the people of God beat down, discouraged, and ineffective. He works hard at it; but remember the words of Nehemiah, *"Our God will fight for us."* James wrote, *"Resist the Devil and he will flee from you,"* (James 4:7).

God encourages us in many ways. Sometimes it is a spoken word such as Nehemiah delivered to the people. Sometimes it is God's written word that touches us and boosts our morale. Sometimes it comes from within as when we sing some favorite old hymn or chorus. God will encourage you because He loves you.

Scripture: Psalm 95:6-11

How long you gonna wander in the wilderness?

Israel wandered in the wilderness for forty years. That's one biblical example you should not emulate. Israel wandered in the wilderness as the result of dis-obedience. Some of us wander in the wilderness for extended periods for other reasons.

Sometimes the time spent in the wilderness is to our benefit. Between the time the Lord told me to quit my job and the time he started me in a new direction I felt I was in the wilderness. Looking back, it was a time of rest and refreshment. I did a lot of scholarly reading I had longed to do. That's one reason for a wilderness journey.

Jesus was led into the wilderness for forty days to be tempted by the devil. Sometimes we are led in the wilderness to be tempted, tempered, and strengthened in our faith.

Sometimes we spend time in the wilderness to learn to *wait upon the Lord*. Of the things I've had to learn *waiting* on the Lord has been the most difficult.

Sometimes we wander in the wilderness because we aren't listening to God's direction for our lives. He may be leading us to go where we don't want to go. So we wander until we give up and give in to Him.

How long we wander in the wilderness often depends upon us. Are you listening for God's direction? Are you ready to be committed to Him? Have you learned what God is trying to teach you in the wilderness? How long you gonna wander in the wilderness?

Scripture: Acts 4:5-12

Anyone familiar with automobiles knows about the fuel gauge. It has two letters E and F. When the indicator is on F the vehicle can go long distances. When the indicator rests on E it's time to refuel. How like the power of the Holy Spirit within us. Perhaps we should have a spirit gauge to remind us it's time to refuel.

In today's text we read about a disciple who once tried running on E but later ran on F. Peter failed to fulfill on his brash words, *"I will lay down my life for you,"* (John 13:37). When the time came he denied knowing Jesus. He was running on Empty (in his own strength).

Now, *filled with the Holy Spirit* Peter boldly addresses his accusers accusing them of crucifying Jesus (v. 10). What a difference between running on E and running of F, between running on his own power and running on the power of the Holy Spirit.

When you and I are operating in the power of the Holy Spirit there is victory in our lives. We perform at maximum ability. We have a sense of destiny. Our confidence is in God. That's how God wants us to function, by His power.

Becoming filled with the Holy Spirit is not like refueling your vehicle. When you received Christ, He filled you with His Holy Spirit.

Becoming filled with the Holy Spirit means yielding to Him, allowing Him to work in your life. Open up, let Him have control now.

Scripture: Ecclesiastes 12:9-14

Satan is making great progress in our terminology to neutralize the word of God. No longer is wickedness wickedness.

When teens commit fornication we say they have become sexually active. Changing the terms supposedly removes the stigma of wickedness and the guilt and the responsibility. Two persons of the same gender involved in a sexual relationship merely have an alternate life style. God destroyed Sodom and Gomorrah because of their "alternate lifestyle". Abortion is classified as *anything* but murder. The list is long and growing.

We have gone from the sublime to the ridiculous. Chairman is now chair person, Flagman is now Flagger. Some would even have all references to gender removed from the Bible.

It doesn't matter to God what terminology we use. *"Because God will bring every act to judgment...whether it is good or evil,"* (v. 14). It does matter to people because neutralized terms lure people into committing sins they might otherwise avoid. Paul warned, *"Let no one deceive you with empty words, for because of these things the wrath of God comes upon the sons of disobedience,"* (Ephesians 5:6).

What can the children of God do? AVOID USING SATAN'S TERMS FOR SIN! Oh, yes, you'll shock some people. Others will regard you as extremely narrow. You will be accused of not caring how other people feel. They will even think you are too old fashioned.

Should you care? No. Does it matter? Yes. It matters because by using God's terminology for sin you may save some from destruction.

Scripture: Ephesians 5:22-31

Dinner out, a dozen long stemmed roses, a special gift for no occasion at all, love notes for him, for her, is all empty if there is no sharing, loving, believing, working, talking, holding, trusting, kissing and giving of one's self. Husbands and wives need time together— intimate uninterrupted time. It may be just a walk around the block or down to the creek by yourselves; or an hour or two together without the demands of children, family, and friends, or the pressing needs of the world.

Sometimes you need to send the children to grandma's, take the phone of the hook, close the shades, and pretend you are somewhere else. Without these times together certain harmful influences creep in. The hot eruptions of "Kiss me quick" begin to cool. The colorful expressions of endearment turn into a dry desert. Before long one or the other begins thinking there is nothing left; but there is.

When it rains in the desert what appeared dead revives, blossoms, and becomes beautiful again. So in a marriage. The refreshing rains of renewed affection brings forth buds of colorful endearments which blossom into "Kiss me quicks". There is a catch, though; it takes rain and ground to receive it. One partner can not revive a dry relationship alone. If rain falls on the pavement of a stubborn heart nothing happens.

Today, renew your commitment, your excitement in your spouse. Let this briar patch be a thunder clap to start you raining love and affection again.

Scripture: Romans 1:28-32

"They're off and running" is a race track phrase. The object is to determine which horse will win. There are many kinds of races: stock car races, foot races, bicycle races, turtle races. In every race there is a winner and some "also rans". There is a race though in which all contestants and participating bystanders lose.

This race is more destructive than a weapons race. This race can destroy more in thirty minutes than whole organizations can build in thirty years.

Innocent bystanders unwittingly get drawn into these races. They get caught up in the rush of things. They hear much conversation and join in not wanting to be left out. All too often, and always too late, they wake up, are embarrassed and ashamed. Those are the bystander participants. There are also the charming champions.

Now you must understand not every charming champion is without a conscience or heart; but many are. They so thoroughly enjoy the sport they'll start a race anytime, anywhere, with anybody. The more destruction and hurt they cause the more they relish the contest.

I'm referring to "tongue wagging" races. Of course the charming champions don't call it gossip, or lying. They are merely sharing the news. Whether the news is based on fact doesn't matter. The point is to be first to tell or first to hear.

In "tongue wagging" races listeners are as guilty as talkers. Not listening is like cutting the legs off a race horse. Are these hard words? Read verses 29-30 again.

Scripture: Hosea 5:8-15

Have you heard the expression, "There's nothing wrong with it." or "Hey, these are modern times". Some very popular ideas become accepted before we check their alignment with scripture. Especially do we find social reforms getting a large following from saints who don't know their Bibles. Some even reinterpret scripture to support their biases. Jesus accused the saints of His day of *"Teaching as doctrines the precepts of men,"* (Mark 7:7).

What happens when God's sense of righteousness conflicts with man's sense of goodness? People figure God made a mistake. Some Christians bypass scripture that disagrees with them. When did it become popular to only believe scripture which agrees with us?

Here's how we begin to accept, then support worldly concepts which are contrary to the Bible. Satan uses every media source to bombard us with his concepts. Our eyes and ears are inundated with worldly ideas. Before long our defenses wear down and we begin doubting that which is not bombarding us, namely the Bible. Soon we buy into man's commands as truth. To be sociable we support man's commands. After all, who would oppose what is proclaimed to be good for society?

There is an inoculation to protect the saints from noxious philosophies. *"Thy word have I hid in my heart that I might sin against Thee,"* (Psalm 119:11). For an inoculation to be effective it must be injected into the system. God's word established in our hearts protects us from falling for worldly concepts.

Scripture: 2 Corinthians 12:19-13:3

In ancient times a shepherd would break the leg of a sheep that constantly went astray. Then the shepherd carried the sheep teaching it to stay with him. By the time the break mended the sheep learned to stay with the shepherd and the flock.

Leg breaking was a severe measure. Sometimes it takes severe measures to correct straying sheep. No shepherd worth his pay enjoys breaking legs. He does it out of necessity. There are distasteful responsibilities in every occupation.

As you study Paul's letters to the Corinthian church you discover he had to break some legs. There were those who absolutely would not submit to the authority of Christ, Paul or anyone. They insisted on doing their own thing (straying).

Shepherds (pastors) today must sometimes break legs, that is, correct the saints with strong measures. It's their responsibility. The pastor is *not* required to give an account to the congregation. He *IS* required to give an account to God, the owner of the sheep. If he fails to take strong measures when strong measures are needed how can he please the One he serves?

Sheep do not like getting a leg broken. Neither do saints enjoy being corrected with strong measures. When preaching and teaching fail what is the pastor to do? He must do what is necessary to redeem the recalcitrant saint.

Why, when the pastor does his job do some want to fire him. Their arrogance prevents them from submitting to correction. In such cases it's not the pastor who should seek another church; but the "straying" saint.

Scripture: Philippians 3:8-14

The great ballerina Agnes de Mille, speaking of her practice regimen, said, "I bent to the discipline, I never sat down. I learned the first and all important dictate of ballet dancing— never to miss practice; miss sleep, meals, rehearsals even but not practice, not for one day under any circumstances except Sundays and during childbirth."

We are not born to anything. The road between desire and accomplishment is paved with hard work, sacrifice, pain, and disappointment. Van Cliburn preparing for the Tchaikovsky Piano Competition in Moscow practiced eight hours a day. He won. Perseverance is the key to doing anything well.

Notable achievement is not gained with a few hours practice a week. Is that why some Christians never amount to much in the kingdom of God; they only practice their faith a few hours per week?

Have you noticed the power of the early church as recorded in Acts? Do we have the power today? We could. The earlier church experienced God's power because they exercised their faith continuously. Luke reports, *"And they were **continually** devoting themselves to the apostles' teaching and to fellowship, to breaking of bread and to prayer,"* (Luke 2:42).

Paul's testimony in today's reading demonstrates what lies ahead for anyone who desires to *"...know Him, and the power of His resurrection and the fellowship of His sufferings..."* (v. 10).

You don't have to be a scrawny defeated saint. With daily perseverance you can become an Atlas for the Lord. Start practicing now.

Scripture: Matthew 7:1-5

Grit! Something very insignificant yet so very powerful producing good and evil. The grit on sandpaper helps smooth rough places. Grit on emery cloth polishes metal. Grit in your teeth is aggravating. Grit in a bearing spells trouble. Grit in the eye blurs vision.

Huck Finn said of Mary Ann, "I never see such a girl. She had more sand in her than any girl I ever see." Grit (sand) here means courage determination, and stamina. He paid her a compliment.

A lot of grit working together smooths a board or polishes metal; but one grain of grit will tear up a steel bearing or groove a cylinder wall.

It just takes a little grit to tear up a church. Just a little grit blurs the vision and purpose of the people.

Big things, too, break fellowship but because they are big they are recognized and dealt with. Forgiveness, time, and patience bring healing in such cases.

It's the grit, the little stupid things slowly grinding away which are most destructive. It's the little irritations that fester and rot until they erupt into a full blown cancer.

If you think there's grit in your brother's eye make sure you are seeing clearly. There's little value in sticking your grimy fingers in to remove the other fellows grit. How do you do that except by confessing your faults to one another, forgiving one another, and *loving* one another. That will get the grit out every time. It's very cleansing indeed. Try it.

Scripture: Psalm 23

Jesus told about a lost sheep saying, "...*does he not leave the ninety-nine on the mountains and go and search for the one...*" (Matthew 18:12). Many songs have been composed about that one sheep needing special attention. Only heaven's records know how many sermons have been preached about that one sheep. What about the volumes of written material? Recall all the artists' renditions of the shepherd searching for the sheep. What are the ninety-nine doing who didn't go astray?

The ninety-nine good sheep were probably doing what comes natural for sheep. They are doing the things mentioned in Psalm 23: grazing in green pastures, refreshing themselves by still waters, enjoying the abundant provision of the shepherd, and all without fear.

Did the shepherd forget about the ninety-nine while he was away caring for just one? What kind of shepherd would that be? It seems totally in character for him to think many times about the ninety-nine while he is busy with just one.

Isn't it wonderful he could trust the ninety-nine to care for themselves during his absence? How could the shepherd concentrate on helping a sheep in need if he must worry about the rest of the flock? From a shepherd's point of view this is important. The shepherd is grateful for the faithful sheep.

If you are a sheep in need you too should be grateful the ninety-nine can be trusted so the shepherd can care for you. As soon as possible the shepherd returns and all have fellowship together.

Scripture: Ephesians 2:1-10

Unless you have received Jesus Christ as Savior and Lord and confessed it to others you remain dead in your sins. Paul wrote, "...*if you confess with our mouth Jesus as Lord, and believe in your heart that God raised Him from the dead, you shall be saved; for with the heart man believes, resulting in righteousness, and with the mouth he confesses, resulting in salvation,*" (Romans 10:9-10). The death of Christ on the cross was not done privately but publicly. Neither will your salvation be effective if kept a secret. You must tell someone. That's my understanding of Paul's words.

Did you notice salvation is the result of believing and telling, not payment or reward for work done. A sinner (which is everybody who has not received Jesus as Lord according to Paul's words in Romans 10) can perform the most beneficial works for humanity, make great personal sacrifices, never cheat, steal, murder, or commit adultery and remain dead in their sins; BECAUSE GOOD WORKS **CANNOT** REDEEM YOU. *YOU ARE SAVED BY GRACE AND GRACE ALONE* (vv. 8-9). Then comes the benefit from good works.

In the Greek, Ephesians 2:8-10 is one sentence. We are created for good works **after** we have been redeemed. It is after we have been saved good works count for something. Not only do they count for something but as Paul says, "...*we should walk in them*". Therefore, shouldn't we be doing good works everyday? What are good works? Doing that which pleases God.

Scripture: Psalm 119:129-136

Driving alone at night through the mountains on old US 66 near Flagstaff, Arizona the head lamps began to dim and wink out. Soon they would shine again and I could continue. Cautiously I crept into Flagstaff. A highway patrolman helped me locate a 24 hour repair shop. After replacing the voltage regulator I had bright head lamps and continued my journey.

How many people must creep through life because they can't see where they are going? How many people travel about in the darkness of this world without adequate illumination? Every believer avoiding daily Bible reading is trying to get around in the dark. You think you're making great progress but you are creeping along because the road is dangerous. If you're not creeping along, you're headed for disaster.

The terrain in Palestine is mountainous, traveling at night without light is dangerous. We understand that. What we fail to understand is traveling the highway of life is just as dangerous without the light of God's word.

The psalmist wrote, *"Thy word is a lamp to my feet, and a light to my path,"* (Psalm 119:105). In today's text, *"The unfolding of Thy words gives light..."* (v. 130). And, *"Make Thy face shine upon they servant..."* (v. 135).

Unless you travel by the illumination of God's word you are walking in darkness. A stumble, or crash, or disaster is unavoidable. Turn on the light of God's word in your life *everyday* by reading, studying, and hiding God's words in your heart.

Scripture: John 17:1-12

The seventeenth chapter of John is really the Lord's prayer. What is often repeated by rote is really the *model* prayer. The model prayer was given as a guide which is discussed in another briar patch.

In the Lord's prayer Jesus confirms something He told Mary and Joseph when he was only twelve. If you recall, the family, Mary, Joseph, Jesus, and his brothers and sisters (Matthew 13:55-56), had gone to Jerusalem to observe the Passover. On the way home they discovered Jesus was missing. They found him in the temple discussing the things of God with the scribes and Pharisees. Upon being questioned Jesus said, "...*I must be about my Father's business...*" (Luke 2:49KJV).

Now speaking to the Father Jesus reports, "*I glorified Thee on the earth, having accomplished the work which Thou hast given Me to do,*" (v. 4). From childhood to His death on the cross Jesus was aware of the work the Father had given Him to do and He did it.

What does this have to do with you?

God also has work for you to accomplish. God said, "*'I know the plans that I have for you,' declares the Lord, 'plans for welfare and not for calamity to give you a future and a hope,*" (Jeremiah 29:11). Those plans are not vacation plans they are plans for service, work, development, growth, and kingdom advance. Will you be able to say at the end of your earthly life, "I have accomplished all that God gave me to do"?

Scripture: Ephesians 1:1-7

Stop complaining! That's good advice for me too.

Do you know *why* we complain? We complain because we have distorted vision. We see things only from our perspective which is tainted, distorted by physical sight. We see someone who appears to be better off than we are. We look at our lack of material abundance. We desire the things of the world to spend them on our own pleasures. Oh, how often we complain without reason.

Paul wrote, *"God...has blessed us with every spiritual blessing,"* (v. 3). The key word here is not *blessing* or *spiritual* or *us* but *every*. What is excluded by the word *every*? That's right, nothing. The second most important word is *spiritual*. We are blessed with every spiritual blessing.

What are those spiritual blessings?

Look at the wonderful list in verses 5-7. We have been predestined to adoption as sons. In Roman law an adopted son had stronger rights than a natural born son. An adopted son could not be disinherited.

God's grace is freely bestowed. His unmerited favor is showered upon us with out restriction. Sometimes our behavior, attitude, or rebellion works like an umbrella keeping God's grace off us (Isaiah 59:1-2). That's our fault not His.

We also have redemption and forgiveness. What would you trade for these things? What earthly glitter or rainbow shiny bubble would you desire more than these things?

Instead of complaining— rejoice! You should be looking with your spiritual eyes at the treasures God has given you.

Scripture: Zechariah 3:1-5

You encounter more opposition from Satan and the forces of hell than you realize. Satan is determined to make your life in Christ as miserable as possible. It's his chief aim to plague you, harass you, pester and aggravate you, destroy your witness, steal your joy, peace, confidence, faith, success, anything to ruin you. He will even turn you against yourself.

How?

Consider this reality in your life. You will agree, I hope, that when you received Jesus Christ as Savior every one of your sins, past, present, and future, was covered and cancelled by the blood of Jesus. Do you ever forget that? You probably do.

Haven't you awakened in the night still regretting some past sin, still hating yourself for having done some ugly wickedness? I have. Haven't you ever felt your spiritual, financial, emotional, or other progress being impeded by some unrighteous act in your past? Don't past *forgiven* sins still try to trip you up, spoil your joy, make you feel defeated, keep you from something God has for you? Does your past cause you to hate yourself?

In Job (1:9) and Zechariah we read about Satan standing ready to accuse. Sometimes he works through people who are eager to remind us of our past.

When Satan accuses you remind him **and yourself** that your sins are forgiven and God remembers them no more. Don't allow the forces of evil to trip you up, pull you down, discourage or depress you. Instead, praise Jesus. Satan will leave.

```
┌──────────────────────────────────────────────┐
│             Scripture: Mark 12:28-34           │
└──────────────────────────────────────────────┘
```

I was a very style conscious teen. At fourteen I began working and buying my own clothes. I examined men's style journals to know the latest fashion. My home town remains conservative. New York styles crossed the Mississippi a year or so after being introduced. A local men's store would special order my clothes at no extra cost. My blue suede shoes were well worn when my cronies began buying them. My mom, a very sharp lady, took advantage of my passion for style. She said, "Roger, good manners, never, but never go out of style." She said it so often I bought an etiquette book for men published by Esquire Magazine.

Now, many decades later, I fully agree with the solid gold truth of that little phrase. Regardless of the latest libertine practice good manners are the style for people with class.

There are books on etiquette to teach what to do in every conceivable circumstance. Few of us have the time nor inclination to read them. Jesus however summed up all good manners in one simple statement, *"...whatever you want others to do for you, do so for them, for this is the Law and the Prophets,"* (Matthew 7:12). Following Jesus' teaching is real style, it's truly FIRST CLASS. Jesus' words imply humility, respect, courage, thoughtfulness, kindness, self-control. In essence *good manners.*

What does this have to do with the child of God? In order to attract people to Jesus you must be an attractive person. Practicing good manners does just that.

Scripture: Psalm 8

The headlines read, *Old Star Has New Companion.* Sounds like a pulp magazine announcement about a change in Hollywood. The star in question predates any old flick crony by a long shot. Both star and companion were created when God spoke them into existence.

The psalmist wrote, *"When I consider Thy heavens, the work of Thy fingers, The moon and the stars, which Thou hast ordained; What is man..."* (vv. 3-4). The psalmist was overwhelmed by the vastness of the universe. We have far greater knowledge of the universe. We can determine the molecular structure of stars and planets. Yet, we too stand amazed. The more we discover, the more we discover how much remains undiscovered. Isn't God neat!

The star's new companion was the first planet discovered outside our solar system. It has a greater mass than Jupiter, a surface temperature of 3000°, and is a mere 126 trillion miles away.

In the midst of this magnificent creation from quarks to the mind boggling vastness of the galaxies, God loves you. What are you or I that God should care? Aren't most of us recalcitrant, contemptible, contentious, and ornery much of the time? Why should God even notice us. No other part of God's creation treats Him as shabbily as man does, yet GOD LOVES US.

God loves us so much He sacrificed His Son, Jesus, on the cross to redeem us from certain death. That should make headlines; but we read instead about insignificant stuff like new planets. Go tell the real news, OK?

Scripture: Romans 8:5-11

When you pour instant coffee into a cup the crystals dissolve, permeating the water changing its color and flavor. There is a spiritual lesson here.

You began with a cup of hot water. The water was clear and rather tasteless. Many things can be done with a cup of hot water. You can make flavored gelatin, add it to a dry soup mix, drink it plain. The uses are only limited by your imagination. Upon adding the coffee crystals the tasteless liquid becomes something more. The water now has color and flavor. Anyone can see something has happened, a change has occurred. You can still use it for gelatin or soup but the end result will be affected by the coffee.

Every person without the permeating life changing indwelling Holy Spirit is like a cup of hot water, plain, tasteless, boring. That life can be used in any way the imagination directs. Life without the indwelling Holy Spirit is plain, tasteless and boring because it is dead.

Add the permeating Holy Spirit and real changes occur. The Spirit gives life (v. 11). Immediately people will notice a change because something vital has happened. Something marvelous has occurred. The once dead in sin is now alive toward God. There has been a name change from nobody to Christian. Yes, a Christian is really somebody. The Christian life is colorful, delicious, fun.

When the Spirit life is used in any endeavor it has a wonderful affect on the end result. What affect does your life have?

Scripture: 1 Kings 20:35-43

Many denominations and individual churches have annual meetings to determine their priorities and set commendable goals. They choose to work for world peace, eliminate hunger, house the homeless, seek brotherhood between the races, and many other socioeconomic wonder works. What follower of Jesus would take issue with such humanitarian ideals and goals?

In sincerity and love we must ask have they missed the mark? Too often not one word is mentioned about evangelism, missions, preaching, or starting churches in unchurched neighborhoods.

Satan has deceived us into thinking busyness is next to godliness. Of course he wants us involved in these excellent works or any kind of work as long as we aren't winning people to faith in Jesus Christ. While the church is engaged in humanitarian busyness it is no threat to the kingdom of Hell. People are helped materially but still die in their sins.

"While your servant was busy here and there..." (v. 40) will be the cry of many churches on judgment day. While the church is busy here and there people are dying and going to hell.

Ahab, trying to be a humanitarian, gave Benhad -ad II life and freedom. Had God brought the Syrians to destruction so Ahab could glorify himself? The prophet's message sunk in. Ahab went home epinastic (v. 41).

Let us keep our focus and our attention on winning souls for Jesus Christ. The other things will then take care of themselves. Don't be deceived into thinking good works is the same as good evangelism.

Scripture: 1 Chronicles 19:1-9

Best intentions are often turned about. A young minister counsels a teenaged girl about family and school problems. The young lady begins coping. Then some wicked persons suggest there are amorous activities between counselor and counseled.

A single teacher helps a colleague with a foreign language course. It isn't long until *rumor* has her trying to steal someone's husband.

True to the sons of Ammon no direct accusations were made. The nefarious work was propagated by simply casting doubt. Nahash, who had just died, had been David's friend, helping David while he was a fugitive from Saul. Thus David sent messengers to console Nahash's son, Hanun. Hanun's wicked advisors cast doubt on David's intentions (v. 3).

No one made direct accusations; but such deceitful remarks resulted in shame, embarrassment and ultimate defeat for Hanun and his army.

It is very hard to live down a lie. There shall always be jealous people itching to tear down the righteous. There are just as many itching to hear innuendo whether or not there is basis for it. There are a few who believe it is their responsibility to keep a check on the righteous. What egos they have!

Regardless of the safeguards one exercises liars will find a way. When you know in your heart you are innocent keep your head held high and face down mischievous mouths. Don't expect any changes soon. Sometimes it takes years before the community realizes it believed a lie. And some will never believe anything but the lies.

Scripture: Luke 4:1-13

At a pastor's conference the speaker was reading his text, stopped suddenly, paused, then said, "That wasn't in there last night." How fresh God's word continues to be. My maternal grandfather knew his Bible so well he could tell you where on the page your answer was. He maintained, at age 86, the Bible was a brand new book everyday. It is if you read it.

Sometimes we forget, other times we learn things others have known for a long time but then we may know things they haven't discovered.

An example is in today's reading. We've often read about the temptation of Jesus. Much focus is given to the three examples recorded. There has even been emphasis on how Satan only left Jesus *"until an opportune time,"* (v. 13). Many miss that Jesus was being tempted continuously *the whole forty days* in the wilderness (v. 2).

What were the temptations Satan launched at the Son of God. No one knows, it doesn't matter, really. We know he was *"tempted in all things as we are..."* (Hebrews 4:15). Even that is hard to understand for what tempts you may not tempt me. Jesus suffered every temptation that every human since Adam has suffered. You can be sure every temptation can be categorized into one of the three examples given.

Avoid the temptation of thinking you know the Bible. As you read it you'll learn new things, gain new understanding, discover a new application of scripture to your life. You'll also be equipped to combat temptation with scripture as Jesus did.

Scripture: Isaiah 62:1-5

If you have White clover in your area no doubt you have seen or yourself made clover crowns, chains, necklaces, and rings. Children believe themselves to be beautiful princes and princesses or kings and queens wearing golden crowns instead of clover ones. Something happens to our self image as we mature. Those childhood imaginations fade.

Yet, notice what Isaiah says we shall be in the hands of the Lord, *"a crown of beauty...And a royal diadem,"* (v. 3). And when will this come to pass?

Paul wrote to Timothy, *"in the future there is laid up for me a crown of righteousness,"* (2 Timothy 4:8). James wrote, *"Blessed is the man who perseveres under trial; for once he has been approved, he will receive the crown of life, which the Lord has promised to those who love Him,"* (James 1:12). We receive our crowns on the great day of reward. Peter wrote, *"And when the Chief Shepherd appears, you will receive the unfading crown of glory,"* (1 Peter 5:4).

Clover crowns last but a few hours. Even gold crowns of this earth are not eternal. The crown of life James mentions is *eternal life*. It is, as Peter says, *"unfading"*.

It's time to renew those childhood imaginations because God will make them reality for those who remain faithful, for those who belong to Jesus Christ. They will wear those abiding crowns scripture describes.

Are you in line for a crown? Have you trusted Jesus for forgiveness and eternal life?

Scripture: Numbers 11:31-35

"...the name of the place was called Kibroth-hattaavah..." (v. 34), that is, **The graves of greediness**. Greediness leads to a grave even while one lives. Greedy people bury themselves in sorrow, sadness, anxiety, discomfort, and hatred. They are never satisfied, never at peace, never comfortable because in their distorted vision somebody always has more or is better off than they.

How did the Israelites get into this predicament? Distorted memory. They forgot that while they were eating fish from the Nile, and leeks, and onions they were also slaves under severe task masters.

Distorted vision and memory is of the devil. He will twist whatever he can to deceive you. Then you, being deceived, act upon that distorted vision or memory creating dissatisfaction for yourself.

In Chaucer's *Canterbury Tales* we read in *The Pardoner's Tale* about three rioters searching for death and finding it through greed. Speaking through the Pardoner (also a greedy man) Chaucer says Satan, "the Fiend", gave the youngest the idea to poison his friends. The "friends" have already plotted to kill the youngest. The youngest is stabbed to death, the others drink poisoned wine. All die being greedy over eight bushels of gold coins.

The Israelites, Chaucer's three rioters, and we suffer greediness because we have not learned as Paul *"to be content in whatever circumstances"* we are in (Philippians 4:11). We cause our own discontent by listening to Satan and refusing to believe God's provision is sufficient.

Greed will get you into a grave, avoid it.

Scripture: Titus 3:1-7

Some people misinterpret John 14:26 to mean believers can't understand the Bible without attending Bible schools or seminaries or by listening to those who have because Jesus was addressing the apostles. One person even wrote in a religious publication that our job is to "determine what the apostles taught" and "there are Bible schools and seminaries that do a good job of that".

Praise the Lord that writer is mistaken. The apostles certainly needed the Holy Spirit to help them understand *"all things"* (John 14:26); but they did not record all their understanding. The Holy Spirit is given to every believer (v. 6) to help him or her *understand all things*.

Wouldn't it be wonderful if every book you read had the author alongside to explain difficult passages? You have that privilege when reading God's word *if* you have been born again.

There have been many fine preachers, expositors, evangelists, and Bible teachers who never darkened the door of a Bible school or seminary. Don't fall for the fallacy that Bible school or seminary is required before one can understand the scriptures.

Bible schools and seminaries certainly aid anyone in their understanding of scripture. A scholarly approach is a great asset and should be acquired if at all possible. I strongly recommend getting all the formal Bible training you can.

When you get it, don't be deceived into thinking you know it all, that your understanding is superior, or that no one can interpret scripture without *your* help.

Scripture: 2 Timothy 1:5-11

When a lad has parents faithful to the Lord as Timothy had his grandmother, Lois and his mother, Eunice; the result is a man who will serve the Lord. *"Train up a child in the way he should go, Even when he is old he will not depart from it,"* (Proverbs 22:6).

The word my mother instilled in me as a small child remains after five decades. Each afternoon she would read of a Bible hero before I took my nap. It wasn't a watered down children's story but straight from her King James version. The list of heros reads like the eleventh chapter of Hebrews.

"There was Moses and Elijah,/and of course young Samuel;/there was Andrew, Peter, Paul,/and the Lord Emmanuel./I could see the fire on Mt. Carmel,/hear the roar in the lions' den,/I felt the heat of Sinai/near the wilderness of Sin./I wore the coat of many colors./I gave the fish and bread./She made those heros live for me/as each afternoon she read."[1]

It was mom who gave me a love for the Bible and especially the Old Testament. Mom was born in this date in 1908. She was nearly 83 when she crossed over to her real home. Only heaven knows the full extent of her influence on one boys life. Everyone touched by this book, by my teaching and preaching are part of the investment she made. Her grandchildren bear fruit to her testimony.

What kind of investment are you making for the Lord? What are you doing to ensure your testimony will bear fruit?

---

[1] Faber, Roger Alan, from *My Mother Read to Me*, (Beaufort, MO, White Stone Books).

Scripture: Ruth 1:6-14

How many people make commitments that last only until they are faced with the reality of what they promised? Do we have church members like that? They promise to perform a special task but renege at the last moment. Are there those who get caught up in the moment of inspiration, commit themselves to do great things but never fulfill? Sure, you may have done it yourself.

In verse 10 both daughters-in-law proclaim, *"No, but we will surely return with you to your people"*. They were sincere, they loved Naomi, thought well of her, and apparently enjoyed being with her. Facing the reality of separation they committed themselves to go with Naomi.

However, when Naomi faced them with the reality of "no husbands" it made a difference to Orpah. As Naomi prepared to leave Moab, *"Orpah kissed her mother-in-law, but Ruth clung to her,"* (v. 14). Orpah returned to her people and we hear no more of her. Ruth went with Naomi fulfilling on her original commitment..

God blessed Ruth with a husband and she became the great-grandmother of King David thus becoming an ancestor to Jesus. She is mentioned again in the genealogy of Jesus (Matthew 1:5).

In the Garden of Gethsemane Judas kissed Jesus while the other disciples remained faithful for a while and later stood boldly for Jesus.

Have you made a commitment to the Lord but have not fulfilled it? Just as the disciples returned so can you. Today, renew your vows and begin to fulfill them.

Scripture: Numbers 9:15-23

From other passages about the journey from Egypt to the promised land we can surmise that all was not as agreeable as these verses imply. Being obedient to the Lord is not easy. Did each Israelite agree with the times to go and the times to stop? Was there total cooperation when the stop lasted longer than some thought it should?

It's human nature to think we know more about what to do than God does. Surely there were some in the camp complaining about how long it took to get to the promised land. Surely some children were asking, "When will we get there?" There may even have been those wondering why God was keeping them in the wilderness so long.

They stayed together and they obeyed the Lord which many congregations need to learn to do today. We fail to stop when the Lord says stop and we fail to go forward at His command because we lack faith.

Many churches fail to really blossom and mushroom because the people lack the vision of the pastor. *"Whether it was two days, a month, or a year...the sons of Israel remained camped and did not set out,"* (v. 22). Churches also fail by getting involved in things that are not of the Lord.

Israel was stubborn and stiff necked yet they started and stopped by the Lord's leadership expressed through Moses. What does that say about congregations that don't start and stop by the Lord's leadership expressed through the pastor?

Scripture: 3 John 1-8

The Gentleman from San Francisco by Ivan Bunin 1870-1953 tells of a man who made every preparation for an extended vacation except one. He failed to prepare his soul for death. Just like millions of people who spend fortunes on their bodies; practically torturing themselves for a fine physique; and pamper their flesh extravagantly; they have never read about Gaius.

With John the Apostle one thing ranked higher than all other concerns. It is the prosperity of the soul. Spiritual wealth must be excellent for anything else to have value. How do we know this?

In verse 2 John writes, "*...I pray that in all respects you may prosper and be in good health, just as your soul prospers*". John is fully assured of the prosperity of Gaius' soul and desires his physical well being to match. For John the prosperity of the soul is the governing factor. The two cannot be reversed.

In this letter we see Gaius doing the work of the whole church. He is housing, supporting and supplying, the missionaries that pass through. The congregation is doing little or nothing because of the influence of wicked Diotrephes. Thus we get a picture of what a remarkable man Gaius is. We see where his heart is. We see his devotion and faithfulness.

What would our condition be if John prayed for our physical well being to match that of our spiritual prosperity? Could we even survive on such meager sustenance? Is it time to make some changes?

Scripture: Lamentations 3:19-25

Who's life is without sorrow and sadness? When we are children we are convinced we've suffered the greatest of tragedies. In old age we look back wishing all of life's ills and sorrows had been as mild. Also in old age we recall how the Lord has dealt with us over the years.

Jeremiah had warned Jerusalem of the coming of God's wrath; but the people refused to believe. Instead they harassed, imprisoned, and sought to get rid of God's spokesman. In Lamentations Jeremiah weeps for his prophecy had materialized. His heart breaks because of the suffering he has seen and himself experienced. Surely he has tasted wormwood and bitterness.

Even in the darkest hour there is hope for the one who trusts in God and waits for Him. Jeremiah, referring to God's constant lovingkindness says, *"This I recall to mind, Therefore I have hope,"* (v. 21). He not only *"recalls to mind"* God's lovingkindnesses; but His compassions and faithfulness.

The casual reader unfamiliar with how God works may question such terms as lovingkindness and compassion. How do these terms describe the God Who just allowed His people to be destroyed or carried into captivity?

Every time upon repentance God withdraws His punishment. His lovingkindness always overrules His anger and wrath when men repent. His compassion continually reaches out to man in his rebellion hoping men will turn to Him in repentance. See how faithful God is to those who humble themselves and seek His face? There's hope for you too.

Scripture: Matthew 6:8-13

Though you've repeated this model prayer often the very familiarity of it may have caused you to miss some important points.

First, note that Jesus does not command us to pray *this* prayer. Rather He tells us to pray *"in this way"* (v. 9). What Jesus has provided is an outline for praying which I'll not restate here. It's so simple you can outline it yourself.

A second thing to note is that the last phrase is not in the best Greek manuscripts. The words, *"For Thine is the kingdom, and the power, and the glory, forever. Amen,"* probably originated with Jerome's Latin translation; but may have been added by some earlier scholar.

Third, there is a grave danger in repeating this prayer by rote. The danger is we'll lose any sense of what we are saying. We all have little phrases we repeat from time to time that no longer hold any meaning for us.

Finally, what this model teaches is superior to our repeating it. When praying we should yield ourselves entirely to God as the prayer indicates. *"Thy will be done On earth as it is in heaven,"* (v. 10). Are we not on the earth? If God's will is performed here it includes everything we are, right?

We must trust God for our entire provision (v. 11). And then we open ourselves up to a difficult task by repeating verse 12. What if God only forgave us accordingly? Ouch!

It's best to use this prayer as a guide.

Scripture: Deuteronomy 11:13-17

Did anyone ever do you a favor without you asking them and it turned out to be more hindrance than help? I've done it and had it done to me. Either way both parties suffer as a result. The one doing the favor feels badly for messing up and the one receiving the favor feels badly they had to be honest about your uninvited help.

We eventually learn to avoid such errors in our human relationships; but do we forget when it comes to serving the Lord?

Few of us have difficulty understanding the first few verses of today's reading. We do perhaps need some application of verse 16 as it relates to our doing favors for God; favors He neither needs nor commands.

The words *"lest your hearts be deceived and you turn away"* is the first sign to watch for. When you get an idea or notion to do God a favor ask yourself these questions: Why am I doing this? Does God need this done? Has He told me to do it? If you can't answer yes to the last two forget it.

Then consider these words. *"...and serve other gods and worship them,"* (v. 16). When we get an idea or notion to do God a favor just *whom* are we serving? Are we serving our egos? Perhaps. Are we trying to gain points with those who will notice the *favor* we did for God?

Just be careful to be obedient and stay out of trouble.

Scripture: Haggai 1:1-6

Opposition to advancing the kingdom of God is not always external. Often the greatest opposition to church growth, church planting, evangelism, extension, additional building space come from within the congregation. Those who oppose kingdom advance may not even know the real reason. Some do and are usually the most ardent resisters campaigning against growth.

In Haggai's day the people were saying, *"The time has not yet come...for the house of the Lord to be rebuilt,"* (v. 2). Of course it wasn't time for them to rebuild the temple just as it is not time for us to advance the kingdom work today. The reason is the same. People are too preoccupied with their own projects.

"If I must get involved with rebuilding the temple it will take time away from my business and the things I want to do." This attitude is very apparent in what God asks them. *"Is it time for you yourselves to live in paneled houses while this house lies desolate?"* (v. 4). They had time to build houses and panel them for themselves. They had time to pursue those things that interested them. As a result they didn't have time to rebuild the temple of the Lord. Don't we always do what really interests us?

God invited them to take inventory, to take an honest look at their circumstances. In verse six God is asking one basic question: Are you really prospering as much as you think you are?

Surely you aren't avoiding kingdom work because it would interfere with your plans and progress?

Scripture: Nahum 1:1-8

We must constantly be reminded of the awesomeness of almighty God. Today's reading paints for us a marvelous picture of the nature of our God. Some of the attributes may seem discordant. He is avenging yet slow to anger. His wrath is poured out yet He is good.

By His word the sea becomes a wilderness. The rivers become an arrid canyon. The most verdant foliage withers and crackles by His wrath. The mountains quake, the hills dissolve in His presence. Should this surprise us? Not really. How were all these things made in the first place if they did not come into being by His spoken word (Genesis 1 & 2). The prophet asks, *"Who can stand before His indignation?"* (v. 6).

Modern man has lost a very important principle. He has ceased fearing the Lord God. Man's pride and arrogance have deceived him. He thinks he is something. The lies of New Age philosophy tells man *he* is god. Woe to that person who thinks himself all sufficient to meet his own needs. Woe to anyone who thinks the answer to man's dilemma is within himself.

God is all Nahum says yet he is *"A stronghold in the day of trouble"* (v. 7) for those who take refuge in Him. He is unfathomable. He is awesome. He is God.

Rejoice God cannot be comprehended nor understood. If we understood Him, if we could explain Him, would He be worthy of our devotion, praise, and adoration? BUT HE IS WORTHY!

Scripture: Matthew 12:30-37

Don't let them hedge. When advocates of non-Christian religions come do you, don't let them hedge. That is, don't accept ambiguous and noncommittal statements about Jesus Christ. The witness who comes to you must either accept or deny that Jesus Christ is the Son of God, that He came in the flesh, died on the cross to redeem man from sin and rose again victor over sin and death, and that He presently lives and is seated at the right hand of God.

It is not a matter of interpretation or understanding. There are no gray areas, or nebulous concepts. This is a matter of absolutes. Either Jesus is *ALL* these things or He is not the Savior. A person must either receive *ALL* that Jesus is or have none of Him.

When the Mormon or Jehovah's Witness missionaries come to you ask them if they accept *ALL* that Jesus is. If they hesitate, ponder, wish to explain, they are hedging. They must either answer "Yes" or "No".

If they hedge, wish to explain, or say anything but "yes", DO NOT LISTEN TO THEM. Anyone, regardless of his affiliation with a religious organization who denies even one part of all Jesus is does not believe in Him and serves the anti-Christ. Satan's goal is to reduce Christ. Those who deny one bit of Who Jesus is serve Satan.

Is this narrow, bigoted, scriptural? You bet it is. One either believes it all or none of it does him any good.

Scripture: Zechariah 2:10-13

A little fellow was smiling at the folks behind him in the sanctuary. His mother corrected him. As tears streamed down his cheeks she said, "That's better."

Should we be morose in church or joyful? Should we be gloomy or glad before the Lord? God says through Zechariah, *"Sing for joy and be glad..."* (v. 10). We should sing and be glad because the Lord dwells in the hearts of those who believe on Jesus Christ. We should rejoice and be delighted because of what God has done for us through His Son, Jesus.

There are times when singing, shouting, raising our hands, even dancing in the Spirit are appropriate. This can be at church during worship or while you are alone. God accepts our joy and praise, our thanksgiving and adoration regardless of time or place.

There is another verse in today's text that many should memorize. It is uplifting to sing and shout to the Lord. We enjoy praising Him; but there is also a time to be silent.

After the time of singing joyfully we must be quiet. How can we hear Him if we are constantly making a racket? God doesn't shout! In His infinite patience He waits till we are quiet before He speaks.

Therefore we should strive to have a balance. A time of singing, praising, and adoration. AND time of silence.

Being quiet is not easy for many people; but we must do it anyway. Be still and know that He is God.

Scripture: Luke 5:1-10

There is a colorful character in the New Testament with whom Christians and sinners alike identify. He's outspoken, as many of us are, speaking first, thinking later. He seemed to live for the moment and adjusted readily to circumsatnces. For example: between the crucifixion and the sea side breakfast with Jesus this man returned to his old way of making a living. He suffered other human traits; defending Jesus when Jesus needed no defence. Jesus told him to put away his sword.

From what we know about Peter he was rambunctious, energetic, ready to rough house and even swore on occasions (Matthew 26:74). Nearly everyone likes this multi-faceted person because part of him is like some part of each of us. There is nothing amiss in boosting our ego identifying with Peter. In fact there is probably no grave sin involved in using Peter as a pattern for your life. The super-righteous may criticize; but that's their talent—criticizing.

Let's look at a trait of Peter's that is not well known. He and his companions (perhaps even business partners) had fished all night to no avail. Jesus had them move into deep water and let down their nets. True to form Peter had to comment (v. 5). Though he balked he obeyed. That's worth our notice.

Peter was so overwhelmed with the results he again opened his mouth saying, *"Depart from me for I am a sinful man."* (v. 8).

Jesus loved Peter just as he was, and He loves you just as you are.

Scripture: Ecclesiastes 1:9-11

Human beings are always enamored with every *new* thing. Product packages splash the word "NEW" across the label to improve sales. Articles are written in technical journals about *new* discoveries.

Putting things in perspective the ancient Inca people performed successful brain surgery. Pretzels were first baked in Italy in A.D. 610. Around 1400 B.C. the Egyptians had crude water clocks. So what's new?

Today many health minded folk strive for a "high fiber", "low cholesterol" diet. My grandmother, born in 1874, encouraged me to get plenty of "roughage". A very elderly doctor in Jackson, Mississippi ate real butter, the fat on pork chops and all manner of cholesterol. I, a youth, warned him. He told me it wasn't fat that hurt but not getting enough strenuous exercise.

Isn't it amazing how soon we forget our past? Not really. *"There is no remembrance of earlier things..."* (v. 11). And forgetting we think we have discovered something new. How much energy and expense could be saved if we would stop thinking we know better than the old people?

Consider how many millennia have passed since Ecclesiastes was written. Yet, the writer asks, *"Is there anything of which one might say, 'See this, it is new'? Already it has existed for ages Which were before us."* (v. 10).

It is better to side with the Bible than to stand by your finite knowledge only to be embarrassed when history proves you wrong. Knowledge, opinions, ideas are in constant flux; the Bible remains dependable.

Scripture: Romans 8:18-25

Being a large person myself I like large animals, for example, Belgian horses. Our cat, Steubben, is fair sized. While lying on the bed with him I dozed off thinking about lying down with tigers and lions. And why not? If you have the Bible view of things your whole perspective of the world is set aright.

Adam may have used a Bengal tiger for a pillow. The Bible doesn't say but that doesn't rule out the possibility. Before Adam sinned all carnivores were herbivores. Why not have a 400 pound feline pet?

Isaiah, quoting God, wrote, *"For behold, I create a new heavens and a new earth; And the former things shall not be remembered or come to mind. But be glad and rejoice forever in what I create..."* (Isaiah 65:17-18). Paul explains, *"For the creation itself was subjected to futility...the creation itself will be set free from slavery to corruption..."* (vv. 20-21).

Works like Frederic Church's *Twilight in the Wilderness* 1860, Albert Bierstadt's *Domes of Yosemite* 1867, and Ashur Durand's *Kindred Spirits* 1849 give some idea of a pristine world. Yet they are tainted with dead trees and signs of erosion and decay. We can not imagine God's original creation nor what He has in store. *"...as it is written, 'Things which eye has not seen and ear has not heard, And which have not entered the heart of man, All that God has prepared for those who love Him.'"* (1 Corinthians 2:9).

Wait with me for God's new pristine creation.

Scripture: Luke 18:18-23

It seems the greater one has been blessed with material possessions the more difficult it is to give. This is not to say there are not generous wealthy people, there are; but they are a small percentage. This is illustrated so well by the widow who gave all she had. The rich gave meagerly from their abundance. The poor widow gave her whole existence.

Do we measure a person's worth by how much they give? Do we tend to cultivate relationships with those who may benefit us? Do we admire folks who are better off than we are? If you answer yes to any of those questions you are thinking like the world thinks.

God is more interested in the attitude of the heart than the amount in the offering plate. Paul wrote, *"Let each one do just as he has purposed in his heart; not grudgingly or under compulsion; for God loves a cheerful giver,"* (2 Corinthians 9:7).

A man committed his business to the Lord promising to tithe if the Lord blessed him. God blessed and the man's tithe reached thousands of dollars per week. Distraught he asked his pastor to pray with him that God would release him of his promise. The pastor said, "No, but I'll pray the Lord will reduce your business until you can afford to tithe." Like the rich young ruler the man left sorrowing.

How is it with you? You may be rich or you may be poor, regardless, the tithe is the Lord's.

Scripture: Job 15:20-35

In Coleridge's *The Rhime of the Ancient Mariner* we read, "But Oh! More horrible than that/Is the curse in a dead man's eye!/Seven days, seven nights, I saw that curse,/And yet I could not die." Many are those racked with sin who, if they knew what lay beyond death, would not wish to die.

They try to pray; but as the ancient Mariner says, "I looked to heaven, and tried to pray;/But or ever a prayer had gushed,/A wicked whisper came, and made/My heart as dry as dust." Satan is quick to prevent prayers of repentance. His demons stand at the ready to quench the spirit of anyone who looks heavenward.

Eliphaz says, *"Let him not trust in emptiness, deceiving himself..."* (v. 31). The ancient Mariner reports, "A speck, a mist, a shape, I wist." The hope of rescue was only a ghastly ship with no life or help in it. All of Satan's comfort is "a mist, a shape" with no substance to it.

All the sailors aboard the ship died from the same sin that plagued the ancient Mariner. At first the sailors accused him of evil for killing the Albatross but later became accomplices saying, "'Twas right, said they, such bird to slay". Sin is a killer. Eliphaz says, *"For the company of the godless is barren,"* (v. 34).

The Mariner said, "In stead of a cross, the Albatros/About my neck was hung." Is your guilt like an Albatross about your neck? Is all about you barren and hopeless? Turn to Christ.

Scripture: 1 Peter 4:1-6

Has believing in Jesus made a difference in your life? It should. Even if there is no obvious external modification there is a change inside, in your heart. Many sinners live good moral lives, helping their neighbors, being forgiving, and upholding high standards. They eschew all manner of blatant wickedness yet remain lost because "goodness" on the part of man just won't save him. When this kind of person receives Jesus there is not an obvious outward change.

Peter is writing to those who have been redeemed from a different life style. He's writing to those good ol' boys and girls who enjoyed their alcohol to excess, who partied until they dropped, and who with good intentions always meant well; but now are washed by the blood of Jesus. For these believers there will be an obvious alteration in their pattern of living.

Peter says their former cronies *"are surprised that you do not run with them into the same excess of dissipation..."* (v. 4). When one of the "good ol" boys or girls gets saved and stops carousing, people notice. Instead of partying their senses away they read the Bible, pray, go to church, worship the Lord, and serve God instead of the flesh. When they do the old cronies malign them. They accuse them of being fanatics, of carrying this religion stuff too far, of being weird.

Are the cronies not carrying the party spirit too far? Do they not pursue pleasure too far? Keep in mind the end result: life or death.

Scripture: Esther 6:1-9

Hadassah's cousin Mordecai was a man of integrity not a glory seeker. Upon hearing of a plot to assassinate the king he made it known through proper channels. Thus he saved the king and protected his own neck from the noose.

Too many people seek glory or recognition for every little thing they do. Like a small child they cry, "Look at me, look at me." Consequently, no one looks and fewer care what meager feats they perform. Don't look at them, the least bit of recognition fuels their ego even more.

Those, like Mordecai, who do the right thing because it is the right thing generally receive their reward down the path. They don't care that no one notices. They don't do it to be noticed.

Mordecai certainly was not expecting King Ahasuerus to keep a record of what he had done. And the honor poured out upon him (Esther 6:10-14) was furthest from his mind.

We have here the same lesson Jesus taught in the parable about sitting down to dinner. Those seeking places of honor may be humbled to take a lesser position. Those not seeking honor may be asked to take a higher position. Where one sits at dinner is an outward sign of any inward attitude.

It is not the act of informing the king which makes the difference but the reason for doing so. Didn't Jesus say when giving alms don't sound a trumpet (Matthew 6:2)? When your attitude is right your actions are right. Right?

Scripture: Ruth 3:8-13

The writer of Proverbs asks a very important question, *"And excellent wife, who can find? For her worth is far above jewels,"* (Proverbs 31:10). Instead of looking for an excellent wife, many men seek a woman who is attractive, sexy, alluring, or possesses certain physical qualities. All physical qualities, age, gray, become wrinkled, sometimes plump up; they never stay the same.

How many men seek the Lord when seeking an excellent wife? If men and women sought the Lord when seeking a mate there'd be a big drop in the divorce rate. In my limited (fifty plus years) experience I have seen something hold true, "What God joins together man does not put asunder." Those marriages that began by obeying the Lord's will in a mate endure.

When desiring something like a life's mate don't we heap all manner of restrictions on God convinced we know more than He does? "Oh Lord, gimme a man/woman who..." and we give God a list. Then we shut our eyes to God's possibilities. When I dispensed with *my list* I saw the girl He had for me in a brand new light. She's not blonde, blue eyed, nor five foot ten, and weighs over one hundred ten pounds; but the one request I made He fulfilled. She loves me.

If you're seeking a life mate put your silly list in the trash. Say to the Lord, "You pick her/him out. You know who's best for me." I believe Boaz asked the Lord for a wife and got Ruth.

Scripture: 1 Corinthians 5:9-13

Satan has certainly twisted this scripture to hinder our witness. Have we not read about those with whom Jesus associated? Have we forgotten what He said about who needs a physician? To cloister yourself away from the world in some protected place is not God's intention for your life. If one is to be effective in the world one must be in the world yet not be of the world.

Salt kept in the salt shaker has no effect on the food and preserves nothing but itself. Just as the light hid under a bushel has little value in showing men the way of salvation, or a testimony hidden in a cloak of fear.

Verse ten we misunderstand. Verse eleven we ignore. Whom are we to avoid? Look what he writes, *"...I wrote to you not to associate with any so-called brother if he should be an immoral person, or covetous, or an idolater, or a reviler, or a drunkard, or a swindler— not even to eat with such a one,"* (v. 11). Ooo! That can cause vacant seats at church dinners.

We are accomplices if we allow wicked persons to remain in the fellowship of the church. By allowing them to stay we approve of their conduct. Do you fear removing them because they give great offerings, or because of their influence in the community?

We mess up understanding verse ten, we ignore verse eleven; but we better heed verse thirteen, *"Remove the wicked man (woman) from among yourselves."* God doesn't tolerate unrighteousness in His people why should we?

Scripture: Galatians 5:16-25

We gain a better understanding of the word if we know something about the people involved. In Galatians, Paul is writing to Celtic people. The Celts (Keltoi) had occupied Galatia from 276 B.C.[1] The Celts were a warlike people placing great value in physical ability, physical beauty, and were great revelers. Whatever they did they did it with all their might, whether eating, drinking, fighting, or worshipping. They practiced all those things mentioned in verses 19-21 and they relished doing them. For example: an *"outburst of anger"*, for the Celts could become a destructive rage.

No wonder Paul wrote, *"...I forewarn you just as I forewarned you that those who practice such things shall not inherit the kingdom of God,"* (v. 21). Then Paul mentions the *"fruit of the Spirit"* all of which was foreign to them except perhaps faithfulness. They did maintain a strong code of honor among themselves. See the difficulty Paul had in trying to get them to be spiritually minded?

One of their favorite pastimes was boasting and challenging one another to a fight to the death. Can't you see these Celts, now redeemed boasting and challenging one another over who is the most righteous? Paul wrote, *"Let us not become boastful, challenging one another, envying one another,"* (v. 26).

It is unlikely that you live life to the extreme as did the Celts. Therefore it will be much easier for you to live by verse 25. *"If we live by the Spirit, let us walk by the Spirit."*

---

[1]Herm, Gerhard, *The Celts*, (New York, St. Martin's Press), 1976, pages 39 & 53.

Scripture: Acts 2:14-21

Previously you read about the necessity of the Old Testament in fully understanding the New Testament (p. 111). Today's reading is partial fulfillment of an Old Testament prophecy.

The pouring out of the Holy Spirit upon all peoples was planned before creation. God knew man would sin, would need the Savior, and need inner light (Holy Spirit) to guide him in life. What God knew before creation Joel prophesied by the impetus of the Holy Spirit. Only selected persons received the fullness of the Holy Spirit in Old Testament times. "*...the prophets who prophesied of the grace* (GK: kharis)*...seeking to know what...time the Spirit of Christ within them...*" (1 Peter 1:10-11). The Old Testament prophets were filled with the Holy Spirit.

Joel announces something brand new for man, planned for eons by God; but brand new for man. Joel writes, "*I will pour out my Spirit on all mankind...sons ...daughters...old...young...male and female servants.*" (Joel 2:28-29). What God planned before creation, what He announced through the prophet Joel, He fulfilled in Acts 2 and afterwards.

Peter confirms that what happened to the hundred twenty was the fulfillment of Joel's prophecy. The speaking in tongues, the power, all the works of the fullness of the Holy Spirit became available to *everyone who believes*. Was speaking in tongues limited to the first century? Many claim it was; many claim it was not.

Since the first part of Joel's prophecy quoted by Peter was fulfilled, you can trust the second part is yet to come.

Scripture: 2 Samuel 16:15-19

Everyone is capable of being deceived making Satan very successful in his work. Perhaps you won't be deceived in your area of expertise; but what about areas in which you must trust the knowledge or reporting of others?

When a publication is usually dependable for accurate reporting we get trapped. We begin believing everything it reports. We get deceived because we don't take time to think things through, or check them out. Most deception bears no eternal significance. Sometimes the publication itself has been deceived.

Some time ago a popular news journal reported some Bible scholars don't think Jesus said most of what scripture records. Such information comes from the brain of Satan to reduce our confidence in Jesus and the Bible. When you read something like that a red beacon should flash in your eyes.

There is always some misinformation propagated by secular journals to reduce, destroy, twist, or cast doubt upon the authority of the Bible. Satan is very busy.

In today's reading Hushai deceived Absalom for good reason, to save David's life and turn the kingdom back to him. Absalom is deceived because of Hushai's established integrity. Absalom trusted, did not check out; but believed Hushai.

We get deceived the same way. A person, publication, or other information resource has established a history of integrity. When a deception spews forth we swallow it.

Whenever you read or hear *anything* which denigrates the Bible, reduces Jesus, denies God, fight back. Write and tell them the truth. Christians MUST speak up.

Scripture: Matthew 10:16-23

Followers of Jesus create a bad image for themselves by not following Jesus' teaching in verse 16. Often the secular world sees **and portrays** Christians as being illiterate, incogitant, gullible, and in general rather stupid. All too often the behavior of some believers give this impression. I'm sorry but it's true.

Face the facts. Some folks are still accusing atheist O'Hair of trying to ban Christian broadcasting. There NEVER was any truth to that lie. Other hoaxes causing Christians to say and do foolish things involve corporate logos, vanishing messengers, missing days, etc. Things like this get propagated by Christians who are NOT as shrewd as serpents, though they may be gentle as doves.

Such Christians get bent out of shape over the weirdest stuff. One Christian publication received several angry letters because of a photograph of a river baptism service. In the photograph a few women were wearing Bermuda length shorts waiting to be baptized. Should they have worn white dresses with lace bodices?

The world is convinced some Christians never read. They swallow whatever the TV preacher proclaims, never questioning, never checking to see if it's right. That is laziness.

If we are going to WIN people to faith in Jesus Christ we must have our brains turned on, tuned in, and demonstrate fine intelligence. We do not live in an uneducated society.

My pastor son said there are too many unfamiliar words in this book. Good, it's the teacher in me. Look them up. Learn something. Knowledge is free.

Scripture: 1 John 4:7-21

There is a children's Sunday School song that goes, "Praise Him, Praise Him, all you little children, God is love, God is love." To make it easier for children and some of us adults to understand, it should say, "Praise Him, Praise Him, all you little children, God loves you, God loves me."

Throughout John's writings we read about love. In these verses John portrays God as love in all its essence. Earlier John describes God as light (1 John 1:5-10). Isn't it interesting that God is described as love and light; two realities man can't really explain.

Agur wrote there were four things which he did not understand. One was, "...*the way of a man with a maid,*" (Proverbs 30:19). Scientists think they understand that chemistry but do they really? Love is wonderful and un-explainable. Right?

The light we see is a minute band on the spectrum. What we know about God is also infinitesimal. If He revealed Himself fully we haven't the capacity to comprehend Him. So He makes Himself known in ways we can understand. "...*He loved us and sent His Son...*" (v. 10).

John also wrote, "...*if God so loved us, we also ought to love one another,*"(v. 11). At least the children of God ought to love one another.

Do they? Do God's children love each other across denominational barriers? Do Pentecostals worship with Episcopalians? Can a Baptist preach in a Lutheran pulpit? Is a charismatic welcome in a Methodist church? Think and pray about these things.

Scripture: 1 Corinthians 12:27-31

There has always been much discussion about the gifts of the Spirit, the variety of these gifts, who sincerely exercises these gifts, and even some have denied the existence of the gifts of the Spirit in the modern day church.

Let's be clear and honest. I believe in all the gifts of the Spirit being active in today's body of believers. The gifts of the Spirit were given for the edification and building up of the body of Christ. They were not given to be wasted on the world. Jesus commanded us, *"Do not give what is holy to dogs, and do not throw your pearls before swine,"* (Matthew 7:6).

That means if you have the gift of healing you heal those in the body of Christ. The speaking and inter-pretation of tongues is for the church not the world. In fact, the Bible is for Christians. God gave us His word to edify, strengthen, encourage, correct, exhort, guide, and sanctify His own.

What does the world get? FIRST it must get right with God by believing on His Son Jesus Christ. Then, and only then should the world redeemed by Jesus' blood reap the benefits of the gifts of the Spirit.

Not everyone enjoys exercising the gifts of the Spirit and no one possesses them all. They are given as the Holy Spirit wills (v. 11). Not all have the same gifts (vv. 29-30). Has the Holy Spirit gifted you? Shouldn't you be using it?

Scripture: Song of Solomon 6:4-9

An Ojibwa love poem begins, "Awake! Flower of the forest, sky treading bird of the prairie. Awake! Awake! wonderful fawn eye one." Song of Solomon 2:10 says, *"Arise, my darling, my beautiful one..."* The bride compares Solomon's breath to apples, *"the fragrance of your breath like apples,"* (SOS 7:8). The Ojibwa says, "The breath of your mouth is the fragrance of flowers in the morning, Your breath is their fragrance at evening in the month of fading-leaf."

Solomon writes, *"you have made my heart beat faster, my sister, my bride..."* (SOS 4:9). The Ojibwa says, "Do not the red streams of my veins run toward you as forest streams to the sun in the moon of bright nights?"

The bride wrote, *"My heart went out to him as he spoke. I searched for him, but I did not find him; I called him, but he did not answer me,"* (SOS 5:6). The Ojibwa wrote, "Earth smiles— the waters smile— even the sky of clouds smiles— but I, I lose the way of smiling when you are not near."

In both poems the lovers call each other beloved. In both poems they compare each other to the beauties of God's creation. Both express sparkling quivers in the heart, desire for one another, and the joy of being together.

Love is like that. Love remains like that for those who truly love. My parents were still kissing in public after their fiftieth wedding anniversary. Remember, *"...perfect love casts out fear..."* (1 John 4:18).

Scripture: Philemon 8-20

Each of us is raised with a specific set of beliefs, prejudices, doctrines, attitudes, work habits, likes, and dislikes. Some things are so ingrained in childhood they are nearly impossible to change in adulthood. That's good in some respects but a hindrance in other respects.

To have love for the Lord and belief in the sovereignty of God and the absolute truth of scripture ingrained in childhood is wonderful. If that's you, you possess a great treasure. Hang on to it.

Other attitudes, especially prejudices likely need to be altered. A favorite book of mine has been banned because people don't understand the author's intent. *The Adventures of Huckleberry Finn* demonstrates the stupidity of prejudice. The slave, Jim, is superior to every white man in the book. He's loving, faithful, kind, generous, thoughtful, and the only father figure Huck has. We also see in this story the position slaves had and how they were treated by others.

In Paul's letter to Philemon he is making the same appeal Mark Twain was making in *The Adventures of Huckleberry Finn*. Paul writes, *"...I have enough confidence in Christ to order you to do that which is proper, yet for love's sake I rather appeal to you..."* (vv. 8-9). Philemon was being asked to accept as a brother, Onesimus, a slave who had run away (v. 16).

Do you have some prejudices against people different from you? What about those of a different ethnic background, or religion, or social standing? Isn't it time to change?

Scripture: 2 Timothy 1:15-18

By what's been said in this book about gossip you may wonder if Paul is gossiping about Phygelus and Hermogenes. Paul mentions them by way of a bad example. These two demonstrated cowardice in the time of testing. Frankly they failed to be what believers should be. Paul names them to make a comparison of what a true believer and disciple is and does. By contrast Onesiphorus is a hero.

Onesiphorus often refreshed Paul, was not a-shamed of his chains, and actually sought out Paul when Paul was in prison in Rome. Jesus said, "...*I was in prison and you came to me,*" (Matthew 25:36). Onesiphorus remembered these words. How well do you remember the words of Jesus? Keep in mind this second imprisonment of Paul's was not in a house allowing visitors but in one of the dungeons under deplorable conditions.

Paul is giving these examples to Timothy il-lustrating what he wrote earlier in this letter. "*For God has not given us a spirit of timidity, but of power and love and discipline. Therefore do not be ashamed of the testimony of our Lord or of His prisoner...*" (2 Timothy 1:7-8). Confessing Christ in Rome put one's life in danger. This is what Paul is talking about.

We have it so easy today. Confessing Christ may garner odd looks, or you may hear some ugly things said about you. Even with such mild mannered opposition Christians hide their faith. Perhaps we need stronger persecution to bolster our courage and separate the sheep from the goats.

Scripture: John 13:1-4

Often when I would told my students something one of them would say, "Are you for real, Mr. Faber?" Yes, I was for real, that is, I meant what I said and I said what I meant. When you do that it can cause some difficulties.

So many people are not "for real". They constantly hide behind a facade, a smoke screen of pretense. "Unreal" people resist accepting others as genuine.

There are probably three basic reasons people pretend. First, they don't know who they are. Second, they don't like who they are. Third are those who have set unreachable goals for themselves.

The Christian should never feel the need to pretend. The Christian, the devotee of Jesus, should be the most genuine person in the world. He should be like Jesus. There was no pretense with Jesus at anytime under any circumstances because He knew Who He was, He knew from whence He came, and He knew where He was going (v. 3).

The follower of Jesus *should* know who he is; namely a child of God (John 1:12). The follower of Jesus has nothing to hide because his sins are forgiven (1 John 1:9). And he should know where he is going (1 Thessalonians 4:16-17). Finally, pretense of your identity fools you more than anyone else.

The world is looking for genuine earthy folks and only the Christian has that capacity. All the rest fake it, being dead in their sins they pretend to live. Be yourself in Christ.

Scripture: 1 John 2:25-29

When asked if they are saved or know they are going to heaven many reply, "I think so" or "I hope so". That is really very sad. Someone who spent his entire life serving the Lord can indeed be anxious about life after death.

On his death bed, Rabban Jochanan I, wept because he did not know what he would meet after death. Here is what he said. "If men were about to carry me before a king of flesh and blood, who today is here and tomorrow is in his grave,...his anger is not everlasting,...his bonds are not eternal; if he should kill me, his killing would not be eternal: and I might perhaps pacify him with words or soften him with a gift. But they are ready to lead me before the King of kings, the Lord, holy and blessed, who lives and lasts for ever...his anger is eternal,...his bond is eternal; and whom I cannot either appease with words or soften with a gift. There are two ways before me, one to paradise, another to hell; and I know not which way they will lead me."[1] That is so sad and unnecessary.

There is no need to be anxious about life after death. The Bible clearly says it's not a matter of "hope so" but a matter of "KNOW SO" (v. 28). Can assurance of salvation be stated any plainer than 1 John 5:13 or Romans 11:29? Put your confidence in Jesus not your piddling works.

[1]Lightfoot, John, *A Commentary on the New Testament from the Talmud and Hebraica*, (Peabody, MA, Hendrickson Publishers), 1989, 1:36f

Scripture: Job 6:14-23

What kind of friend are you? When your friend is hurting spiritually, emotionally, physically, how do you respond? Do you reach out in love or level accusation? Do you pray for or prey upon? When your friend's relatives have fled, do you remain faithful?

Job was hurting in all the ways a person can hurt. His heart was crushed by the loss of his children and his wealth. His body was racked with sickness. His spirit wrestled with his Redeemer craving understanding of his predicament.

Three of his friends came: Eliphaz from Teman, Bildad decendent of Shuah the son of Abraham by Keturah, and Zophar from Naamah. All were very wealthy and considered wise men. Eliphaz's reasoning is superior. His philosophy of life hinges on a dream he had. Of the three, Bildad shows less sympathy for Job's suffering. He is so traditional he fails to see Job as a person. Zophar is considered the youngest and was probably an Arab chief. He exercises more common sense than the others and was a man prudent with words. None of them console or provide the least bit of comfort for Job.

Job says of them, *"My brothers have acted deceitfully...* (v. 15). They disappointed him, he looked for consolation but was given condemnation, he needed solace but got censure.

Are you like Eliphaz, Bildad, or Zophar? If so, what good is your friendship? When your friend is beat down, love your friend for all you're worth. Help carry his burden the best you can.

Scripture: Judges 11:12-15

Do we wonder that no one can bring peace to the middle east? All efforts to establish peace between Israel and her neighbors are fruitless. From Abraham to the present there has been and will be enmity between Arabs and Jews.

In today's text the Ammonite king accuses Israel of taking land from his people. Doesn't that sound like the Palestinian argument of the latter twentieth century. Listen to what he says, *"Because Israel took away my land when they came up from Egypt, from the Arnon as far as the Jabbok and the Jordan...* (v. 13).

Ammon was not as closely related to Abraham as the Ishmaelites, who were direct descendants. Benammi, father of the Ammonites, was the incestuous son of Lot by his youngest daughter (Genesis 19:30-38). Lot was Abraham's nephew. Though all these people are related they continuously fight and war to the bitter end.

Jephthah, the ninth judge, sought to explain that God was the one who gave the land to Israel. We have here the sovereignty of God being accepted by the one who benefits and rejected by the one who suffers loss.

Don't we vacillate between these extremes in our Christian lives? When miracles are happening in our favor we proclaim God is Sovereign, He is still on His throne. When hardship, trial, and tribulation are our lot we begin to hedge on our former declaration.

We must decide, either God is sovereign all the time or He never is. What do you think?

Scripture: John 17:19-23

Sometimes brothers haggle fervently about politics, sports, or some other life and death matter. They do not love each other any-the-less. They do not cease speaking or fellowshiping together except in rare cases. They are sons of the same father having a family bond whether they like it or not.

Children of the same father can be quite different. Being a father and grandfather, I know. At an awards banquet two brothers were receiving awards. One was clean shaven and dressed in a three piece suit; the other was bearded, had long hair, wore jeans and a flannel shirt. There were differences in the behavior of the children. One man's children sat quietly, ate politely, disturbed no one. The other man's children had poor table manners, crawled under the tables, upset chairs and were a general disturbance. The father of the unruly and undisciplined children wore the three piece suit. These brothers were successful partners in business, enjoyed great camaraderie and had a sincere appreciation for each other.

Every born again believer is a child of the same Father, despite differences in dress, attitude, opinion, political party, theology, or exercise of faith. Brothers heatedly arguing do not reject their sincere beliefs in order to love each other. Why isn't this true in God's family?

Jesus desired and prayed for us to be one (John 17:11. 21 & 23). Where is this unity, this oneness? Christ desired it, we must pursue it. Our lack of unity hurts the cause of Christ.

Scripture: Numbers 13:25-33

A fellow pastor trying to persuade me said, "The Lord is not the author of confusion". Since I wasn't confused I let the matter pass. He was right of course. God is the author of order, Satan the author of confusion.

Where God works, Satan works. Here's proof. Caleb and Joshua were not confused regarding conquering the promised land. The remaining ten spies were confused and confused the congregation. This confusion led to disobedience and forty years of wandering.

Nehemiah, governor of Israel, was not confused regarding rebuilding Jerusalem; but Satan caused confusion through a man named Sanballat. As Satan's pawn Sanballat caused much confusion and a delay in the work.

A church I knew very well called a new pastor. He began leading the church to new heights. The leadership of the new pastor was very orderly but Satan wouldn't leave it alone. Satan stirred up a bunch of Sanballats to confuse the work. Factions arose. The mettle of the new pastor was sorely tested but he stuck by his belief in God's call. Eventually many of the Sanballats left. It's interesting but sad that every church accepting the dispersed Sanballats had trouble. With the Sanballats gone and under the leadership of the new pastor the church became unified and grew to be one of the great churches in the state.

When there is confusion among the saints it's the work of Satan. Confusion delays, hinders, and sometimes halts the advance in God's kingdom. Pray for God's order to dominate.

Scripture: Romans 1:21-27

Some people awaken instantly. The alarm goes off, fully alert they swing their feet over the side of the bed. Others, upon hearing the alarm groan, doze off, make a feeble attempt to move, collapse, try again, and after a while attain a semi-erect position albeit a slumped one.

Life apart from God can be compared to being asleep. Those dead in sin are asleep to the things of God. They are not aware of what is going on in their lives. God calls; but the sleeper sleeps on. God pulls off the covers— no response. He nudges them with problems and set backs— still no response. On and on it goes until finally God dumps them out of bed.

How does God dump them out of bed? By allowing some calamity to shake them up. Is this scriptural? Yes, God asks, *"What more was there to do for My vineyard that I have not done in it?"* (Isaiah 5:4).

Some people awaken, realize God is calling but never accept Jesus. They soon return to the stupor of sin and remain dead.

What does God do then? He may give them up as Paul writes in today's text. In which case they have forfeited every opportunity to be redeemed. God may, by His grace and mercy awaken them anew, giving them another opportunity to receive Jesus as Savior. God is not required to offer second, third, or more chances.

Has God reawakened you giving you another chance to be saved?

Scripture: 2 Corinthians 5:1-10

The most successful student I had in over twenty years of teaching high school English was a fellow who failed. He was successful because he attained his aim. He aimed at nothing and succeeded.

Praise the Lord, every believer has an aim and a goal to last a lifetime of growing, attaining, and succeeding. Paul wrote, *"Therefore also we have as our ambition, whether at home or absent to be pleasing to Him,"* (v. 9). The words, *"Therefore also"* causes us to examine what he wrote previously.

To begin, Paul is referring to 2 Corinthians 4:18, *"...we are keeping our eyes on the things not seen."*[Lenski] One of those things not seen is our *"building from God, a house not made with hands, eternal in the heavens,"* (v. 1). Another unseen but equally real manifestation is the Spirit given to us as a pledge (v. 5).

What affect do these unseen realities have on us as we live our lives striving to please the Lord? We are always of *"good courage, and knowing that while we are at home in the body we are absent from the Lord—"* (v. 6).

Our goal then is to live a life with one objective, one ambition, to be pleasing to the Lord. We can do this if *"we walk by faith and not by sight—"* (v. 7).

Here then is the whole key to successful Christian living. It is a life of faith walking day by day in obedience to the Master. No other lifestyle should appeal to us.

Scripture: Isaiah 38:9-20

Each of us is a little nation of Israel within ourselves. We are complex and do not understand the things we do. Like Israel we turn aside from focusing on the Lord. We do this despite our previous commitment to please Him in every way.

When we change our focus, reverses begin to appear in our lives. We begin to worry, get depressed, wonder what's going on. Once in such state I asked the Lord, "Is everything all right?" He said, "No." I was devastated. I meant was everything going to be all right in my life and family. He was telling me everything was already not all right.

When Israel took their focus off God, chased other gods, oppression came upon them. Usually when things got severe enough Israel would repent and God would restore. It happens thirteen times in the book of Judges.

How does this happen? Life begins going entirely too well; we take our eyes of the Lord and focus on our successes and blessings. This happened to Hezekiah. God gave him military victories, things were going well, then instead of trusting God for deliverance of Jerusalem he considered and alliance with a military power. He had changed his focus.

Often undetected by us things begin going awry. They keep going awry until we refocus on the Lord. It involves repentance. Hezekiah tells how things went badly for him until he returned to the Lord (vv. 19-20).

If things are beginning to go awry for you, is it time to repent and re-focus on the Lord.

Scripture: 2 Corinthians 6:14-7:1

George Washington, in his farewell address, September 17, 1796, said, "Tis our true policy to steer clear of permanent alliances, with any portion of the foreign world." If it seemed important to Washington for the United States to remain free of foreign alliances how much more important is it for believers to remain free from alliances with foreign powers?

Who is the foreign power but Satan and the world? We must keep constant vigil, we must keep constant alert, we must be constantly aware that we are strangers in a foreign land. Devotees to Jesus Christ are at war with the devotees to Satan and the things of this world. None of the practices of this world, the lust of the flesh, the lust of the eyes and the pride of life are from God.

During the American revolution those who sided with the British were turncoats. They traitorously switched alliances. Are not the followers of Jesus who make alliances with the world also turncoats?

Paul makes it so plain saying, "...*what has a believer in common with an unbeliever, or what fellowship has light with darkness?*" (v. 15). Paul is referring to more than marriage between believers and unbelievers. He is warning us against *any* alliance with the world, against partnerships with unbelievers. He is warning us against spiritual fornication, of having idols in our hearts, (v. 16).

If you have made such alliances. Pray God will give you the wisdom and strength to break them.

Scripture: Acts 10:44-48

There are two points made here that have caused a great deal of controversy among believers. I believe the controversies have arisen because too often with many scriptures we apply our preconceived theology to the Bible. We should be applying the Bible to make our theology agree with scripture.

There are some fine folks who argue that one must be baptized to be saved. This cannot always be true for it is not true in the evangelistic response in Cornelius' house. They who received the Holy Spirit, were indeed saved. Peter asks, *"Surely no one can refuse water for these to be baptized who have received the Holy Spirit just as we did, can he?"* (v. 47).

There is another group of fine folks (both groups are born again believers) who cling to the teaching in verse 47 but refuse to accept in modern times verse 46. This second group accuses the first of not accepting scripture at face value then are guilty of the charge themselves. It reminds me of the Puritans leaving England because of oppression then becoming oppressors themselves in the American colonies.

Granted, there are some things in the Bible each of us has difficulty accepting, believing, and with which we totally agree. So let's not put each other down because someone else's understanding differs from our own. If the Bible says it, accept it. If someone gives more emphasis to one verse and you to another, love each other, accept each other, and serve the Lord.

Scripture: 1 Corinthians 9:24-27

Do you know any sports pagans?

Sports pagans put athletic contests before God. Who would do that? Millions of people. Here is how they do it.

Parents who never satisfied their athletic prowess push their children to succeed in athletics at the expense of their spiritual growth.

Paul loved sports. He used athletics to describe spiritual truth in today's text. And he wrote to Timothy, *"...if anyone competes as an athlete, he does not win the prize unless he competes according to the rules,"* (2 Timothy 2:5). There is no harm in athletic contests *UNLESS* they retard spiritual development.

What are families who drive many miles, spend large sums of money to participate in sports on Sunday going to tell the Lord on Judgment day? What are coaches going to say who insisted on starting times that kept team members away from church? It will be a sorry day for them because athletic prowess, games won, learning team spirit carries no weight with God.

God is not interested in one's commitment to sports. He is interested in how much commitment you or your children have to His kingdom and His righteousness.

Everything about sports is in honor and praise of man. Paul warned, *"For they exchanged the truth about God for a lie, and worshiped the creature rather than the Creator..."* (Romans 1:25). A sports fan said that.

If every Christian, athlete, regardless of age, refused to play or practice on Sunday it would be a great witness. Is God your priority or is your priority your god?

Scripture: Genesis 1:5-13

God's day always ends in light!

How often do we lie awake at night anxious about one thing or another? How often have our burdens been greater at night than in the day? Humans have an expression about the light at the end of the tunnel. For the Christian, light at the end of the tunnel is the beginning of God's day.

Throughout scripture we read about God's deliverance in the morning. Lot was urged to leave the city in the morning (Genesis 19:15). All night the homosexuals strove to get to the beautiful men who had come to Lot's house. God's destruction of Sodom was imminent; the angels urged him to escape.

Israel left Egypt in the morning (Exodus 12:31ff). In the night Pharaoh called Moses and told him to take the people, cattle, everything and get out. By dawn they were on their way.

God gave deliverance to Abimelech and Israel in the morning (Judges 9:33). Daniel was called from the Lion's den in the morning (Daniel 6:19ff). Jesus arose from the grave in the morning (Luke 24:1ff).

For all believers we have this wonderful promise. *"The Lord's lovingkindnesses indeed never cease, For His compassions never fail. They are new every morning..."* (Lamentation 3:23). Isn't it wonderful that His mercies are new every morning?

Our lives, through trial, turmoil, and tribulation, even the brief respites are all night and darkness. At the end is the eternal light of glory. God's day indeed ends in light and so will yours.

Scripture: Acts 6:1-7

Many of my Christian associates like to know if a person is filled with the Holy Spirit. A Spirit filled life is remarkable. It's dynamic, joyful, fulfilling, evangelistic, Christ centered, etc.

Look at these seven laymen chosen to serve tables. There service went far beyond assuring everyone had an equal share. Stephen became a martyr, Philip held evangelistic meetings. In verses 3 and 5 we read the words, *"full of the Spirit"*.

These men were full of the Spirit and controlled by the Spirit. **It's not how much of the Holy Spirit you have but how much of you does the Holy Spirit have?** That is, how yielded are you to His control in your life?

Look at it this way. Your life is a large house with many rooms. You put a wood stove in one room and shut the doors. The only room heated is the room with the stove. If you open the doors the heat begins to permeate the whole house. The same is true of the Holy Spirit, if you keep Him confined to a small part of your life that's all He affects. He doesn't force Himself into locked rooms.

To be filled with the Holy Spirit as those from the first century until now you must yield to Him, open the doors, give Him control. Then your life will be as effective as Stephen or Philip or Peter or Paul. Witnessing boldly for Jesus is one indicator of being filled with the Holy Spirit.

Are you witnessing boldly? Are you yielded to the Holy Spirit?

Scripture: Isaiah 61:4-9

Where do you live? I don't mean your geographic location on the earth. Where do you live in your spiritual life? Some live in the wilderness, some in the fertile valley, some on the mountain, or among the rolling hills.

In another *briar patch* you read about living in the wilderness. Living in the fertile valley may be compared to living in the midst of God's blessings of peace and tranquility. Living on the mountain may mean living close to God and His glory. Living on the rolling hills is probably where most of us live. We are spiritually up for a while, then we descend into the swale for a while before climbing the hill again.

In Isaiah, chapters 59 and 61 we have a contrast. Chapter 59 immediately informs us that sin makes a separation between sinner and Holy God. We learn that God is still able to bless but sin blocks the blessing. The chapter clearly describes the world today. Verse 9 describes spiritual frustration, verse 10 spiritual condition, verse 13 reveals what lay at the base, *"...denying the Lord and turning away from our God..."*

What a contrast with today's text. From iniquity to being *"called the priests of the Lord;"* (v. 5); from devastation and destruction to *"eating the wealth of nations..."* (v. 6); instead of humiliation— joy! (v. 7).

Let me ask again, "Where do you live?" If in chapter 59 you need not stay. You can move to chapter 61 by repentance. Do it.

Scripture: Luke 15:25-32

The focus here is not the son who went astray and returned home to a loving forgiving father. The focus is on church members who behave as the prodigal's brother behaved. You think we don't have such church members? As Buck Grangerford asked Huck Finn, "Why where was you raised?"

Some congregations may be blessed by not having anyone like the prodigal's brother. Truth is, not all congregations are so blessed. Your's may not be as blessed as you think. Jealous brothers (and sisters) may be rooted in the finest church in the kingdom. How are they identified?

Jealous brothers and sisters are often very difficult to detect. Few are as open as the brother Jesus mentions in this parable.

Here is what happens. A church begins to grow by winning sinners to faith in Jesus Christ. These new believers are really on fire for the Lord. They begin doing work the old timers have let slide or have ignored. The pastor recognizes the potential of these fired up believers and taps it for various positions in the church as he deems them capable. The dynamics of the enthusiastic new believers begins to agitate the pew sponges, those thinking themselves corner stones, and the dead wood pillars. So they grumble about the changes. Oops, did I step on some toes?

Believe me, most believers are thrilled to see sinners saved and become active participants in the work of the church. I hope you are. If not, get that way, it'll please Jesus.

Scripture: Revelation 1:9-20

Strange ideas arise because we don't really read God's word. We get a notion in our heads that blinds us from what God is really saying to us. One such notion should be dispelled by today's text.

Haven't you heard devout, sincere, committed Christians mention how they are going to run up to Jesus and give Him a hug on that Great Day. There are even artists' renditions of a saint arriving in heaven hugging Jesus. While all this may be comforting to the heart it is contrary to scripture.

What disciple was nearer to Jesus' heart than the Apostle John? Who do we read of being with Jesus during private times? Which of the disciples lay his head on Jesus' breast at the Pascal meal? To whom did Jesus commit the care of His mother? John knew Jesus better than anyone before or since except God the Father.

Yet, when John saw Jesus in all of His glory what did he do? Did he run up and give Jesus a hug? Read John's own testimony, *"When I saw Him I fell at His feet as a dead man..."* (v. 17). Who are we to think we'll run up and hug Jesus when we see Him? What egos we have.

Our silly notions have reduced the glory, power, authority, and awesomeness of the Lord Jesus Christ. Our silly notions have weakened our reverence and respect for Who Jesus is. When we see Jesus we too shall fall at His feet. Remember that!

Scripture: Mark 3:20-26

As you see, the concept of a nation divided against itself being unable to stand did not originate with Abraham Lincoln. Jesus spoke those words showing His work was not the work of Satan.

When an organization such as the Ku Klux Klan asks the American Civil Liberties Union to intervene you have proof Satan's kingdom is in tact. When any organization of violence, oppression, or one opposing Jesus joins hands with another you know Satan's kingdom is alive and well. Repeatedly we see evidence of Satan helping Satan.

What are you, who are citizens of the kingdom of God, doing about it? What can you do?

First, of all pray God's victory and authority to reign over your community. Second, pray for the leaders of Satanic organizations to be saved. Third, support your political leaders who stand up to and oppose wickedness and denounce those who support evil by word, vote, or lifestyle. Finally, write to your political leaders expressing your concerns and encourage them when you agree with their decisions.

These four simple acts of resistance on your part will make a terrible impact on the kingdom of Hell. Be prepared! Satan will attack you when you interfere. JUST REMEMBER, you, as a child of God, have been given authority over the forces of evil. *"But resist him (Satan), firm in your faith, knowing the same experiences of suffering are being accomplished by your brethren who are in the world,"* (1 Peter 5:9). Remember, Satan is defeated.

Scripture: Hebrews 10:26-31

Often conversations between my public school students and I would turn to church. Invariably one of them would ask, "Is you been sanctified, Mr. Faber?" To which I usually answered, "I'm in the process." There was always a bit of discrepancy about the meaning of the word "sanctified".

In one understanding, every believer is sanctified, set apart, made holy by the blood of Jesus as expressed verse 29. Indeed, every believer is set apart from the world. When we are washed by the blood of Jesus we cease being citizens of earth and become citizens of heaven. It's guaranteed!

Another understanding of the word sanctified could be "made holy". That was the sense I meant when I said I was in the process. In other words I am growing in holiness. Here too, are two ways to look at holiness. First, when we are washed by the blood of Jesus we are *holy* in the eyes of God. He sees us through the blood of Jesus. Second, the living of our daily lives are not entirely holy. John wrote, *"If we say that we have no sin, we are deceiving ourselves..."* (1 John 1:8). However, the sin count should be decreasing day by day.

A third understanding given by my students was that of being filled with the Holy Spirit.

Let me ask, "Have you been sanctified?" Have you been washed by the blood of Jesus? Are you growing in holy living? Have you been filled with the power of the Holy Spirit?

Scripture: Numbers 12:1-10

Every time I read this passage I think of an earthly father dealing with three children. Doesn't God sound that way saying, *"You three come out to the tent of meeting,"* (v. 4)? Miriam and Aaron should have felt a little knot in their stomachs when God called them. And as children often express, they probably thought, "What'd we do now?" as if they didn't know.

This is an interesting study with many lessons. Every person anointed by God for ministry is special to God. Whether we agree or not we must treat God's anointed with respect or suffer the discipline of the Lord.

Moses was special to God. Yes, God has favorites as earthly fathers have favorites. The child who pleases, who obeys, who makes the father proud should be the favorite. With earthly fathers this isn't necessarily so. With God it is. God is perfect, His judgments are perfect.

Note, Moses was the most humble man on the face of the earth (v. 3). As you study the life of Moses you discover a man with a heart for God's people, a man of obedience, and faith. Dr. Ira Peak Sr., my pastor during my youth, met those qualifications. No other man in my experience ever came close to him in humility and spiritual strength.

Miriam became leprous because she spoke against the Lord's anointed. Miriam was shut up for seven days to let God's words soak in. When we get off too easy we forget. Moses interceded and she was healed.

Scripture: Proverbs 4:10-19

Before retiring at night I make sure toys, etc., are under the furniture so if I or someone else must go through the house in the dark we won't stumble over something.

The writer of Proverbs gave his son instruction so he wouldn't stumble over something. He wrote, *"I have directed you in the way of wisdom; I have led you in upright paths. When you walk, your steps will not be impeded; And when you run you will not stumble,"* (vv. 11-12). Sons and daughters who have been instructed in wisdom and right paths do not stumble in life unless they choose to sin.

As this father wrote in Proverbs bad company can cause one to stumble. Speaking of the wicked he wrote, *"...they are robbed of sleep unless they make someone stumble,"* (v. 16). The world is never interested in encouraging you in righteous living. Paul wrote, *"Do not be deceived, 'Bad company corrupts good morals,'"* (1 Corinthians 15:33). I've never seen those words disproved.

Notice this difference, the path of the righteous is like the light of dawn and growing brighter, (v. 18). We are not likely to stumble if we walk in the light. The way of the wicked is darkness and he doesn't know what tripped him, (v. 19).

Prepare for each day by filling your heart and mind with the Word of God and your spirit with prayer. Then you can go forth on a clear path and not trip or stumble in this dark world.

Scripture: Mark 14:66-72

Peter followed at a distance and began warming himself at the fire of the world (Mark 14:54).

It's when the followers of Jesus begin following at a distance they get themselves into trouble. Becoming irregular in church attendance and missing Bible reading and prayer are just two ways of following at a distance. No Christian can resist the devil for very long while following at a distance.

Peter would have never denied his relationship to Christ had he not been at the fire of the world. Many believers today deny their faith in Jesus not in words, perhaps, but in deeds. Instead of being in God's house and with God's people they go to the wrong places for the wrong reasons and associate with worldly people. Soon they are inundated with temptation and succumb. There is the fire of the world and there is the fire of the Lord.

In John we read how the disciples sat around the fire Jesus made for preparing breakfast (John 21:9-12). Here Peter is in the right place with God's people. His entire demeanor is different from being at the fire of the world with worldly people.

Peter was adamant in his denial at the fire of the world. At the fire of the Lord he was just as adamant in proclaiming his love for Jesus. Between the two fires lay bitter repentance.

If you're at the fire of the world Jesus is calling you to breakfast. Even if you must walk through the valley of repentance— go!

Scripture: Jeremiah 7:21-26

When the Lord told me to quit my teaching job it was a time of testing. We had been praying for the Lord to provide a way for me to make a living working at home. I thought He would provide the way then I could quit teaching. God chose the reverse order. In seeking to validate His word we began searching the scriptures. My wife, Robyn, was reading Jeremiah when she was assured that indeed God had spoken.

Between Jeremiah 1:1 and 27:22 God says, one way or another, *"Obey my voice"* more than twenty times. In today's text He says, *"...obey my voice and I will by your God and you will be my people...they did not obey my voice or incline their ear...and went backward and not forward,"* (vv. 23-24). We chose not to follow Israel's example;but to go forward.

The reward of obedience is always the same. Finishing verse 23 we read, *"...walk in all the way that I command you that it may be well with you."* At no point in biblical history did God ignore obedience to Him. I bear testimony that it has been more than well with us.

Do not fear. God will not tell you to do something He won't give you the faith and grace to do.

When God tells you to take a certain step of faith *first* make sure it's God not some inner desire. Then, regardless of how drastic it may seem, DO IT! God rewards obedience every time, it's guaranteed.

Scripture: Acts 20:29-38

It's our nature to hold on, to keep control of something for which we've been responsible. It is difficult to let our children make their own way, to let them make mistakes and take the consequences. It's difficult leaving a job where you were in charge. I didn't like turning classes over to substitute teachers for long periods. It's difficult for pastors to retire. Some never do they just slow down. When we must make these separations we should do as Paul did.

Paul had become very much attached to the Ephesians. For three years he lived among them, taught, preached, and encouraged them. They were his spiritual children. He had won them to faith in Jesus Christ. He had taught them the principles of Christian living. With tears he had struggled and encouraged them to be committed to Jesus. Now he must leave them. Notice his concern. *"I know that after my departure savage wolves will come in among you...men from among yourselves will arise speaking perverse things to draw away the disciples..."* (vv. 29-30).

Therefore he must leave them in God's care. He said, *"...I commend you to God..."* (v. 32). That is, he deposited (entrusted) them with God. The Lord now is responsible for their safe keeping. He commended them to the word (commands, counsels, and promises[Ampf]) of God's grace.

We must do that. After we have labored raising a child, or performing a ministry, there comes a time to let go and entrust the work to the Lord.

[Ampf]*The Amplified New Testament*, The Lockman Fondation (Grand Rapids, Michigan, Zondervan House), 1958

Scripture: 1 Peter 1:3-9

More people dream of receiving a large inheritance from a relative than actually do. Many families have a wealthy person in the family. Just what many would do with a great amount of money is anyone's guess. Like so many who win a million dollar lottery, it could ruin their lives.

Those who believe on the Lord Jesus Christ for eternal life have an inheritance that can not ruin their lives and which has no end of enjoyment.

Earthly inheritances can be used up, stolen, wasted, and so on. Even if invested these things can happen to it. The inheritance Peter mentions is *"...imperishable, undefiled, and will not fade away,"* and is reserved by God in heaven (v. 4). It is protected by the power of God (v. 5). Just how secure is that? You tell me.

There is something quite unique about an inheritance. You can't earn it, get it by wishing, or deserve it. An inheritance is only secured one way— by relationship. You must be related to the one providing it.

How does one acquire this inheritance? Peter writes, *"Jesus Christ...has caused us to be born again to a living hope through the resurrection of Jesus Christ from the dead, to obtain an inheritance..."* (vv. 3-4). Through Jesus we are born into the family of God. *"As many as received Him, to them He gave the right to become children of God, even to those who believe on His name,"* (John 1:12). Are you in line for an inheritance from Jesus?

Scripture: Mark 8:11-19

When depressed, discouraged, wondering; is it all right to ask, "Why"?

"And sighing in His spirit, He said, 'Why...'" (v. 12). Again in verse 18 Jesus expressed discouragement. He is speaking of spiritual matters; the disciples insist on focusing on physical matters. Jesus asked, *"Having eyes, you do not see? And having ears, you do not hear?"* (v. 18).

We get ourselves depressed, discouraged, even disgruntled, worrying about our physical condition while ignoring our spiritual condition. We are no further in faith than the disciples worrying about a loaf of bread instead of seeking the bread of heaven.

Jesus taught us saying, *"Consider the lilies how they grow; they neither toil nor spin; but I tell you, even Solomon in all his glory did not clothe himself like one of these,"* (Luke 12:27). The lily works growing, blossoming; but it doesn't worry about how it looks. No lily ever said, "I wish my leaves were as green as her leaves," or "My bloom is bigger than your bloom." It's too busy being a lily to act like a human. The lily does its part and leaves the rest to God. That's why the lily is better clothed than Solomon.

If Satan can, he will discourage you so you won't do the work God assigned you. We resist him by doing the work of God with determination and faith, consciously leaving the results to God. If you're doing His work *"God will bless you in all your...work..."* (Deuteronomy 16:15). Ignore Satan's lies.

Scripture: Romans 12:17-21

John Heywood in his 1546 collection of English proverbs wrote, "Tit for tat". It means simply "payment in kind". All of us have experienced tit for tat from childhood upwards. On any school playground you can hear, "He hit me so I hit him."

Difficulty arises as we grow older. Many begin to add a plus to tit for tat. They not only want to make payment in kind, they want to make payment in kind plus. For most of us tit for tat is difficult to avoid. The times the Lord has prevented me from bopping someone on the nose are innumerable. We too often believe we can win an argument by losing our temper. Worst of all we wreck our witness for Jesus.

The Christian should never get involved in tit for tat. It's against the word of the Lord (v. 19). We all agree and say "AMEN!" when we are not nose to nose in conflict. Wait until you cross swords with some cantankerous, contentious character who really stirs your ire then say "Amen". Romans 12:19 will probably not even come to mind unless you've hid it in your heart.

Do you think you can play tit for tat and call yourself a child of God? Listen to what Jesus said, "...*love your enemies, and pray for those who persecute you IN ORDER that you may be sons of your Father who is in heaven;*" (Matthew 5:44-45). The words I've capitalized carry great weight. Got any questions?

Scripture: 1 Kings 6:1-7

It was Wednesday night prayer meeting. My childhood church had three sets of pews and four aisles. I was sitting in the middle of the middle section with a girl on each side chattering away when Pastor Peak said from the pulpit, "Roger, you can talk to the girls after church." I didn't. Dad collared me and I sat in the car after church.

I relate that because many parents do not control their children or teach them to respect the worship center. Too many kids exit and enter at will during the service. They squirm, rattle paper, chatter, as I did, creating a disturbance. My dad is in heaven but I still thank God for a father who cared for his church and his son. And I thank God for a pastor who diligently corrected his sheep.

I doubt your church building is overlaid with gold, or was built without the sound of hammer or axe within its walls. Does that mean you have the right to be disrespectful in it. The building itself holds no magic.

Have we over emphasized the church as the people not the building to the extent we show disrespect for the building? Does this modern attitude please the Lord when we allow our children to dash in and out of the service, run up and down the halls, and be careless with furnishings? You'll have to convince me.

We must demonstrate respect for God and His people and the building in which we worship. It's the parent's responsibility to teach the children to respect and be respectful in our houses of worship. Did they learn poor behavior from the adults?

Scripture: Titus 2:1-6

To the chagrin of many, it is God and the Bible that gives respectability to women. It is the world that treats them less than persons. This is a hard concept to get across. Scripture teaches a man should honor his wife not brow beat her. Though she is to be subject to her husband she is not inferior to him.

A boy in a class I was subbing during my planning period struck the girl across the aisle. Students who knew me said, "Oh oh". In no uncertain terms I told him he was less than an animal. "But she cursed me," he defended. "I don't care what she did, you are never to strike a girl." This led to a discussion of how a man should treat a woman.

A science teacher, a biologist, and a veterinarian all agreed that even in the animal kingdom the male does not beat up on the female. There may be a rare instances when this is not true but none of my sources knew of it. So when a human male strikes a female he is less than an animal and worse than a coward.

The girls were enjoying this until I reminded the boys that a real lady will not do anything to provoke a man to hit her. They had to agree.

A very little fellow asked, "What if she's bigger than you?" "Then you run man and you run fast." Expediency is often the better part of valor.

Scripture: Joshua 24:14-18

Robert Frost 1874-1963 remains one of my favorite American poets. My students were required to memorize his poem *The Road not Taken*. What Frost says in this poem can be applied to many areas of life dealing with making decisions.

As followers of the Lord Jesus Christ we must make right decisions everyday. You may ask, "Doesn't the world need to make right decisions?" Not really. Until a person receives Jesus Christ it doesn't matter what decisions he makes except as his decisions affect the children of God. In making right decisions we need to know what the Bible says. We need to understand the consequences of the decisions that people made in the Bible. These results must remain upper most in our thinking.

The decision Joshua lay before Israel reminds me of Frost's poem. In the poem there are only two possible routes. For Israel there were only two possible routes. For us there are only two possible routes. The routes are obedience and commitment to the Lord or rejection and disobedience. How each person decides makes a world of difference.

The last three lines of Frost's poem says it all:

"Two roads diverged in a wood and I—
I took the one less traveled by
And that has made all the difference."

Joshua declared, "...*as for me and my house, we will serve the Lord,*" (v. 15). Israel answered Joshua, "*Far be it from us that we should forsake the Lord...*" (v. 16). What is your decision?

Scripture: Mark 9:1-8

Driving around as young folks do we drove by the bottom of lover's leap south of Hannibal, Missouri. The other fellow and his girl decided to climb it. We drove to the top and met them. Unusual? Yes, it was after ten o'clock at night.

When Jesus, Peter, James, and John ascended the mountain it was daylight. Verse 2 says *"six days later"* not six nights later. It's important for you to remember the transfiguration took place in bright sunshine. What God does, He does in the light. The appearance of Moses and Elijah was not ghost-like but real. Ghosts, goblins, and other phenomena appear in the dark. When Jesus walked on the water it was night and the disciples thought they saw a phantom.

Do not try to make this incident seem ghostly, dark, and unreal. Yes, there was a cloud but notice when the cloud appears. Jesus' robes are radiant *in the sunshine* (v. 3). Elijah and Moses were visible *in the sunshine* (v. 4). Peter, of course, had to comment about it's being good they were there and should build "sacred tents" for Jesus, Elijah and Moses (v. 5). Following all this the cloud of God overshadows (επισκιαζω = over shadow not surrounds or engulfs) them (v. 7).

The disciples with Jesus when He was transfigured were given a taste of heaven's glory. Had not Jesus said six days before, *"...some...shall not taste death until they have seen the kingdom of God..."* (v. 1)?

Scripture: Genesis 25:1-11

Many people are interested in their ancestry. In a special Ethnic Studies class in cooperation with Washington University in St. Louis my students did genealogical studies of their families. They all made neat discoveries.

Old Testament genealogies vary by purpose. The earliest biblical genealogy lists people by occupation (Genesis 4:25-5:32). Genesis 10 begins the long list of nations descending from Ham, Shem, and Japheth. Chapter 11 narrows the focus to God's chosen people.

In today's reading Abraham was 137 years old when he married Keturah and had twelve more children (vv. 1-4). Those are actual fifty-two week years.

Genesis 29 begins Jacob's family, chapter 36 records Esau's family. Samuel, Kings, and Chronicles distinguish between northern and southern kings. The king's mother is always mentioned for southern kings; but not for northern kings. In Ezra and Nehemiah we have genealogies of those who returned from the exile in Babylon. Also Ezra lists those who married foreign wives.

The New Testament doesn't emphasize physical genealogy like the Old Testament. There's the genealogy of Jesus and references are made of someone being "the son of" but no long genealogies.

The New Testament emphasizes spiritual descent. The Pharisees and Sadducees claimed Abraham as their father. John the Baptist said, *"God is able from these stones to raise up children to Abraham,"* (Matthew 3:9). *"...it is those who are of faith that are sons of Abraham,"* (Galatians 5:7).

There are only two spiritual families on earth. God's and Satan's. Have you been born into God's family through Jesus Christ?

Scripture: 2 Corinthians 11:24-31

At most farm sales you can buy an old tobacco can of used screwdrivers. By examining them you can guess how they were used. The bent one served as a pry bar, the one used as a chisel has the corners of its blade missing, the rusted one was ignored in the elements for a while. The screw drivers were not purposely abused; but in the press to get the work done the screwdriver was pressed into service for which it was not equipped.

A Christian totally committed to Jesus is much like a well used screwdriver. He may be bent or misshapen or have corners missing. He may be pitted or disfigured but when called into service he did what he could according to his ability and God's provision. Paul aptly describes his sufferings for the sake of Christ: whipped, beaten, stoned, ship wrecked, he suffered hunger and thirst, was exposed to the elements and in constant danger of robbers while bearing concern for all the churches (vv. 24-28).

Used screwdrivers get thrown into a bucket to be sold for a pittance; but used Christians receive a crown of glory. Both suffered abuse in their line of duty but only the saint gets a reward. Both bear the marks of service but only the saint receives a resurrected body. Amen!

You may be called upon to perform tasks beneath your dignity. So what if you're persecuted, reviled, ill-used, harassed, treated shabbily; thank the Lord you're not a screwdriver. You have a guaranteed reward.

Scripture: James 5:13-18

James' oft quoted words, *"The effective prayer of a righteous man can accomplish much,"* (v. 16) has been a banner of commitment to many great servants of the Lord. James gives the example of Elijah (vv. 17-18). Alfred Lord Tennyson 1809-1892 has King Arthur say, "More things are wrought by prayer than this world dreams of." William Carey 1761-1834 said, "Prayer— secret, fervent, believing prayer lies at the root of all personal godliness."

William Carey must have been a man of prayer. Look at his life. He learned the cobbling trade but after his spiritual conversion spent part of his time preaching. He cobbled at night and pastored and taught school during the day. During this time he taught himself Greek, Hebrew, Latin, Dutch, and French.

He had a heart for lost people the world over. In 1792, at the ministers' meeting he established the saying, "Expect great things from God and attempt great things for God." This inspired the birth of the Baptist missionary movement.

He went to India in 1793. By 1798 he had translated the New Testament into Bengali. Around 1801 he was made professor of Sanskrit, Bengali and Marathi at Fort William College in Calcutta. He also translated the Bible in whole or in part into twenty-four languages and dialects.

By prayer you too can accomplish much in the kingdom. Isn't that what the brother of Jesus, the Apostle James wrote? Carey accomplished more than he dreamed of because he was a righteous praying man. What can you accomplish by prayer?

Scripture: John 8:31-36

My cousin, Wayne, said of being in the United States Marines, "I'd never do it again, but I wouldn't give anything for the experience." That's often said of many experiences.

To read or hear of something is one thing, to experience it is entirely different. You don't know pain until you hurt. You don't understand kindness until someone is kind to you. Love, hate, forgiveness, friendship are all understood by experience.

You can't understand freedom until you have first been captive. Neither can you understand captivity until you've been set free. That makes it difficult for all who are slaves to sin to realize they are slaves. Didn't the Jews claim, *"We are Abraham's offspring, and have never been enslaved to anyone..."* (v. 33)? Had they forgotten four hundred years in Egypt? But that was not the point.

Jesus said, *"...every one who commits sin is the slave of sin,"* (v. 34). Every one who is a slave to sin can be set free by believing on the only begotten Son of God. Satan deceives his own into thinking they are free and accepting Christ will put them into bondage. The opposite is the truth.

There was no doubt in Wayne's mind about what he had experienced. He knew he'd been in the Marines. Neither is there any doubt about being set free from sin by Jesus. Every believer and follower of the Lord can remember the time Jesus removed the shackles of sin and set them free. Can you?

Scripture: 2 Samuel 3:17-21

There are numerous males in the Bible who qualify as men, others less than men. In the life of David are examples of each. Joab wasn't much of a man, murdering everyone who might be a threat to his position. There is also Abner. A man of integrity and good sense. When he realized Israel could not stand against David; when he learned God had anointed David king over all Israel he turned the followers of Ish-bosheth to David.

Abner demonstrated manly qualities: courage, honor, respect, commitment, and integrity. Other great men of the Bible demonstrate other characteristics.

Jeremiah was a man of great courage, having a tender heart for God's people. He let us know it's all right for a man to cry (Jeremiah 9:10, Lamentations 1:16). He is called the weeping prophet; but it doesn't diminish his manhood.

A real man believes God and is obedient. There are numerous examples; but consider Ananias (Acts 9:10ff). He not only believed God and obeyed Him, he accepted the work God had done in Saul calling him *"...brother Saul..."* (Acts 9:17).

Real men are humble. What man bore greater bearing and took more abuse in the Old Testament than Moses, yet his outstanding trait is his humility (Numbers 12:3).

The world ignores these manly attributes honoring instead physical prowess, athletic performance, achievement, etc.

Christian men are giants because they can say, "I'm sorry" to a child and weep over a lost soul. They also stand for righteousness facing down the world.

Scripture: 2 Samuel 7:10-17

Nearly a millennium ago a significant event happened on the southern shores of Britain. On this day in the year 1066 William of Normandy defeated Harold II of England. The Battle of Hastings was the last time the British Isles were attacked and conquered by a foreign power. The English have not had peace all this time. There were wars with Spain, the American colonies, and Germany to name a few.

Legend reports William of Normandy chose Tuesday to attack Britain because it would give him success in battle. In the pantheon of the North, Teutates is the god of war and is the first element in forming the name Tuesday. Another myth says Teutates (Tues) would gather the souls of fallen soldiers. All through man's history the mythical and mystical have guided his decisions.

Only under David and Solomon did Israel actually control everything from Dan in the north to Beersheba in the south. God elected David to bring peace militarily to His people. He elected Solomon to build the glorious temple. Under Solomon's reign Israel reached the apex of its glory.

God gives peace for a purpose. The British along with other nations need to examine and see if they have fulfilled God's purpose. Or have they, like America and others, turned away from the Lord?

God has revealed in His word how He deals with wicked nations. He also reveals His mercy and grace on those nations that repent. Pray for repentance and revival in your nation.

Scripture: Judges 3:4-8

Paul wrote, *"No temptation has overtaken you but such as is common to man; and God is faithful, who will not allow you to be tempted beyond what you are able, but with the temptation will provide the way of escape also, that you may be able to endure it,"* (1 Corinthians 10:13). The difficulty is not that God allows us to be tempted, the difficulty is we don't seek the way to escape.

God allowed the Philistines, Canaanites, Sidonians, and Hivites to remain in the land to test Israel. As mentioned in a previous *briar patch* the testing was not so God would discover something about Israel; but that Israel would discover something about itself.

God gave specific commands not to intermarry with the heathen because the heathen wives and husbands would turn the hearts of Israel away from the Lord God who had rescued them from Egypt (Deuteronomy 7:3-4). The very thing God commanded them not to do they did and the results were as God said they would be.

We read these reports in the Bible and think it won't happen to us. We fool ourselves into thinking we are smarter, wiser than those ancient Jews. If we were Paul would not have had to write 1 Corinthians 10:13.

Just as Israel suffered the consequences of disobedience so we too bring suffering upon ourselves. Yes, God forgives upon repentance; but between disobedience and repentance we suffer. Praise the Lord, it's the suffering that leads to repentence.

Scripture: Ruth 4:13-17

Years ago on this day at age 48 the Lord blessed us with a baby boy. When we learned a child was imminent we were perplexed. I complained to the Lord explaining (as if He didn't know) that I already had enough children and was looking forward to not having that responsibility. When God had heard enough of my complaining He said, "He will be a joy to you in your old age."

Those words from the Lord have served to comfort me many times. They promise I am to reach old age and my youngest son will remain alive to give me joy. He already gives me joy as do each of my children.

Do I know the purpose and plan God has for Peter? No; but I'm confident His plans are for His welfare and my joy. God is so good.

As a result of this child I can understand Jacob's joy in Joseph and Benjamin. I have better insight into Abraham's attitude in Genesis 17:17 though I was half his age. Scripture does not say; but I'm confident Boaz rejoiced over the birth of Obed as did Naomi and the other women folk.

The children John wrote of were spiritual children yet he expressed what every parent whose children follow the Lord should express. He wrote, *"I have no greater joy than this, to hear of my children walking in the truth,"* (3 John 1:4). I can say that of my children. Can you say that of your children?

Scripture: Hebrews 4:14-17

There was a bull named Noal (pronounced Know-all) who won blue ribbons at all fairs. The accolades were so profuse his horns began to spread. A bovine rumor claimed Noal was an expert in everything. This made him bow in respectful humility while the rest of him shivered with pride.

After returning from another fair with ribbons and trophies Noal decided to apply his expertise in other fields previously unknown to him. The other farm animals applauded his decision.

After studying the work of a spider building a web in his stall Noal began advising the spider on web building. The spider followed Noal's advice because Noal was a very exceptional bull. This pleased Noal no end.

One day while grazing near the hen house Noal looked in the window. Day after day he watched the hens lay eggs. Each afternoon while chewing his cud he contemplated egg production. Soon he was advising the hens on how to lay eggs.

In our society we have a number of Noals who presume to advise, predict, guide, teach, and recommend about things they've never experienced. Their qualifications are impressive so everyone listens.

A well known Christian speaker gave advice on dealing with teens in an inner city school. His advice was ludicrous, he had no experience. If followed, his advice could get someone hurt if not killed.

All this is to say, when seeking guidance or advice, go to someone with experience. That's what makes Jesus the perfect High Priest.

Scripture: Psalm 103:1-14

Many congregations sing the grand old hymn *Count Your Blessings*. It's a good thing to do. The psalmist wrote, *"Bless the Lord, O my soul, And forget none of His benefits;"* (v. 2).

Satan never ceases pointing out your problems, aches, pains, mistakes, misfortunes, disappointments, sorrows, worries, and anxieties. He brings these things to your remembrance to depress and discourage you. When depressed or discouraged your commitment is weak and you're not sure of God's promises. Not being sure of God's promises puts you at sea and you don't do what God has commanded. Never underestimate Satan's craftiness or purpose.

The psalmist knew what to do. He began listing God's blessings. The greatest of which is forgiveness of our sins (vv. 10-12). Shouldn't we do that too, list our blessings.

Take a piece of paper and pen or pencil and begin listing all the good things God has done for you that you can remember. One blessing will probably remind you of another. Don't quit until the page is full. Use the back if necessary.

Now when Satan begins enumerating your woes counter attack by enumerating your blessings. You will get glad and Satan will get mad. He despises joyful Christians, hates them with a passion. Goad him by praising Jesus and thanking God for your many blessings.

When ol' slue foot hits me hard I remind him how I'll dance with joy when he is cast into the lake of fire. He usually leaves for a while. Try stomping Satan, it's fun.

Scripture: Ecclesiastes 12:1-7

Life is often compared to the seasons of the year; Spring being youth, summer the productive years, autumn middle age, and winter old age.

It is a grand thing to approach the autumn of life with satisfaction, with peace in your heart, and your joy in the Lord. To accomplish it you must follow the advice of the first few words of today's reading. *"Remember your Creator in the days of your youth..."* Though it's never to late to begin serving the Lord the sooner you begin the better.

Youth rarely if ever thinks of old age, of being decrepit or disabled. A teenager climbed the stairs slowly at school. I raced passed saying, "What will you do when you're my age." She responded, "I won't live that long." Those who love and serve the Lord He satisfies with good things and renews their youth (Psalm 103:5).

Consider his latter days the psalmist wrote, *"Do not cast me off in the time of old age; Do not forsake me when my strength fails,"* (Psalm 71:9). If you live long your strength will fail. All those things described in Ecclesiastes will creep up and conquer you.

The believer has God's promise, *"Even to your old age I shall be the same, And even to your graying years I shall bear you, I have done it and I shall carry you; And I shall bear you, and I shall deliver you,"* (Isaiah 46:4). Take God's promise to heart trust Him to do what He says.

Scripture: Exodus 31:12-17

Did you know the word Sabbath does not mean "seventh"? The word Sabbath comes from the root 'shabath' meaning *brought to an end, to cease, to rest.*

Let me illustrate it this way. Think of sitting on a porch swing in summer. No one is mowing, hammering, or driving by. A fly is buzzing nearby, grasshoppers tune exchange seats and tune again. It is a quiet and peaceful afternoon with absolutely nothing to do but sit quietly and listen to God's creation. Those not taking a nap converse quietly or not at all.

It is probably impossible to recapture the essence of an old fashioned Sunday afternoon. Today's world buzzes like an alarm clock, people scurry like ants bumping into each other. TV's and radios pierce the air. Children no longer take naps.

When the Lord established the Sabbath rest He did it for our benefit not His. He doesn't need a day of rest, we do. His Sabbath is not a diversion. We all need to do something different occasionally, hobbies, gardening, sports, reading, any break from the daily routine. A diversion still engages the body and mind.

A Sabbath rest means doing absolutely nothing and feeling good about it. It's a time without schedules, obligations or competition. It's a time to think or not think. It's a time of quiet fellowship with one another. Sadly, we are so oriented toward busyness we find it difficult doing nothing.

Some Sunday soon try having a real Sabbath, God's intended Sabbath.

Scripture: Jeremiah 11:1-5

Often the Lord asks His people, *"Why are you testing me?"* Israel tested God forty years in the wilderness. How did they test God? By continually asking God to prove Himself. We read about the Exodus from Egypt and wonder how those ancient Jews could be so mistrusting. Then we follow in their foot steps. It's one thing to review how God has worked and another to live day by day in the midst of God's works.

Look at God's word to Solomon (2 Chronicles 7:17-18), "If you will (v. 17)...I will (v. 18)." It's never the other way. God always asks us to believe Him, to trust Him, to step into the Red Sea (Exodus 14:15) or the Jordan River at flood (Joshua 3:15-16). God said through Jeremiah, *"Listen to My voice, and do according to all which I command you; so you shall be My people, and I will be your God,"* (v. 4).

As late as Jeremiah's day God was saying, "If you listen and do I will take care of you." Israel responded, "Take care of us and we will do." The problem was they didn't and God knew they wouldn't.

We are no different. We constantly seek assurances, put out the fleece, beg for provision even before we need it. Are you like that too?

Let us try doing what Jesus said to do (Matthew 6:33). Let us practice in life what we claim to believe in our hearts. God doesn't ignore true faith and obedience. He never has.

Scripture: James 2:14-26

Don't you appreciate a little sarcasm in the right context? I do and dish it out on occasion. One of the most sarcastic writers of the New Testament was James, pastor of the Jerusalem church. His letter makes very delightful reading.

One of the most sarcastic verses in the Bible is James 2:19. Listen to it in contemporary English. "You believe in God? Wonderful! You're just like the demons because they also believe in God; BUT THEY FEAR HIM." The implication is the reader should also fear God if he wants to move up in belief to the level of a demon.

James mocks those filled with pious platitudes and nothing else (v. 16), asking, "...*what good is that?*" In a Peanuts cartoon Charlie Brown tells his dog Snoopy, "Be warm, be filled," then leaves him shivering in the snow.

James' point is faith without works is dead. And remember, works without faith in Jesus Christ is dead (Ephesians 2:8-10).

Isn't this what Jesus said, "...*you will know them by their fruits,*" (Matthew 7:20)? It doesn't matter how much one proclaims, "I believe, I believe." If there is no change in that person's life we must ask, "What do you believe?"

James gives two examples of faith proven by action (works). Abraham offered up Isaac, Rehab hid the spies.

If you are truly born again there will be a difference in your life. If you have said, "I believe," but there's been no change in your life you better examine *what* you believed. Be sure before it's too late.

Scripture: 2 Peter 1:1-8

Many dedicated, committed followers of Jesus Christ often fail trying to achieve the growth pattern Peter outlines in verses 5-7. They fail because they try to acquire these *"qualities"* through the power of the flesh. The flesh, of its own power and desire, can not accomplish anything for the Lord.

If you've been experiencing failure let me ask, "What role is the Holy Spirit playing in your life?" Surely you are not like those who told Paul, *"...we have not even heard whether there is a Holy Spirit,"* (Acts 19:2).

Peter gives the secret for acquiring these qualities in verse 3. *"seeing that His divine power has granted to us everything pertaining to life and godliness..."* What power is Peter talking about? He is talking about the power Jesus promised in Luke 24:49 and delivered in Acts 2. That is the power of the Holy Spirit.

Should the believer then be lacking in anything pertaining to life and godliness. NO! Not if he is allowing the Holy Spirit to empower him, guide him, equip him, use him.

How do you begin living in the power of the Holy Spirit? First by realizing the Holy Spirit began abiding in you the instant you received Jesus Christ as Savior. Second by asking Him to exercise His power in your life. After asking Him to take control go forward in faith.

As you begin to acquire these qualities you'll become useful and fruitful *"in the true knowledge of our Lord Jesus Christ,"* (v. 8).

Scripture: 1 Samuel 8:10-18

A nanny told the boy he couldn't have it. He began screaming, "I want it, I want it." The mother called from downstairs, "For heaven's sake let him have it." The nanny obeyed and an even louder wail burst forth from the child. The mother rushed into the room, "What has happened to my baby?" The nanny said, "He wanted to grab a wasp on the curtains and you said to let him."

Ouch! Have you asked for things then regretted receiving? Israel demanded a king. They wanted a king because all their neighbors had kings. They rejected God as their King (2 Samuel 8:7). Wasn't God able to do a-bundantly more than all the neighboring kings combined? Did they remember?

God told Samuel, *"Listen to their voice; however, you shall solemnly warn them..."* (1 Samuel 8:9). Samuel warned but they did not believe him. The were bent on having their own way and God gave it to them. Many years later they sang a different tune. The Israelites begged King Solomon's son Rehoboam to lighten their burden saying, *"Your father made our yoke hard; therefore lighten the hard service of your father and his heavy yoke which he put on us..."* (1 Kings 12:4). Isn't this what Samuel warned in verse 18?

It has been my experience after hard lessons to let God decide what I should ask of Him. You do that by saying, "Lord, put your desires in my heart." I've never regretted HIS CHOICE and you won't either.

Scripture: Romans 5:1-10

We run our lives by the clock even eating by the clock when not hungry. We manipulate time to our advantage. Very soon now the United States will go back to Standard time.

In the New Testament there are two words for time *chronos (GK-cronos)* clock time, and *kairos (Gk-καιροσ)* the right time. Chronos appears fifteen times in the gospels while kairos appears thirty times. "Kairos is not the quantitative time of the clock, but the qualitative time of the occasion, the right time."[1] The early church spoke of the right time for Christ to come. Jesus came in that special moment in history when everything was in order for His coming. There was peace under Rome, the right language, the star God started on its journey in creation was in the right place to shine over Bethlehem, etc.

Paul wrote, "...*at the right time (kairos) Christ died for the ungodly,*" (v. 6). Later he wrote, "*for He says, 'At the acceptable time (kairos) I listened to you, And on the day of salvation I helped you'; behold, now is the 'acceptable time (kairos),' behold, now is the day of salvation'*" (2 Corinthians 6:2).

While Paul witnessed to Felix, "*Felix became frightened and said, 'Go away for the present and when I find time (kairos), I will summon you,*" (Acts 24:25).

When it comes to accepting Jesus as Savior and Lord it is always the kairos, the right time. What better kairos do you expect than now. Believe on Him TODAY.

---

[1]Tillich, Paul, *A Complete History of Christian Thought*, (New York, Harper and Row), 1968, p. 1

Scripture: Deuteronomy 25:17-19

God doesn't administer retribution at the moment of sin and rebellion. T. S. Elite wrote, "Between the idea/And the reality/Between the motion/And the act/Falls the Shadow/*For Thine is the Kingdom*"[1] Between the sin of Amalek and the annihilation lie about 500 years of dormancy.

Amalek cowardly fought Israel by attacking the weak, feeble, sick, and aged who had difficulty keeping up with the tribes. They harassed the people of God because they did not fear God.

God told Israel, "*...you shall blot out the memory of Amalek from under heaven; you must not forget,* (v. 19). Then He reminded Israel when He instructed Saul to utterly destroy the Amalekites (1 Samuel 15). The shadow (death) was about to fall on them.

Scripture makes it clear that punishment for sin is sure unless repentance intervenes and God by His grace forgives, which He does. Scripture also teaches the world can not mess with the children of God and expect to get away with it.

God has not changed. The world has not changed. Everything is as it was when Amalek attacked Israel. The world despises and persecutes the children of God because it does not fear God. The world does not fear God because it does not know God. The world does not know God because it rejects the gospel of God as revealed through Jesus Christ.

Throughout the Bible we see God is Sovereign and in control. As Eliot wrote, *"For Thine is the Kingdom"*.
We must remember that.

---

[1]from *The Hollow Men*

Scripture: Amos 5:1-7

As we approach the Christmas season manufacturers and retailers begin promoting their guarantees. Each claiming their guarantee is trustworthy. One company said, "You can rest on our guarantee." We accept such statements at face value but doubt the word of the Lord.

God said through Amos, *"Seek Me that you may live,"* (v. 4). *"May live"* doesn't mean avoid dying but to obtain true life. God said it. Why can't we rest in it? Why don't we rest in EVERYTHING God said?

Amos warned Israel not to resort to the shrines of Gilgal and Bethel. Both cities had become places of idolatrous worship (Amos 4:4). Gilgal and Bethel were celebrated because holy events had happened in them. Gilgal means "circle of stones" suggesting a pagan foundation. Here Joshua circumcised Israel, Samuel sent Saul there to be confirmed king. Bethel (Lud) is God's meeting place with Jacob, the Ark had been kept at Bethel, Jeroboam established a worship center there, etc. Beersheba in southern Judah had become a shrine for similar reasons. Israelites made pilgrimages there. Amos warned visiting idolatrous places of worship does no good. Instead seek the Lord.

God warned through Amos that Gilgal would go into captivity and Bethel come to trouble which of course happened. God's word is guaranteed. What He says will come to pass. Guaranteed!

As you read God's word remembering the promises; remember also the warnings. God said, *"I am watching over My word to perform it,"* (Jeremiah 1:12). That's your guarantee. Believe it.

Scripture: 1 Kings 20:1-11

Young people and older ones too need to learn to draw the line. As parents we need to draw the line (set limits) for our children; teachers must do the same.

King Ahab was a rather willy nilly fellow allowing Jezebel, his queen, to control (see 1 Kings 21). When the enemy began making demands on Ahab, he didn't resist. Ben-hadad increased his demands until Ahab finally said, "*...this thing I cannot do,*" (v. 9). He meant it. Ben-hadad, king of Syria threatened to make dust of Samaria. Ahab answered, "*Let not him who girds on his armor boast like him who takes it off,*" (v. 11). Ben-hadad was defeated (1 Kings 20:21).

Most of us grow up defying and conquering as Ben-hadad did. Then someone draws the line and we threaten to cross it.

In the twenty years I taught in room 301 at McKinley High School (St. Louis) I had many Ben-hadads in class. Something I read; but also learned from experience, young people like to know what the limits are. In 301 we had few rules but each one was enforced. Outside the scope of Faber's Law students were free to do as they pleased. Rarely did we have an altercation, theft, or need the administrators to intervene. Many attempts were made at breaking the rules but few succeeded.

You can experience this in your own life. God's rules are few, really. Use them to draw the line in your life and the lives of your children.

Scripture: Colossians 1:13-20

We must keep in mind that Jesus is pre-eminent in ALL THINGS. He is the first born of all creation and the first born from the dead. JESUS IS FIRST!

It is easy for us to understand Him being first born of all creation. By His own testimony He was before Abraham. John wrote, *"In the beginning was the Word..."* (John 1:1).

How is He first born *"from the dead"* (v. 18)? What are all those who were raised from the dead before and after Calvary? How do we classify the widow of Zarephath's son, the Shunammite women's son, Lazaras, Tobitha, and all the others?

The difference is to what they were raised. All those raised from the dead in the Bible, except Jesus, were raised up in their old fleshly bodies only to die again. Like Hezekiah who only came to the point of death when he got an extension on life, those resurrected only got an extension on earthly life (2 Kings 20:6).

Jesus was raised to a glorified body. His resurrected body was not limited to the forces of this world. Didn't He appear in the midst of the disciples on two occasions, the doors being shut and barred (John 20:19 and 26)? No earthly body could do that.

Jesus is *"first born from the dead"* first to receive a resurrected body. The resurrected body cannot die. It has eternal life. Every one who believes in Jesus Christ shall receive a resurrected body on the great day of the Lord.

Scripture: Luke 14:1-15

Many today play a game the Pharisees played. It's called "one upmanship". What one person does another must do it better. The old song says, "Anything you can do, I can do better, I can do anything better than you." A musical argument ensues and it's fun. In life it's not always fun.

The Pharisees persistently reminded people of the law and the tradition of the elders. They put others down by reminding them of their failure to meticulously keep the regulations. They constantly sought the better seats at dinners and craved being honored on the streets. The reason the woman caught in adultery was taken to Jesus was to put her down, trap Jesus, and inflate their egos (John 8:5-6). The Pharisees were not enamored with the law of Moses except as they could use it to denigrate others. Do we do that?

Pharisees enjoyed being critical thinking it enhanced their own image. What is our motive in criticizing someone else? Isn't it to make them look bad and us good? Isn't that really why we point out the faults and failings of others? Sure it is. If it wasn't we'd do what Paul says.

Paul, a Pharisee of the Pharisees, proved his conversion saying, *"Brethren, even if a man is caught in a trespass, you who are spiritual, restore such a one in a spirit of gentleness; each one looking to himself lest you too be tempted,"* (Galatians 6:1). Which method do you think Christ would have you use? How does He want you to behave?

Scripture: Galatians 4:8-11

There is *NOTHING* Christian about Halloween. It is a pagan celebration from before the time of Christ on earth. Pagan peoples the world over observed October 31 /November 1 one way or another. Since many of the gentile members of the Galatian churches were Celts we'll look at their observance of October 31/November 1.

This holiday, called Samain (also spelled Samhain and Samon) marked the end of summer and beginning of winter. The Celtic world observed four special days throughout the year, Samain - November 1, Imbolg - February 1, Beltene - May 1, and Lughnasadh - August 1.

They believed Samain to be "a time outside of time...a temporary resumption of...primordial time."[1] That almost sounds like modern day science fiction. Samain was a "...dissolution of established order as a prelude to its recreation in a new period of time."[2] "The eve of Samain was the great time for commemorating the dead..."[3] Samain was "dedicated to all the gods and denizens of the Celtic otherworld."[4] From my understanding Samain was a time of renewal, rebirth; in a sense a kind of salvation. The Celts measured the year by nights (renewal) not days therefore festivals began on the eve of the holiday.

The converted Jews wanted to reinstitute Hebrew festivals. The redeemed Celts wanted to incorporate their ancient celebrations. Thus Paul writes, "...*how is it you want to turn back again to weak and worthless elemental things...You observe days...months...years.*" (vv. 9-10).

Should we then be careful about the purpose and observance of holidays?

[1-2]Mac Cana, Proinsias, *Celtic Mythology*, (London, The Hamlyn Publishing Group) 1970 pp. 126-128

[3]Ross, Ann and Robins, Don, *The Life and Death of a Druid Prince*, (New York, Summit Books) 1989, p. 141

[4]Ibid. p. 35

Scripture: 1 Corinthians 3:1-9

Kenneth Hagen said, "If we are *'laborers together with God'* we must be workers of miracles because God is a miracle working God." We hear such great truths, rejoice, and then look about us for the miracles. Where are they? The questions should be "Why aren't they?"

You'll find one clue in verses 1-8. We think because we live in the flesh we must operate as fleshly people. And we do. What church is totally free of Paul's accusations here? Haven't we seen great churches crumble in the past because the shepherd went astray? Were those congregations built upon faith in Jesus Christ or faith in the man in the pulpit? Are we then any different from the Corinthian bunch?

Considering all the preaching we hear, all the books we read (or should read), and all the opportunities to grow in the spirit we remain babes. Many shoutin' believers would choke on real spiritual meat. Not all, but a fair majority.

Another clue: we forget Paul's words in verse 16, *"Do you not know that you are a temple of God and that the Spirit of God dwells in you?"* Then we should be working miracles, right? Why not? We suppress the Spirit within us. We are great fans of our own busyness and worldly accomplishments. Our minds and hearts are not on spiritual matters.

Brother Hagen's words challenge us to be *"...God's fellow-workers..."* (v. 9). To be God's fellow miracle worker operate by the power of the Spirit within you.

Scripture: Colossians 1:9-12

A survey revealed three in every one hundred teenagers knew the ten commandments. Do you know them or where they are found? Who was Esau's grandfather? Who was Jesus' cousin? Where was John when he wrote the Revelation? Can you name the books of the Bible from Genesis to Revelation?

Perhaps churches should institute an assessment program to measure the effectiveness of all the time, money, and energy invested in the Bible teaching program. The results may be shocking; but then we could take corrective measures.

Our school system altered the English program, ten years later the expected results had not materialized. The curriculum was changed. Without testing the failure of the program would have continued.

Without testing we know there are people who have attended Sunday School for years who are functionally illiterate about the Bible. This is a travesty, a shame, and a sham.

Paul prayed the Colossians would walk in a manner worthy of the Lord (v. 10). He wrote to the Philippians, *"Only conduct yourselves in a manner worthy of the gospel of Christ..."* (Philippians 1:17).

He also prayed and admonished the Colossians to be *"...increasing in the knowledge of God..."* (v. 10) Apparently there is some correlation between knowledge and the ability to walk in a manner worthy of the Lord and the gospel.

Be brave, assess your teaching program then make necessary changes. God will be glorified and the people will be equipped to walk in a manner pleasing to the Lord.

Scripture: John 3:1-15

Early in my teaching career I would assign an essay in November to encourage students to think of things for which they were thankful. At first I was alarmed how many were thankful to be alive. The experience of teaching in the inner city taught me life is fragile for these teens. The life of a friend may be senselessly snuffed out in an instant. It was brought home to me when one of my students, a beautiful, sweet, studious, black girl was shot to death going home from a school dance.

Thankful for life? Yes, each of us should be thankful for life. How many families experience untimely often tragic deaths in a year? Look back over the last twelve months; how many close encounters have you had with death but the Lord spared you life? No one is guaranteed of returning home from a journey. Physical life is precious.

There is another life for which we can be thankful. We are not as aware of it as we are physical life but it is far more valuable and enduring. Those born into the kingdom of God through faith in Jesus Christ know I speak of eternal life.

We must be thankful everyday that God loved us and sent His Son to cancel the charge of sin against us. Without the death of Jesus on the cross and His resurrection from the dead we would be without hope of eternal life. Be thankful for eternal life and live like it.

Scripture: 1 Kings 17:17-24

Isn't it amazing how we survive for long periods on the miracles of God's provision then tragedy befalls us and we're ready to blame God? Or in the case of our text, God's servant got blamed.

By Elijah's prayer it had not rained and would not rain until the three and a half years were completed. The ravens fed him bread and meat twice a day until the brook dried up. By God's direction he moved in with the widow and her son. God provided meal and oil for bread for the duration of the drought. Suddenly her son took ill and died.

Listen to the widow's accusation, *"What have I to do with you, O man of God? You have come to bring my iniquity to remembrance, and to put my son to death!"* (v. 18). Had she forgotten how near death both of them were before Elijah came? Had she forgotten the never failing meal and oil? Before being hard on her, do we follow in her footsteps?

Elijah took the boy to his room, prayed over him and the Lord restored the boy's life.

We must note the widow did not turn away from the Lord. She remained submissive allowing Elijah to take her son to his room. She never imagined Elijah would bring her son down alive.

What would you or I have done in like circumstances? Would we do as many have, turn away from the Lord? If so, where then is there help for distress?

Scripture: 2 Kings 15:27-31

Today is Guy Fawkes Day in Britain. James I was king of England in 1605. A gun powder plot to blow up Parliament was instigated by Fawkes and ten others. Guy Fawkes is the one remembered. Parliament established a day of Thanksgiving. On the night of November 5 the whole country lights up with bond fires and celebration. Old verses are repeated, "Remember, remember, the fifth of November/Gun powder, treason, and plot;/I see no reason why gun powder treason/should ever be forgot."

The Old Testament is full of conspiracy and plot as one ruling family secumbed to the treachery of another. We should note these many battles for control because as believers we too are in a struggle for control. Our struggle is a spiritual struggle for the control of the heart and mind of man.

Just as rebels have plotted against authorities and kings, so Satan plots and conspires against the followers of Jesus Christ. His purpose is no more noble than that of Elah in today's reading. Destruction and death are the aim of all conspirators. Satan is no different.

Just as the old verse says, "...I see no reason why gun powder treason/should ever be forgot." There is no reason for you or I to forget we are engaged in spiritual combat with a powerful, cunning, and totally wicked conpirator.

Fawkes conspiracy was detected and Parliament spared. By being spiritually alert demonic conspiracy against you can be detected and you spared. Peter warned, *"Your adversary, the devil prowls about...seeking someone to devour."* (1 Peter 5:8).

Scripture: Isaiah 58:1-5

Are you a pew sponge?

In today's reading the Lord is hurling accusations against the pew sponges of Israel. Pew sponges are those who never miss a service. They delight in singing and listening to good "old fashioned" preaching. That's good. Pew sponges enjoy church fellowship. They like getting together down at the church for all manner of activities. That too is good. Many of them are real honest to goodness tithers. That's commendable. Pew sponges delight in the nearness of God. Shouldn't we all?

Then why is God indicting them?

God indicts them for *being* pew sponges. Though they hear the word preached with power and persuasion they remain unaffected by it. Though they sing with gusto the great hymns or praise choruses it only provides an emotional high. When they get together down at the church are all relationships seasoned with love and forgiveness? In their hearts they sing, "I'm saved to sit, I'm saved to sit. Oh, don't bother me, I', saved, saved, to sit." Pew sponges rarely make an impact on the world for Jesus.

Mark Twain said something like this: We brave miles and miles of bad roads and bad weather to go to church, worship the Creator and criticize each others clothes.   God said, "*...this people draw near with their words...but they remove their hearts far from me...their reverence consists of tradition learned by rote,*" (Isaiah 29:13).

The only cure is repentance and real effort in growing as a Christian. Pew sponges are capable of that.

Scripture: Nehemiah 6:1-9

Satan will do anything to lure you away from doing the work of the Lord. He had Sanballat and his cronies send messengers to Nehemiah to lure him away from finishing the walls around Jerusalem. Nehemiah wisely answered, *"I am doing a great work and cannot come down. Why should the work stop while I leave it and come down to you?"* (v. 3).

Notice their persistence in verse 4. They tried fear on their fifth attempt coupled with an offer to help avoid trouble that did not exist. Nehemiah knew the plot was to lure him into a trap and kill him.

The enemy even hired Shemaiah to prophecy a lie (1 Kings 6:10-12). The object was to strike fear in Nehemiah's heart so he would seek refuge and not continue the work.

Remember this: Offers from the world to save the believer from trouble are dangerous. Should not the believer seek help from the Lord?

Isaiah wrote, *"Woe to those who go down to Egypt for help, And rely on horses, And trust in chariots...but do not look to the Holy One of Israel, nor seek the Lord,"* (Isaiah 31:1). Uriah feared and fled to Egypt was pursued, captured, returned and put to death (Jeremiah 26:20-23). The examples in scripture are abundant.

When Satan tries luring you away from your calling be wise and courageous as Nehemiah not stupid and fearful as Uriah. In real trouble seek the Lord not the help of man. God is our Deliverer!

Scripture: Nehemiah 13:10-14

You can, if you ask, receive a financial statement from most TV, radio, and other ministries. Trinity Broadcast Network has broadcast their financial statement explaining where and how their income is distributed and used for the glory of God. I believe they will send you a printed financial statement upon request. Not all ministries are as open to scrutiny.

The Billy Graham Association has never, to my knowledge, asked for your tithes though they do ask for financial support as do other ministries.

The tithe belongs to the local church. Today's text and Malachi 3:10 direct us to bring our tithes into the *"storehouse"*. I understand that to be the local church where you regularly worship. The local church provides a printed financial statement on a regular basis. It explains where and how the money was spent and used. In most churches the people also have an opportunity to express their opinions regarding expenditures, recommending some be decreased others increased.

When contributing to other Christian work make it an offering above and beyond the tithe. You can't outgive God, but it's fun to try. The Bible speaks of both tithes and offerings. The tithe belongs to the church. Offerings can be made to the church or other work.

What about civil aid programs? That's up to you; but you can't count what you give to United Way or other civil aid programs as part of your gift to God. God's gifts are for God's work through the ministry of the gospel.

Scripture: 2 Corinthians 4:1-6

If one is alert to the voice of the Spirit some of the most mundane things speak to us about God and our relationship to Him. A potato had tumbled out of the box in our cellar and had not been noticed. When found it was a pitiful sight all shriveled from finding neither light nor soil. The frail roots had pushed hard against the cement floor. Their tips had pressed and pushed until they were bent and misshaped. A few withered leaves had struggled upward in the darkness seeking the light. How like mankind without the word of God for nourishment and the light of the Spirit to synthesize the Word.

Man, like a potato in the dark on a cement floor, is struggling to survive. He presses his roots downward searching for some fulfilling nourishment, some answers to life's dilemma. He reaches up for help but finds only darkness until someone comes to him with the light of Jesus Christ. Unless he is given the Word for his roots and the light of Jesus Christ for his leaves; he, as the potato of the earth he is, will shrivel, wither, and die.

If caught in time and buried in good soil the potato would not only survive; but flourish and reproduce. The sinner, if caught in time and buried in Christ will also survive, flourish and reproduce.

Do you know any struggling potatoes seeking the light? Get busy planting them in Jesus. There are plenty of potatoes waiting for you.

Scripture: Psalm 34:1-7

One of Satan's powerful weapons is fear. He not only uses it against the saints, he uses it against everybody. The saint of the Lord has the advantage because he can cast out fear in the name of the Lord.

While on a mission trip in Elko, Nevada I was driving over the mountain from Spring Creek where we were staying to hand out evangelistic tracts at a carnival. Fear attacked to prevent me from going. Suddenly I felt afraid of some criminal element that *might* choose to do me harm. The Holy Spirit revealed the cause of the fear so I cast out fear in the name of Jesus. I then went happily and peacefully to the carnival and had a great time handing out tracts.

At other times fear has attacked simply to disturb my rest, or a peaceful afternoon. Haven't you suddenly worried about someone without cause? Haven't you awakened in the night fearful for one of your family or friends?

In such circumstances take time to pray for the person on your mind. Often I've arisen in the night and spent hours praying for someone I feared for. God hears and answers such earnest praying.

The psalmist wrote, *"I sought the Lord, and He answered me, And delivered me from all my fears,* (v. 4). Instead of fearing the pain, tragedy, and conflict of the world, fear the Lord. *"The angel of the Lord encamps around those who fear Him, and rescues them,"* (v. 7). HE DOES!

Scripture: 2 Samuel 7:18-23

For years at eleven O'clock on the eleventh day of the eleventh month the British, Canadians, and Americans celebrated the signing of the armistice ending World War I. The British and Canadians still call this day The Day of Remembrance. In American it was called Armistice Day but is now called Veterans Day. Since World War II it's a day for honoring those who gave their lives in all wars.

Those who fought on our behalf should be remembered. Memorials of stone, marble, and bronze are erected in honor of our dead soldiers. Public buildings display plaques or framed documents listing the local heroes who died in various wars. This is as it should be. Our military men and women gave their lives that we might live in freedom.

Britain, Canada and the U.S. have been blessed in all their wars. Though we lost thousands of lives we were victors. Do we think God did not have a hand in it? Are we so egotistical we think it was by our might or strategy we won?

In today's text David gives honor to the Lord for all his military victories. David realized it was not by might, nor by power, but by the Spirit of the Lord the battles were won.

In remembering those who gave their lives on the battle field for you; remember it was God who gave the victory. Be reminded of God's intervention when you see a war memorial and say a prayer of thanksgiving.

Scripture: Daniel 9:20-23

Have you ever watched water on a window after a rain? Not the rain striking the window but the little droplets that formed as a result of the rain. Pretty soon a little drop descends and joins another. The new heavier drop descends more quickly to join another. And so it goes until the first little drop, now large, is racing down the glass. Prayer is like that.

Children requesting favors from parents don't give up after asking just once. They ask repeatedly until they get an answer, even if the answer is, "No".

Daniel had been praying fervently constantly for twenty-one days when Gabriel brought an answer. Delay in answered prayer is not always your fault. Gabriel explained *"At the beginning of your supplications the command was issued..."* (v. 23). In Daniel 10:13 we are told how Gabriel was delayed. *"...the prince of the kingdom of Persia was withstanding me for twenty-one days..."*

By the time Gabriel arrived Daniel was exhausted from praying. *"...Gabriel...came to me in my extreme weariness..."* (v. 22). Are you serious enough in your praying to pray until you are exhausted?

Fervent effectual prayer is work and not work for the weak and dying. Paul wrote, *"Epaphras...is...always laboring earnestly for you in his prayers..."* (Colossians 4:12). It is the fervent exhausting serious and sincere praying that changes the history of individual lives and the world.

Laboring in prayer gets results. It may take days, even years; but God will answer everyone who prays seriously and continually.

Scripture: Genesis 22:1-8

Dads, like other people, are excellent, good, mediocre, and sorry. I'm grateful God gave me an excellent dad. He wasn't perfect; but suffered normal human frailties. Yet, he was outstanding in every possible way.

All dads should emulate my father's outstanding qualities. First, he was not merely a church "attender"; he took an active part. Every time the church doors were open dad was there, and he was not the custodian. Testing my freedom in adolescence I announced at supper I wasn't going to prayer meeting. Dad said, "Then leave the table." I asked why. He added, "As long as you put your feet under my table, you'll go to church when I go." Guess who ate supper and went to church?

Second, dad exhibited stewardship of his time. He worked ten hour days but always had time for me in the evening. We'd play catch, wrestle, or do something together. He did these things even when there were other things he needed or wanted to do.

Third, dad was a great lover. Even when angry at me for some stupid kid stunt, he loved me. Mom spanked. Dad sat me in a chair and told me what for. As I chewed on his words, hated, and rebelled in my heart I knew dad loved me. He had said so in thousands of ways.

To list all of dad's fine qualities would fill many pages. He was born on this date in 1898. Are there any modern dads like him?

Scripture: Isaiah 60:18-22

There is much conjecture about the new Jerusalem, the new earth, heaven. Looking at some of the things revealed in scripture makes heaven very enticing. What God has created for those who love Him also destroys earthly passions and values. There is really nothing in this life to which heaven can accurately be compared.

We value gold. People hoard it, hide it, murder for it. What is it's true value? God shows us what gold is worth. He treats it as we do common stone. He paves the streets of heaven with it. Shouldn't this teach us there are greater values than material things?

People in every age and in every place have worshiped sun, moon, stars. The new Jerusalem *heaven* has no need of sun, moon, stars. What will the astrologers do? What will they worship? How will they survive? They won't be there.

Even before the new Jerusalem comes down the old order of stars will be no more. *"...and the stars of the sky fell to the earth as a fig tree casts its unripe figs when shaken by a great wind,"* (Revelation 6:13).

Just as in 1 Samuel 5:3 Dagon fell on his face before the Ark of the Lord so all pagan gods shall fall. When the stars fall to the earth everyone trusting the stars (horoscopes) will be put to shame. Those who worship the sun or moon will also see their gods fall.

Worship the eternal God of the Bible and rejoice in Him.

Scripture: Ezra 8:21-23 & 31

Canada celebrates Thanksgiving in October, the U.S. within the next two weeks. The first settlers were a thankful people. When reading the works of William Bradford 1590-1657 you detect a repetitious note of gratitude. He wrote "...many were afflicted with sea sickness. And I may not omit here a special work of God's providence." He then told how an arrogant and disdaining sailor died in an unusual way. "...for they noted it to be the just hand of God upon him." The "they" refers to the non-believing sailors.

Pilgrim writings often mention the hand of God in their affairs. Having disembarked on the wilderness shores without store or shelter or friends to welcome them, and winter hard upon them, Bradford wrote, "What could ...sustain them but the Spirit of God?" It was November 11, 1620.

Before those brave pilgrims boarded ship they asked God's protection over them. It is logical to believe that during the several weeks of crossing the Atlantic there were many prayer meetings asking for God's assistance.

Before beginning the journey Ezra led the people in prayer and fasting. When the journey was complete Ezra gave this testimony. "...*the hand of our God was over us, and He delivered us from the hand of the enemy and the ambushes by the way,*" (v. 31).

We are approaching the holidays when many will travel to visit friends and relatives. Wouldn't it be wise to ask God's protection before you depart and thank Him for His protection when you arrive?

Scripture: Proverbs 6:6-11

These verses have a different meaning for urban folks than for rural folks. City dwellers often do not see the results of their labors. One can become discouraged not seeing tangible results beyond the pay check. Though they work hard there's often little to show for their efforts.

Rural folks have gardens from which they harvest food for the winter. The farmer stores feed for live stock. Many rural homes are heated partially or a totally with wood. Rural folks have an advantage which I call *tangiality*. (You won't find that word in the dictionary, yet.)

Tangiality is many things wrapped into one. It is proudly looking at many jars of beans, or tomatoes you canned yourself. It is realizing you provided that pile of winter fuel. It is appreciating the labor of your hands. It is the reality of labor invested that is expendable but not spendable.

One must work in order to eat and be warm in winter. Some prefer to labor at a job, purchase their groceries and pay the utility company. Others prefer to labor in the garden and hot kitchen to put food by for the winter and cut wood for heat. Either way, it's work.

Poverty overtakes urban and rural folks for the same reason. *"A little sleep, a little slumber, A little folding of the hands to rest,"* (v. 10). Will they suffer? NO! Public assistance has created generations of lazy people. The Bible is explicit regarding whom we should help and it's not the "sluggard".

Scripture: Obadiah 12-17

There is a double message in Obadiah. Through verse 16 the prophet, whose name means "one who serves God" announces God's retribution on Edom. Utter annihilation is the message. Utter annihilation because of Edom's treatment of Israel (v. 10). Beginning in verse 11 Obadiah lists Esau's sin against Jacob.

Following the message of annihilation the prophet reveals the victory of God's children. *"But on Mount Zion there will be those who escape...and the house of Jacob will possess their possessions,"* (v. 17).

Edom loses their possessions. Israel possesses their possessions. This second message then is living the victorious life. We can live victoriously because our confidence is in Him who won the victory on Calvary. Yes, we have victory amid failure, persecution, tragedy, misfortune, and anything else Satan dishes out.

There is victory for each one remaining faithful to the Lord. Though the world may gloat over our misfortune, rejoice over our tragedies, and disdain our very existence God has not forgotten us nor their deeds.

We have here again the theme, "you can't raise your hand against the Lord's people and go unpunished". Judgment is coming on those who despitefully use you. Victory belongs to the Lord and to His own who follow after Him.

Repeatedly God promises believers will possess the land. Perhaps not in this brief earthly existence but in eternity. Hasn't God promised a new heaven and a new earth?

Every believer must remember **who he is** in Jesus and that the strutting world will be destroyed.

Scripture: Haggai 2:4-9

Satan uses discouragement to halt the work of the church. He tried it during the post exilic temple in the days of Ezra and Nehemiah. This new temple couldn't compare to the opulence of Solomon's temple. The people may have wondered, "Is the new building well pleasing to the Lord?" Remembrance of things passed did not compare to the reality of the present. To rebuild Solomon's temple was impossible; but what does God tell Zerubbabel? *"...take courage..."* (v. 4).

Many small congregations get discouraged because they can't do the things the large churches do. The smaller congregation has neither the resources nor the people. Does that mean their service in the kingdom of God is not important nor valuable? Because they can't provide all the programs of a large church is what they provide not worthy? God says to small churches, "Take courage!" Is God's Spirit abiding any less in the small congregation than the large? Listen to Haggai. *"As for the promise which I made you...My Spirit is abiding in your midst; do not fear,"* (v. 5). Isn't God's Spirit abiding in all believers? Hasn't every believer come out of Egypt (slavery to sin)?

The small congregation, the pastor who hasn't the talents of another pastor, the believer who simply sweeps the walk in front of the church are each one precious to the Lord. Therefore, work as if the whole kingdom depended on you.

God is with you. Take courage. God promises, *"...the latter glory...will be greater than the former..."* (v. 9).

Scripture: 2 Kings 2:7-14

How determined are you to acquire what the Lord has for you? God's message to each of us is, *"I know the plans that I have for you...plans for welfare and not for calamity to give you a future and a hope,"* (Jeremiah 29:11). However, God will not force His plans on you. He will not make you into a great anything unless you prepare for it.

I think every believer will be disheartened to a degree on judgment day. How will each one feel when God shows His plan along side the reality of the believer's life? To be sure, some will fair better than others.

When I was in college a dorm mate asked me to make a sign to hang over his desk which read, "Want to enough!" That's the secret to successful Christian living, to attaining and acquiring what God has planned for you.

Elisha greatly desired a double portion of Elijah's spirit. He followed Elijah to Bethel, to Jericho, finally to the Jordan, and across the Jordan *"on dry ground"* (v. 8). Finally Elijah asked Elisha, *"What shall I do for you before I am taken from you?"* (v. 9). Elisha told him. Elijah made Elisha's acquiring his desire conditional, *"...if you see me when I am taken..."* (v. 10).

Elisha did not receive a double portion of Elijah's spirit by chance. He had to pursue it diligently, persistently, faithfully, without distraction thus receiving what he desired. Of course it was God's plan for Elisha. Are you willing to pursue what God has for you?

Scripture: Jude 1-4

Jude begins his letter mentioning first his relationship to Jesus which was that of *"bond-servant"*. Then mentions he is the brother of James. The James mentioned in Galatians 1:19 the physical brother of Jesus, writer of the book of James and pastor of the Jerusalem church.

It's Jude's relationship to Jesus that concerns us here. He mentions his spiritual relationship, not his physical relationship. The physical relationship was not something to be claimed as we might claim relationship to some famous person. Jude mentions a much higher relationship; that of bond-servant.

As we understand the relationship of bond-servant we understand what our relationship to Jesus should be. A bond-servant is a slave and therefore every area of his life is restricted by the master. This is true whether the slavery is voluntary or coerced.

Another relationship expressed in bond-servant is being enthralled, excited about, devoted. Jude was excited about Jesus; as were Paul, Peter and the rest. Are you excited about Jesus? Are you devoted to Him?

Yet, another facet of the relationship is that of dependence. A slave is dependent upon the master for everything. Do you trust Jesus for your every need? Or do you try handling it all yourself except in times of crises?

Every human being is a slave either to Satan who wrecks lives and pays with death; or to Jesus who builds lives and pays with eternal life. Yes, it IS a black/white issue. You are either for Jesus or against Him (Matthew 12:30). Whose slave are you?

Scripture: Titus 2:9-14

Through high school and some of my college years I worked for a large grocery chain. It was common practice among the employees to carelessly damage a package. We then would consume the contents, whether cookies or cheese or some other ready to eat food. None of us considered it stealing; but it was.

In every industry there are losses consumed, carried off, misused by employees. These losses are added to the retail cost of the product so everybody pays. Technically then, the theft was not from the company but from everyone who purchases that companies product.

Titus had a rough group to pastor. They were *"...liars, evil beasts, lazy gluttons,"* (Titus 1:12). Paul advised Titus to *"rebuke them severely"* (1:13).

What Paul writes regarding slaves applies to employees. Employees are to give an honest days work whether they receive an honest days pay or not. Employees are not to argue with their bosses. Neither are employees to pilfer, that is appropriate company supplies, equipment, funds, or reputation for their personal benefit.

True, the company may not have an honest pay scale, the bosses may be ogres to work under, the corporation probably can afford the losses. Pilfering is stealing and you will give an account to the Lord.

Now that you know better it's your responsibility to correct your own behavior if need be. Not all employees are guilty. Most would not take so much as a paper clip or an extra five minutes for lunch. God guarantees their reward.

Scripture: Ecclesiastes 3:1-11

We find significance in the long list of times beginning in verse 2. The list is intended to cover every aspect of life and show that God is in control of life from beginning to end and everything in between.

Some restrict these verses to spiritual life and matters. Others apply them to all of life spiritual and physical. Certainly we experience all of these things both spiritually and physically.

We are born physically and upon accepting Christ we're born spiritually (John 3:5-7). We die physically and if born again put to death our old nature spiritually. Every contrast can be compared in the same manner. The list ends beautifully speaking of war and finally peace.

Isn't God gracious? He gives us birth and though we experience all these contrasts our lives end in peace. We face times of difficulty and tragedy; but they're balanced with times of laughing and joyful dancing. All this is because of God's accurate timing of events in our lives.

Many testimonies have been given illustrating God's work in leading an individual through the valley only to bring them to the mountain top (Psalm 23:4). Could the mountain top be reached any other way? Only God knows. You can be sure He chose the best route for you.

Verse 11 tells us to look at all God has done in our lives and call it *schön und gut* (beautiful and good). To do otherwise accuses God of evil intent. God always has your best interest at heart.

Scripture: Ezekiel 8:1-5

Here is a very powerful warning to everyone who follows Jesus. It warns us against falling into the same trap of deceit gripping the seventy elders of Israel. We must not be deceived by any idol of jealousy.

The *"idol of jealousy"* (v. 3) must be understood as "the anger-image provoking to anger"[1] Israel had again set up pagan images in the temple of the Lord. It was not the first nor last time Israel had so sinned. God will not tolerate the image or worship of any other god in His temple. What the idol was in this instance is not important and never is. The point is God was not the center of their worship provoking Him to anger.

Why is this such a powerful warning to contemporary Christians? It's a powerful warning because we are capable of doing the same thing. God remains adamant regarding "anger-images" in His temple. Do you know where God's temple is today? Paul reveals, *"We are the temple of the living God; just as God said, 'I will dwell in them...'"* (2 Corinthians 6:16).

Surely, followers of Jesus don't have "anger-images" in their temples. Ah, but we sometimes do. If your zeal and commitment for the Lord flags or falters you are in danger of setting up an "anger-image" in your heart, which is the temple of God.

Whatever takes precedence in your heart before the Lord is an "anger-image". You need to chuck it out or be in danger of God's wrath.

---

[1]Brown, Francis, Driver, S. R., Briggs, Charles A., *The New Hebrew and English Lexicon* (Peabody, MA, Hendrickson) 1979 p. 888b

Scripture: Revelation 2:14-22

There are some who advocate Christians not only should but will eventually dominate the world. While this sounds good it requires some major changes in the actual practice of the Christian faith.

Too many Christians are like the Laodicean church— neutral! Jesus accuses them of being *"lukewarm, and neither cold nor hot..."* (v. 16).

As Jesus so ably demonstrated the kingdom of God is a kingdom of *POWER!* This power was bestowed on the disciples, *"...He called the twelve together and gave them power..."*(Luke 9:1). Then Jesus promised that all His followers would receive power through the Holy Spirit. They are to be *"...clothed with power from on high,"* (Luke 24:49). Beginning in Acts 2 we see the exercise of that power through the Holy Spirit.

Some followers of Jesus Christ live and function powerfully through the Holy Spirit. They are a far cry from the majority and aren't even a noticeable minority. Other Christians deem them a strange lot. They are truly as Peter described *"...a peculiar people..."* (1 Peter 2:9KJV). Paul wrote, *"For God has not given us a spirit of timidity, but of power..."* (1 Timothy 1:7). If what Paul wrote to Timothy is true where is the power?

The power is insulated from its source by delusion. We, like the Laodiceans, believe we *"...need of nothing..."* (v. 17). Jesus revealed the facts about our condition and what to do about it: depend on Christ's power through the Holy Spirit and exercise that power *by faith.*

Scripture: 1 Samuel 1:9-18

There is a deadly heart problem common to us all that isn't physical. Christians are not immune. This heart problem is caused by severe long term grief, disappointment, or deep hurt. It's called bitterness of heart.

When we suffer desperately and often unjustly bitterness is a normal result. When our dreams and hopes are suddenly or repeatedly shattered we become bitter toward life, toward others, toward the whole world. Bitterness is a method of coping with pain. If it is not recognized and disposed of bitterness will consume your joy, peace, contentment, and satisfaction like cancer.

Look at Hannah. *"And she, greatly distressed, (literally 'bitter of soul') prayed to the Lord and wept bitterly,"* (v. 10). Hannah's bitterness was being childless. It did not matter that Elkanah loved her more than he loved Peninnah. Peninnah had children, Hannah had none, thus the bitterness.

Bitterness is always brought on by some upsetting circumstance. We discover someone we admired has done a disgraceful thing; a dear friend turns savagely against us; a child dies; a marriage breaks up; a career turns sour; any number of circumstances can cause bitterness. They are things beyond our control.

What can we do to prevent bitterness from destroying us? Paul wrote, *"Let all bitterness...be put away from you,"* (Ephesians 4:3). Therefore bitterness must become a matter of prayer. It was for Hannah and God removed her bitterness by giving her a son. When you have bitterness in your heart ask God to remove it.

Scripture: Luke 2:41-52

No one would argue with Solomon's advice, *"Train up a child in the way he should go..."* (Proverbs 22:6). Let's examine the way parents raise children. Mary and Joseph followed Solomon's advice. *"And Jesus kept increasing in wisdom and stature and in favor with God and Man,"* (Luke 2:52).

Parents normally guarantee three fourths of that growth pattern. They strive for growth in wisdom and stature and favor with man. Leaving religious training up to the child is like the gardener leaving growth up to the garden. The weeds and thistles would smother it. Parents want a child to be in favor with man; but neglect what is necessary for him to be in favor with man. Unless a person is in favor with God he will be out of favor with himself, and/or others.

What do you emphasize with your children? Financial success? Athletic prowess? Business acumen? Good manners? No one finds fault with any of these IF they do not replace establishing a right relationship with Jesus Christ.

Rev. Jesse Jackson said, "Don't come to me, Mamma, claiming you can't control you sixteen year old. Of course you can't 'cause you didn't control him when he was six." Part of that control must be exercised in taking that child to Sunday School and staying with him for worship. Unless you raise up a child by the nurture of the Lord in your local church you are cheating him of the most vital necessity for growth, success, and achievement.

Scripture: James 1:1-8

James knew life and a bed of roses are both laden with thorns. *"Count it all joy, my brethren, when you encounter various trials, knowing the testing of your faith produces endurance,"* (vv. 2-3). Trials come and enduring them pays dividends.

Paul compared life to running a race. A key ingredient to winning a race is endurance. The runner who can keep going will eventually out distance those who fall by the wayside. The winning runner did not wake up one morning to discover he had endurance. Many nights the knotted muscles in his calves and thighs prevented him from sleeping until he built up his endurance. The pains were real but the runner with a desire to win knows the suffering is temporary.

The various trials we encounter cause painful heart aches and real suffering. Often sleep flees as we wrestle with our trials, soothe our hurt hearts, and seek comfort from the Lord.

The follower of Jesus knows the suffering is only temporary. He knows God's promises will not fail. Joshua testified, *"...you know in all your hearts and in all your souls that not one word of all the good words which the Lord spoke...not one of them has failed,"* (Joshua 23:14). The writer of Hebrews testified, *"...He Who promised is faithful..."* (Hebrews 10:23). Jesus said, *"Peace I leave with you, my peace I give to you...let not your heart be troubled, nor let it be afraid,"* (John 14:27).

Endurance will make you perfect, complete, lacking in nothing.

Scripture: Acts 16:22-30

John Bunyan 1628-1688 was born on this date. His masterful work *Pilgrim's Progress*, pub. 1678, has been reprinted more than any English work except the English Bible. Over a hundred thousand copies were sold in his life time. No other non-biblical work is more dependent on the Bible for its phrasing, imagery, and rhythm.

He was a tinker, a mender of pots. As he traveled about the country he preached Jesus to men and women as poor as himself. He was jailed for preaching. Beginning in 1660 the law forbid any preaching except Anglican. He was a Baptist.

His confinement was neither strict nor severe. He could occasionally visit his home. His confinement provided the environment for writing. In *Shepherd Boy's Song* he wrote,

> "My sword I give to him that shall succeed me in my pilgrimage, and my courage and skill to him that can get it. My marks and scars I carry with me, to be a witness for me, that I have fought His battles who now will be my rewarder."

Such testimony reminds us of the imprisonments of Paul, his scars, beatings, stonings, and sufferings for Jesus.

Bunyan and the Apostle Paul differ in many ways. Paul was highly educated, Bunyan was barely educated. Though both traveled in their ministry, Paul traveled extensively. Bunyan's travel was limited to a few shires.

Do you too wish to reach people with the gospel? You can't be a Paul or John Bunyan; but you can be yourself and as committed as they.

Scripture: Ezekiel 29:17-20

What do you own? What is yours, entirely yours, and no one else's? Nothing really! What have you acquired by your own efforts and gained by your own craftiness? Nothing really! We fail to realize we are *not* in charge, God is still in control.

You have what God has allowed or given to you. Perhaps it's not much. If you had more would you continue in faithfulness to Him who provides? Everyone likes to think they would. Then why are churches filled with poor people, working people, average wage earners instead of wealthy folks?

God said, *"Behold, I shall give the land of Egypt to Nebuchadnezzar king of Babylon..."* (v. 19). The Egyptians, like us, ask, what right does God have in giving the nation of one people to the king of another country? God doesn't have to explain, you know, for He is God.

God removed several nations of people to give the land to Jacob and his descendents. Was that fair? Not by man's distorted view; but entirely right by God's standard. Remember, God created everything: land and people. He can do with them as He pleases.

You and I need a bigger picture of Who God really is. We need to understand His sovereignty, power and authority.

This doesn't let you off for who you are. You are free to chose to follow Him or go your own way. God's way leads to eternal life, your own way leads to eternal death— always dying but never dead. What's your choice?

Scripture: Matthew 7:15-23

Winston Churchill 1874-1965 was born on this date. After Rudolf Hess descended by parachute into Scotland, Churchill remarked to Parliament, "This is one of those cases in which the imagination is baffled by the facts." Another such case will be the day of judgment for all those who *thought* they were saved.

Jesus knows what will be said by those who believed with the head but not with the heart. *"Did we not prophecy in Your name, and in Your name cast out demons, and in Your name perform many miracles?"* (v. 22). Surely their imaginations will be baffled by the facts.

Jesus will say to them, *"I never knew you..."* (v. 23). Never means at no time were they ever born again into the family of God. They were never saved in the first place. They had gone through the motions, been baptized, and all the rest with no inward change of heart.

What does Jesus say about being sure of acceptance into the kingdom? *"...everyone who hears these words of Mine, and acts upon them..."* (Matthew 7:24). He then tells of two house builders comparing them to life builders. The life built upon Jesus Christ the solid rock will stand in the day of judgment.

Life in Christ is not a fringe benefit. It is not an occasional pilgrimage into righteous living. It is not a display of religion. It is new life, changed life, guided and controlled by the Holy Spirit. Then you will know it's real.

Scripture: Galatians 6:1-5

Pride prevents us from admitting our mistakes and leads others astray. Few relish admitting they goofed. Here are examples. Karen is divorced and bombastically boasts about her freedom, her happiness; but says nothing about her struggles. Joe strove to succeed in his career and having succeeded found he'd failed as a father. His sons are grown yet he encourages them to be successful. Susie married the one and only guy she ever dated. Does she regret having done so? You bet. Does she warn others. Of course not, she doesn't want people thinking her marriage is the pits.

Paul wrote, *"...if anyone thinks he is something when he is nothing, he deceives himself,"* (v. 3). The only person the pretender really fools is himself.

We are taught to not publicly admit error. It takes courage. It can cost the loss of some "friends". It can be embarrassing, even painful. It will certainly slap down your pride. However, real Christians will support, encourage, love, and pray for you.

There are other rewards. One who is willing to admit to error sleeps better at night, can look himself in the mirror, and is more at ease for being honest. There is the added satisfaction of hoping your honesty will steer someone else away from your stupid mistake.

What is the responsibility of the Christian who hears a brother or sister confess to making a mess? We are to help them carry the load. What do you think Paul means by *"...bear one another's burdens..."* (v. 2)?

Scripture: Isaiah 28:9-13

"Experts are still trying to unravel the many routes by which a memory settles into the brain. But they're pretty sure that repetition is one fairly reliable route."[1] It's still amazing how "experts" continually reject the first book of knowledge insisting on re-inventing the wheel.

The above quoted source is one of many of such reports. Children learn by repetitious exposure to information. It's that simple. There are various means by which the repetition reaches the mind; but it's the repetition that instills it.

Nothing has changed since the days of Isaiah. The "experts" in Isaiah's day mock him for his repetition saying sarcastically, *"Precept upon precept...line upon line..."* (v. 10KJV). Yet this is exactly how God gets His message across. *"And the Lord, the God of their fathers, sent word to them again and again by His messengers, because He had compassion on His people and on His dwelling place; but they continually mocked the messengers of God..."* (2 Chronicles 36:15f).

The "experts" claimed they had not just been weaned from milk, nor just taken from the breast (v. 9). Pretended wisdom and knowledge fills the heart and mind of those seeking to avoid the truth of God's word. Like Isaiah's detractors, modern "experts" claim they don't need God or the Bible.

Isaiah retorts, *"So the word of the Lord to them will be...that they may stumble..."* (v. 13). When you hear the "experts" you can be sure they don't know all they claim UNLESS they are loyal to God and His word.

---

[1]Churchman, Deborah, "Writing to Reach Young Readers." *Writer's Digest*, August 1991, p. 22

Scripture: Deuteronomy 28:1-14

God has promised if we are obedient to His word we will be the head not the tail, we will be the lenders not the borrowers (vv. 12-13). In fact we are commanded to refrain from borrowing, *"...you shall not borrow,"* (v. 12). How many families really try to stay off the credit doom buggy? If you are hopelessly in debt whose fault is it? According to this text and Romans 13:8 we are not to owe anyone anything.

What causes most families to get hopelessly in debt? A desire for things, a desire to dress, eat, and travel, as well as the next person who is dressing, eating, and traveling well on credit to keep up with you. This is not God's plan folks. Plastic money is made easy for the soul purpose of getting you to buy. When going shopping "leave home without it" meaning your credit card.

If not the result will be as God says in 2 Chronicles 28:43-45. For many families this has already happened. Fine, church going, tithing Christian families have become the tail instead of the head because of one point of disobedience— they borrowed. Larry Burkett has sound biblical advice for families riding the debt doom buggy.

Some things must be purchased on time payments, houses, cars; but not clothing, groceries, TV's, etc. Save up for expensive items and while saving for them research the market so you get the best for the least expenditure. You'll be leagues ahead of the impulse buyer and richer.

Scripture: Zephaniah 3:1-8

These verses describe cities in the modern world. Tyranny reigns, the word of the Lord is ignored, and trust in the Lord is something to be scoffed. Many politicians devour widows houses and line their pockets with wealth extracted from the poor. The judges decisions are bent by the influence of big business, money, and prestige. Too often the priests, ministers, and rabbis are detoured from crying out "Thus saith the Lord..."

When a man of God opposes city hall even many Christians disclaim him. Woe to that city that ignores the authority of God. Woe to those "believers" who disclaim the prophet of God because his righteous words are not good for commerce.

The cities are filled with the carefree who live in safety, who protect themselves with wealth, who prey upon the less fortunate. They are headed for ruin because they have ignored the word of the Lord. Though their photographs appear in the Sunday magazines, though they appear well off; they are dead in their trespasses and sins.

Who is going to reach the cities for Jesus? In the midst of the cities are believers, claiming to love Jesus. In the cities are fine large churches. What are they doing to make an impact for Christ on their neighborhoods, their cities, their political leaders, the wealthy society patrons?

The only hope for our cities is for believers to begin witnessing and winning people to faith in Jesus Christ one by one. Begin with your neighbor.

Scripture: Hebrews 10:1-10

My childhood home faced west with a walk along the north side by the alley. On warm evenings I'd sit on the back steps waiting for my dad. Long before he popped around the corner I could see his shadow stretching before him. The sight of his shadow gave me joy for I knew my dad was coming.

All those who believed God in the Old Testament rejoiced because they too saw the shadow of reality in the sacrifices being offered year by year. They too looked forward to the reality of the Messiah knowing by faith He was coming because God had promised.

Just as a shadow can not satisfy so the Old Testament sacrifices could not satisfy. They satisfied neither God nor man; but were given as an indicator (a shadow) of what was coming.

The joy and fellowship among true believers, as rich as that is, is only a shadow of the reality of heaven. The spiritual ecstasy we sometimes experience is but a shadow of the unfathomable rapture of glory. I'm not sure our physical beings could withstand heaven's magnificence and splendor.

Equally, the greatest anguish man can experience in his body is but a shadow of eternal hell. If there is a heaven there must also be a hell. The Bible testifies of both.

In our physical finite bodies we can not comprehend either heaven or hell. What we do know and understand should propel us to the cross, to Jesus, to His gift of eternal life.

Scripture: Jude 17-23

The things people believe and practice baffle me. Hearing something that sounds good people will swallow it and adhere to it. As opportunity allows they will expound on *their* religion.

There is much in the world that *sounds* good. The tragedy is people think all good sounding words have come from the Bible. Larry Burkett calls this religious folklore.

He gives this example. "God helps those who help themselves." It isn't scripture but it sounds good. Mark Twain called such sayings "pious platitudes". The fact is, God helps those who CAN'T help themselves." The Old and New Testaments are replete with examples.

Jude alerts us, "...*remember the words that were spoken...by the apostles of...Jesus Christ*, (v. 17). In other words, if it isn't in the Bible it's probably not so. Scripture must be your final authority.

Jude also provides three exercises to protect you from the plague of pious platitudes. First, build yourself up in holy faith; second, pray in the Spirit; and third, keep in the love of God. The foundation of all this is studying your Bible daily.

Consuming scripture will build up your faith as you read how God has worked in the lives of others. Praying in the spirit has different interpretations. Suffice it to mean *praying earnestly*. Practicing these will keep you in the love of God.

When you hear religious folklore gently ask the speaker to show it to you in the Bible. It will be enlightening for them and a testimony for you. Try it.

Scripture: 2 Chronicles 15:1-8

The United States remembers Pearl Harbor today. The so called "surprise attack" by the Japanese could have been avoided had President Truman and his advisors been believing listeners. In the same war Clark Air Base in the Philippines was captured in one air raid. That was another tragedy resulting from not listening to good advice. I write this cognizant hind sight is superior to fore sight.

Asa learned from his grandfather, Rehoboam, to listen to good advice. Recall how Rehoboam split the nation of Israel as a result of rejecting good advice. Asa also observed the results of forsaking the Lord.

When he became king after the death of his father, Abijah, he immediately began religious reform. *"...he removed the foreign altars and high places, tore down the sacred pillars, cut down the Asherim, and commanded Judah to seek the Lord God of their fathers and to observe the law and the commandment,"* (2 Chronicles 14:3-4). Asa did good and right in the sight of the Lord his God.

When Azariah met Asa returning from war with the Ethiopians he confirmed that God was with Asa. Azariah explains, *"...the Lord is with you when you are with Him. And if you seek Him, He will let you find Him..."* (v. 2).

Could you and I save ourselves a great deal of anxiety and difficulty if we would only listen to honest and good advice? No doubt about it. When good advice is based on the word of God believe and do.

Scripture: Ezekiel 16:44-52

God is here accusing the women of Judah of Lesbianism, *"...who loathed their husbands and children..."* (v. 45). He compares them to the people of Sodom and Gomorrah (v. 48). Yes, God opposes female homosexuals as well as male. *"...for their women exchanged the natural function for that which is unnatural,"* (Romans 1:26). It is one's sexual preference that is an abomination to the Lord not one's gender. Eternal punishment in hell is the judgment waiting for those who practice homosexuality (1 Corinthians 6:9-10). The fire of Sodom has long since died out. The fire of hell is eternal.

What lies at the root of total depravity and abomination? *Arrogance!* Their arrogant and haughty attitude prompted them to commit abominations (vv. 49-50). Arrogance is not always detected by others; but God sees what's in the heart.

Arrogance not only engenders wickedness, it obstructs repentance. Though these verses are aimed directly at Lesbians there are lessons for Christians. (To say one can be a homosexual Christian is tantamount to heating your home with frozen steam.)

The lessons for Christians are these. Arrogance by itself is sin and leads to greater sin (v. 50). Often citizens of the world behave better than Christians who are citizens of heaven (v. 51). And I ask, do Christians use freedom in Christ as a license to sin (see Romans 6:1-2)?

The Bible is written to believers to steer them in the right direction and warn them against those things that are an abomination to the Lord. Apply the Bible to your life.

Scripture: Genesis 19:23-29

Peter wrote, *"and He rescued righteous Lot, oppressed by the sensual conduct of unprincipled men,"* (2 Peter 2:7). Compared to the people of Sodom and Gomorrah Lot was righteous. Our text reveals, however that God rescued Lot because of the righteousness of Abraham. *"...God remembered Abraham and sent Lot out of the midst of the overthrow..."* (v. 29).

Abraham believed God and it was reckoned to him as righteousness. Thus is was the righteousness of Abraham that saved Lot out of the fire. God rescued Lot because of Abraham's righteousness. Who's righteousness is keeping you and me out of the fire?

Those who believe, follow, and obey the Lord Jesus Christ are definitely more righteous than their neighbors by comparison. There are many pseudo-Christians who are actually worse than their unbelieving neighbors; their disobedience to Christ disqualifies them. True believers ARE MORE RIGHTEOUS than their neighbors; but their righteousness has no redeeming value with God.

Those who have received Jesus Christ as Savior and Lord are saved from the fire by the righteousness of Christ; not their own. Our atonement is like Lot's who was saved by vicarious righteousness. Vicarious means one person's deeds substituting for another.

It was Christ's substitutionary work on Calvary that keeps believers from the lake that burns with eternal fire. Only as each person receives Christ and His work on Calvary is he saved by it. It can be said of Christians, "God remembers Christ and keeps us out of torment".

Have you believed in Jesus so God will remember and rescue you?

Scripture: Isaiah 11:1-5

Merchants have long ago begun putting out items for Christmas. Last summer ad campaigns were finalized and sent to the printers. Christmas is a great boon for commerce. So much so that many in industry and sales begin looking forward to Christmas on January 1.

Isaiah began his ministry nearly eight centuries before that miraculous conception in Nazareth. When Isaiah wrote, *"...a shoot will spring from the stem of Jesse, And a branch from his roots will bear fruit,"* he was foretelling of Jesus. Isaiah is known as the Messianic prophet for so much of his book speaks of the Savior. He and others looked forward to "Christmas" for far different reasons and for a far greater length of time.

Children look forward to Christmas for different reasons than merchants or prophets. They anxiously await the receiving of gifts.

So many wait for Christmas that it's date is used as a symbol of something slow in coming. Haven't you heard people say, "You're slower than Christmas"?

Of all those who wait for Christmas the children have the right concept of receiving; the prophets have the right reason; and the rest have missed by a mile.

The right reason is God's gift to mankind, not in a stable but on a cross for the redemption of mankind from sin. It is the receiving of God's gift of salvation through Jesus Christ that makes Christmas Christmas.

To miss God's gift of eternal life is to choose eternal death— always dying but never dead.

Scripture: Romans 7:14-25

From *circa* 400 to the present scholars have disputed the spiritual state of the person described in these verses. Both sides support their position from scripture. Each claims the other is in error.

Simply put the two sides are: One claims the person "I" is unregenerate, not redeemed by the blood of Jesus. The other claims the "I" is saved by grace and struggles with sin. To muddy the water further, many interpretations have arisen in between these extremes.

No born again believer has ever lived free from the struggle with temptation, failure, and consequently sin. If the Christian never sins as some maintain, the Apostle John was certainly confused on this issue. *"If we confess our sins, He is faithful and righteous to forgive us our sins and to cleanse us from all unrighteousness,"* (1 John 1:9). In Romans 7 Paul was writing about the redeemed; he confesses his own struggle with his flesh. Like Paul, we must die daily (1 Corinthians 15:31 and Romans 12:1).

"Justification does not take all the carnal nature out of man at conversion. This is the work of sanctification, which is progressive"[1] Only some holiness sects claim perfection in Christian living. The rest know from experience the truth of Paul's struggle.

There is a caution here! Do not interpret these verses to excuse you from striving toward holy living. Paul is NOT providing a license to sin (Romans 6:1-2) Rather he wrote to encourage you. His spirit strives for righteousness; his flesh struggles to do evil. That's every believer's experience.

---

[1]McBeth, J. P. *Exegetical and Practical Commentary on the Epistle of Romans,* (Shawnee, OK, Oklahoma Baptist University Press), 1937, p. 182

Scripture: Job 3:1-10

How time past can be cursed is mental gymnastics for bored philosophers. Let them deal with such non-sense. Scripture here reveals the humanity of Job.

Recall his declaration, "*...the Lord gave and the Lord has taken away...*" (Job 1:21). Each of us can proclaim our faith in trial and tribulation. Today's text reveals that for each of us there is a breaking point, a time when suffering may overwhelm us. When Job reached the depths of despair he cursed the day he was born. He did not curse his God who made that day.

When we suffer severely; when we reach the extremity of our faith and ability to cope we cry out against someone or something. We must be careful not to cry out *against* God Who has everything under control. Job questioned God but did not accuse God of evil.

Through every trial, in the most painful circumstances you and I must maintain our faith in God, His sovereignty, His compassion, and His lovingkindness. Though Job suffered greater losses than any of us, though he was a physical wreck suffering pernicious pain, though his "friends" pelted him with insults (Job 19:3); yet he says, "*...I know that my Redeemer lives, And at the last He will take his stand on the earth. Even after my skin is destroyed, Yet from my flesh I shall see God; Whom I myself shall behold And whom my eyes shall see...*" (Job 19:25-26). Pray you too will stand on your faith in the Lord.

Scripture: Psalms 1:1 - 2:12

These two psalms serve as an introduction to the entire book. They introduce the two basic fundamentals of the Old Testament; namely law and prophecy. Any reader who rightly understands these two concepts is well on his way to understanding all the psalms. Law and prophecy was basic to the spiritual life of Israel.

The first psalm proclaims true happiness is found by shunning wicked acts and evil people in favor of finding delight in the law of the Lord. We should have an aversion toward sin and we should not seek the company of sinners. To carry out this attitude in a spirit of self-righteousness is to miss the whole point. Some have sought refuge in cloistered places but in so doing have been of little use in building the kingdom of God. We can, by the power of Christ within us, live in the world without being part of it. We can indeed love and cling to God's word in a spirit of humility and gratitude. We who do, shall stand and bear fruit as the tree planted by brooks of water.

The second psalm establishes full confidence in the prophecy, fulfillment and ultimate victorious reign of the Messiah. What a wonderful proclamation to every believer in any age. Despite the thunderings and harassment of rulers Jesus will subdue all.

The psalm closes with a mighty promise, *"How blessed are those who take refuge in Him!"* Make these psalms the ultimate guide and foundation for your life.

Scripture: 1 Peter 3:1-6

Nothing persuades better than a good example. Sure, it may take longer to be effective, especially with a stubborn spirit; but the end result is more firmly established.

Husbands can reject preaching, brow beating, harassment, coercion, and all other methods of persuasion. They will even rebel by being worse in their behavior. None of those methods please the Lord so toss them out in favor of doing it God's way as Peter expresses.

The most hardened, recalcitrant man will actually suffer under the weight of a woman with a gentle and quiet spirit. God will see to it. Let your desire for your husband be smothered in sweetness, devotion, and honor.

The problem is too many women desire to control their husbands. God told Eve, "...*Yet your desire shall be for your husband...*" (Genesis 3:16). This is more than a sexual attraction. It is an attraction, often taking a perverted form, which she cannot root from her nature. The same word "desire" is used of the sin's desire for a person (Genesis 4:7).

Women must also exhibit a gentle and quiet spirit with their children. It will gain their respect and foster obedience. Again, too many women lord it over their children, bossing, and running their lives even after they are grown. I've never seen it produce the kind of relationship the mother or children want.

Take Peter's words to heart. Ask God to help you be the woman He wants you to be. You've everything to gain, nothing to lose.

Scripture: Proverbs 12:8-13

Macho bacho! Solomon compares the macho man and the real man in today's reading.

Why are so many males pretenders? Why do male humans pretend to be bigger, better, smarter, stronger, braver than they really are? It's stupid. Real men see right through their macho bluster and bravado. True women are not impressed with the Chanticleer on the block.

A man praised according to his insight is one who sees himself as he really is. He recognizes his limitations and is not anxious about them. He builds on his strengths. Every man has both strengths and weaknesses. The macho maniac has the perverse mind (v. 8). He has twisted the concept of himself into something fake. The perverse mind makes the man a fraud.

Why can't men see the grinding truth of verse 9? Which is better, pride or provision? Would you rather be esteemed or established? An excellent example of a man honoring himself is Haman in the book of Esther. Read what a fool he was for his pride.

Does it show bravery to kick the dog, beat the horse, pull the wings off a fly? Those who practice such things are deceived by Satan.

The man who works and tends to his business is superior to those who chase after vain things. The workman will be established in his household, his community, and regarded even among his enemies.

My brothers, put away vain trappings, boasting, belching, and bravado. Be yourself. Be the man God made you to be.

Scripture: Mark 2:18-22

The people understood perfectly when Jesus said, *"No one sews a patch of unshrunk cloth on an old garment; otherwise the patch pulls away from it, the new from the old, and a worse tear results,"* (v. 21). They understood so well because all of them were virtually poor. Nearly all of them at one time had worn patched clothing. It was not an uncommon sight to see patches on clothes in Jesus' day.

Today it is rare to see patches on clothes, especially in America. Contemporary children would be mortified if they had to wear a patch on their clothes. What woman today darns socks? None to my knowledge. Are we so well off we can dispose of worn clothes and buy new? Many poor in America dress well, often better than the working class.

Being poor has never been a wonderful life to live. The poor have always been denigrated and relegated to the lowest position. Yet, poverty is not something of which to be ashamed. Some of the world's greatest men and women came out of poverty. Often some of the finest, most dependable people on earth are the poor of the land. The King of Kings was born in a smelly stable. Joseph's offering of two turtle doves was the offering of a poor man (Leviticus 12:8).

No one expects you to be proud of your poverty; but don't be ashamed of it. If you're born again, you are a child of the King waiting for your inheritance.

Scripture: Luke 5:17-26

Seen any miraculous healings lately? Have you been doing what scripture commands? Do you have the faith of the men who carried the paralytic?

They were determined to bring healing to their friend. When the crowd about the door would not yield, did they give up, go home, claiming it couldn't be done? You know they didn't. They lifted some of the roof tiles and got their sick friend to Jesus.

It was no easy task lifting their friend to the roof. It was risky. Suppose they dropped him. I want you to note these men took great pains and gave great effort to getting the paralytic healed.

You who claim the Bible is literally true do you practice James 5:14-15? When one is sick do you call on the elders for prayer and anointing with oil? Some do and are healed. Others claim that was only for the New Testament days. If so when did God cancel that part of His word?

When the elders come do they offer up prayer only one time? Or do they labor in prayer? Have the elders put forth as much effort as the friends of the paralytic? Do they have the faith of the paralytic's friends? Does the sick person have faith Christ will indeed make him well?

My experience has been that often those who claim these things don't work haven't really tried them. There is nothing magical in laying on of hands, praying, or anointing with oil. It's obedience. Try it.

Scripture: 2 Kings 1:1-8, 17

The brief life and reign of Ahaziah teaches us a great lesson. Our future is not in the hands of Baal-zebub (actually Satan) but in the hands of the Lord. Satan would like you to think he is in charge, that he has control, that if we want anything in this life we must get it from him.

Ahaziah's life demonstrates that it just ain't so. God is in control and what we have comes from Him.

Who would seek things from Satan? Many Christians do unwittingly. When you read the horoscopes you are inquiring of Satan. When you use a Ouija board you are inquiring of Satan. If you inquire of a palm reader or crystal ball gazer you are inquiring of Satan. DON'T DO IT! Anyone who depends of crystals, rocks, or anything else in creation he is seeking assistance from Satan. Ahaziah's life proves that seeking from Satan results in death. Paul wrote, *"The wages of sin is death..."* (Romans 6:23).

Apply Elijah's question to yourself. *"Is it because there is no God in* your land *that you inquire of Baal-zebub?"* (v. 2). Isaiah asked, *"Should not a people consult their God?"* (Isaiah 8:19). When Christians do those things mentioned above it makes me question who their god is? Don't even play with Ouija boards, crystals, etc. Can you juggle hot coals and not burn your fingers?

Learn from the life of Ahaziah. Don't think it can't happen to you. Seek the Lord and live.

Scripture: Daniel 6:10-15

Are you aware of what really takes place in your spiritual life? Do you comprehend the effect prayer has? Is your loyalty and commitment to God worth anything? Do you ever notice narrow brushes with tragedy in your life? Does it matter? Let's look and see.

Daniel was a man of prayer regardless of the king's edict. Prayer carries weight with God, *"The effective prayer of a righteous man can accomplish much,"* (James 5:16). I doubt Daniel was praying to be saved from the lion's den. He was praying as a regular part of his daily life, *"...praying and giving thanks before his God as he had been doing previously,"* (v. 10). How is your prayer life? Do circumstances drive you to your prayer closet or is prayer part of your daily routine? The hungry lions had no appetite for Daniel.

How about your loyalty and commitment? Does it matter? Mordecai was a loyal follower of the Lord God. He daily went about his business being loyal to the Lord. He wasn't concerned that his loyalty to God angered the king's chief officer (Esther 3:2). He was not aware that death was stalking him in the form of his enemy, Haman (Esther 6:4). Yet, God not only saved Mordecai but made Haman honor him. Then God arranged for Haman to die on his own gallows.

Just because you don't *SEE* the results of prayer and loyalty doesn't mean God hasn't been taking care of you. What does all this mean to you?

Scripture: Isaiah 56:1-8

Rejoice and be glad. The Lord opened the door of salvation to all nations long ago (Acts 13:47). Salvation was to come from the Jews (John 4:22) but it was never intended to be restricted to Israel. God situated Israel to touch all the nations of the world. The trade routes of many nations passed through Israel opening wide the door of opportunity to tell the world about their God. From the beginning God intended for people of every nation and race to come into His kingdom.

Who then are the foreigners mentioned in today's reading? They are every person who is not of Jewish decent, who join themselves to God through the shed blood of Jesus Christ. They are the non-Jews saved by faith, who love Jesus, who are desiring to be His servants.

When we hold fast to His covenant we too become children of Abraham, children of faith, children of commitment to the Lord.

And the Lord will bring us to His holy mountain making us joyful in His house of prayer. Our offerings are acceptable to Him because our desire is to serve Him because we love Him. Therefore rejoice in the good news that we foreigners have been invited to partake of God's glorious salvation. Rejoice as did the first gentiles to hear, *"...when the Gentiles heard this, they began rejoicing and glorying the word of the Lord..."* (Acts 13:48).

Rejoice constantly being assured your name is written in the Lamb's book of life.

Scripture: 1 Chronicles 15:16-24

By now the air waves undulate with the sounds of Christmas. I do NOT refer to *Rudolf the Red*, or *Here Comes Santa*, but to *Hark the Herald Angels Sing, Gloria in Excelsis Deo*, and *Silent Night*. What music thrills the soul, stirs the heart, and lifts one to his feet better than Handel's *Hallelujah Chorus*?

This is about the only time of year when the world listens to Christian music without bristling. Saint and sinner alike enjoy the vibrant sounds of Christmas. It is a time of rejoicing, yes, even for the world. Though Jesus was probably born in late April or early May we celebrate His incarnation in just four days.

To offer joyful praise with voice and instrument dates back centuries before Jesus and even before King David. In today's reading David calls for musicians to raise sounds of joy. In addition to the singers there were three men playing loud bronze cymbals, eight tuned harps, six tuned lyres, and seven trumpeters.

Why sounds of joy? David was moving the Ark of the Covenant to Jerusalem. To those ancient Jews it was tantamount to God Himself coming into the city.

God Himself did come physically in the person of Jesus Christ. The Christian faith is the only religion whose God has come down to man in the form of man to experience the human predicament (Hebrew 4:15). That is cause for rejoicing.

Even greater is the rejoicing of those who have believed on His name. Rejoice in the Lord.

Scripture: Revelation 11:15-18

The child whose birth we celebrate in three days, who gave a flesh and blood living example of what man *should be*, who gave His life for the ransom of many shall indeed rule and reign upon the earth. How does that affect your life?

Suppose you lived in a land with an autocratic king. Now suppose this king forgave every evil doer of misdeeds upon request thus cancelling the charge of death against them. Suppose all he asked was for you to trust him and his promises. Now suppose you reject his forgiveness and refuse to believe his promises. When the time of judgment comes what will your fate be?

Would you say anyone who rejects such an offer was really stupid? You're right. Everyone who rejects the forgiveness God offers, who refuses to believe His promises is abysmally stupid. They think they are wise, smart, in control. They think they are rich; but Jesus warns, *"...you say, 'I am rich and have become wealthy, and have need of nothing,' and you do not know that you are wretched and miserable and poor and blind and naked,"* (Revelation 3:17).

Those who reject God's forgiveness and promises are deceived. Satan has blinded their eyes. Break free, hear what God's word says. Unless you are a child of God born into His family through the blood of Jesus Christ, you are a child of Satan.

When Jesus comes and rules on the earth, what will your fate be? God says your reward will be given to the saints (Revelation 11:18) and your judgment of eternal death will be upon your own head (Ezekiel 18:20).

Scripture: 1 Corinthians 12:1-11

Do you have all your gifts wrapped? No other time of year brings forth the idea of gifts more than Christmas. In some families there are gag gifts between certain members. One of my uncles consistently gave someone an empty box for Christmas.

Charles Dawson gave the scientific community a great gag gift when he gave it Piltdown man. Scientists the world over wrote papers and made speculations about the life and times of Piltdown man. In 1953 the skull and jaw (upon which the farce was built) were proven to be faked. The skull was a modern day human skull and the jaw was that of an orangutan. The truth made the scientists look ridiculous.

There is a gag gift perpetrated on Christians by a greater trickster than Dawson. The giver is the great deceiver, which should alert you to watch out. Satan has given many Christians the gift of an outright lie. He has given them the concept that there are giftless Christians. Like Piltdown man the species has never existed.

How shamed you should be if you have accepted Satan's hoax. Paul states plainly, "...*to each one is given the manifestation of the Spirit for the common good,*" (v. 7). Paul then gives examples of the gifts given by the Spirit to _EVERY_ believer. YOU HAVE A GIFT to be used for the common good of the church— use it!

Of course if you want to look ridiculous go on believing you are a giftless Christian. Satan loves a good laugh.

Scripture: Luke 2:8-20

The report of the birth of Jesus is probably the most famous scripture the world over. It certainly is the greatest news the world has ever had. It is the good news that God Himself came down to dwell with man and redeem him from his sins.

There are few places in the world failing to observe this greatest of events in history. All time is divided by the birth of Jesus. Yet, God haters, Jesus deniers, and other of Satan's workers seek to destroy the truth of God's word.

The birth of Christ is the only time in all history when the angels appeared en masse to praise God (v. 13). Even then we often miss the most important point in the angelic chorus. We often quote the first part of what they sang but leave off the qualifier. Read again *ALL* of what they sang. *"Glory to God in the highest, And on earth peace among men with whom He is pleased,"* (v. 14).

It's true too! Those with whom God is pleased have peace. Not the peace the world gives but the peace of Christ in their hearts. Jesus promised, *"Peace I leave with you; My peace I give to you; not as the world gives, do I give to you,"* (John 14:27).

Do you have the peace of Christ in your heart? Please God by accepting Jesus Christ as Lord and Savior and His peace will reign in your heart. Accept God's gift to you this Christmas.

Scripture: Luke 1:26-35

Isn't it amazing how many scientists and other scholars can't read? Perhaps they are so biased that when they read what disagrees with them their minds twist the meaning. Or do they not know anything about conception? As a result of not being able to read, or being biased, or not understanding conception many have sworn that Jesus was not born of a virgin.

It never ceases to amaze me how complicated scientists who don't believe the Bible make it seem. They go to great lengths to prove theories refusing to accept the facts.

The Bible clearly states that Jesus was conceived in the "womb". Even many non-degreed people know that conception occurs in the fallopian tube not the womb. After conception the microscopic child migrates to the womb and there begins developing. No, it doesn't mean Doctor Luke was wrong in his reporting. It means the conception of Jesus Christ in the womb of Mary was JUST AS SCRIPTURE SAYS— in the womb.

Verses 31 and 35 are key to believing in the virgin birth. Indeed, later Mary had other children (Matthew 13:26; Luke 8:19; John 2:12; John 7:3,5,10; Acts 1:14 Galatians 1:19; and Jude 1). All His brothers and sisters were conceived in the natural way— in the fallopian tube.

The virgin birth was merely the fulfillment of Isaiah's prophecy, *"Behold a virgin will be with child and bear a son, and she will call His name Immanuel,"* (Isaiah 7:14). Since Jesus fulfilled all prophecy (Luke 24:27) we must believe also in the virgin birth.

Scripture: Malachi 1:6-11

In Canada and Britain (except Scotland) today is boxing day. It's a day when Christmas gift boxes were regularly expected by the postman, dustman, and generally all those functionaries who serve the public at large without receiving payment from any individual. Boxing day is celebrated the first working day after Christmas.

How would these civil servants feel if you offered them shabby hand-me-downs, or broken stuff? Would you even consider giving such truck? Oh, of course not. What would they think of you if you offered them junk?

Yet, consider what you offer to God. When I look at the service rendered by many Christians; when I see shoddy church signs, unkempt church property, hear preachers slaughter the language, or observe unprepared Bible school teachers I am reminded of God's accusation against Israel.

Do we care what God thinks of us? Does it matter to you what God's opinion is of your service to Him? It should. If you wouldn't give the postman a moldy candy bar is God less important to you than your postman? Hey! Let's stop playing games with ourselves. We must radically altar our opinion about God.

Do you want to spend eternity with someone you have grandly offended for twenty, thirty, forty, or more years? God does not expect better than you can give, but He expects and deserves your best effort; always and all the time.

As we approach a new year, why not begin now to practice giving God your best everyday in every way?

Scripture: Luke 24:44-53

The last promise and command Jesus made to His disciples and us was, "...*I am sending forth the promise of My Father upon you; but you are to stay in the city until you are clothed with power from on high,*" (v. 49). He has sent the power as promised. The early church operated in the power and victory of the Holy Spirit. Luke testifies, "*And with great power the apostles were giving witness to the resurrection of Jesus Christ...*" (Acts 4:33). We should note that it was not just the apostles who received power but the whole 120 who tarried.

One of the secrets to operating in the power of the Holy Spirit is found in the command Jesus gave with the promise. It is the words "wait until you are clothed with power". In our eagerness to serve, in our eagerness to win souls, in our eagerness to go and do we fail to "*wait upon the Lord,*" (Isaiah 40:31). When we go and do in the Spirit of God we go and do with *power!*

More than five hundred disciples saw the Lord after His resurrection (1 Corinthians 15:6). Only 120 tarried and received the power from on high. Shall we be like the 380 who couldn't wait? And where do we read about them accomplishing anything for the Lord? I'm sure they lived for Him but without the power from on high.

Just so, the greater multitude of Christians today are living for the Lord but without the power. ARE YOU?

Scripture: 1 Corinthians 15:50-52

Remember your youth, your vitality. Remember how you could play or work all day then go out at night and enjoy having a good time. You seemed to never tire. You could eat anything you wanted without worrying about weight gain.

If you're past fifty you know your get-up-and-go has got-up-and-gone. Sure you're still active but you have slowed down. The energy seems to play out about three in the afternoon. It doesn't get any better this side of Jordan.

All through this fifteenth chapter of 1 Corinthians Paul talks about the resurrection, about a new body. *"It is sown a perishable body, it is raised an imperishable body...it is sown in weakness it is raised in power..."* (1 Corinthians 15:42-43). Those who believe on the Lord Jesus Christ have something to look forward to.

"Behold I tell you a mystery: we shall all be changed, in a moment, in the twinkling of an eye..." (vv. 51-52). The resurrected body of the believer will be perfect, faultless, without spot or blemish inside and out. It will be eternally free of disease, sorrow, discouragement, boredom. Believers will abide in heaven where the trees bear twelve manner of fruit. Glory hallelujah, I'm glad I'm headed there. Paul says the dead in Christ shall be raised first. The sinners too shall be raised to an eternal existence. They do not get glorified bodies. They spend eternity in hell with their resurrected physical bodies.

Where are you going?

Scripture: Jeremiah 2:20-25

Have you ever known anyone who constantly washed her hands. When I was a young pastor a girl in our community developed a strange rash. She confessed to her doctor that she took three and four baths a day. He limited her to a bath every other day until the rash cleared up.

People do many strange things to make themselves clean either in their own eyes or in the eyes of others. My favorite literary author wore white in his effort to be clean. God tells His people, *"Although you wash yourself with lie And use much soap, The stain of your iniquity is before me,"* (v. 22).

Dr. Charles Stanley demonstrated what most photographers and physicists know. When you see a red dot on white paper it stands out clearly. When you look at the same red dot through a red filter the dot disappears. The red pigment in the filter cancels out the red rays being reflected from the red dot.

That illustrates the way God looks at those who have believed on His Son Jesus Christ. He looks at our sin stain through the blood of Jesus and the sin stain is cancelled out. Isaiah wrote, *"'Come now let us reason together,' says the Lord, 'Though your sin are as scarlet, They shall be as white as snow; Though they be red like crimson, They will be like wool,'"* (Isaiah 1:18).

What can wash away your sin and make you clean? Only the shed blood of Jesus Christ.

Scripture: John 6:34-40

America is a nation of over fed under exercised folks. There are many 'lose weight' methods on the market. What about our spiritual weight? Do you know any fat souls?

None of us is overweight spiritually. When was the last time you skipped eating because you were too busy? When was the last time you skipped Bible reading because you were too busy? When it comes to feeding our souls by reading God's Word many of us suffer malnutrition.

Do you ever feel dissatisfied? You look in the fridge, you search the pantry for something to satisfy. Could it be your soul is starved for the Word of God? Recall what Jesus said, *"Man shall not live by bread alone but by every word that proceeds out of the mouth of God,"* (Matthew 4:4). Jesus also said, *"I am the bread of life, he who come to Me shall not hunger, and he who believes in me shall never thirst,"* (John 6:35).

Unless you have believed on Him Whom the Father has sent and feed on every word that proceeds from the mouth of God you are not living in all the fullness God intends for you.

When that feeling of dissatisfaction gnaws at you feed on His Word. Start listening to your heart instead of your stomach. Start a spiritual revolution in your life.

God's Word is rich, tasty, and has no calories or cholesterol; but oh how it builds strength in the inner man. You never need to diet spiritually.

Scripture: Philippians 2:1-8

Resolutions! Resolutions! We hear resolutions proclaimed. We make them at the New Year and what are the results? Resolutions are usually forgotten before we get home. And what about New Year's resolutions? Those surviving until January 31 are on the critical list. We don't need New Year's Resolutions, we need New Year's Revolutions.

A resolution is a bland sort of half promise that carries no pizazz; but a revolution, now there is something with some action to it. A revolution has fireworks, it's filled with activity that stirs the heart and gets something accomplished. Resolutions are not expected to mean a general overhaul of the way you do things but a revolution is going to be noticed by everyone. A revolution will make news. People talk about revolutions. Let the resolutions rest. This year make a revolution that will honor Christ, fill your life with pizazz, and make those around you take notice.

Paul wrote, *"Walk in a manner worthy of the Lord, to please Him in all respects,"* (Colossians 1:10). Now brother, if that's not a revolution... Do you think people would not notice the fresh ecstasy of your life, the new bearing in your walk, the new vitality in your work, the new you?

Paul wrote, *"Let this attitude be in you which was also in Christ Jesus,"* (v. 5). Christ's attitude was to please the Father in all things (John 8:29). Resolutions? Bah, hum bug. Let's have a revolution! Come on, revolt, live for Jesus Christ every day next year.

Scripture Index

Scripture Index

Scripture Index

Scripture Index

Scripture Index

Scripture Index

Scripture Index

Scripture Index

Scripture Index

Scripture Index

Scripture Index